America's Failing Economy and the Rise of Ronald Reagan

Eric R. Crouse

America's Failing Economy and the Rise of Ronald Reagan

palgrave
macmillan

Eric R. Crouse
Tyndale University College
Toronto, ON, Canada

ISBN 978-3-319-70544-6 ISBN 978-3-319-70545-3 (eBook)
https://doi.org/10.1007/978-3-319-70545-3

Library of Congress Control Number: 2017962434

Cover illustration: nsf / Alamy Stock Photo

Printed on acid-free paper

This Palgrave Macmillan imprint is published by Springer Nature
The registered company is Springer International Publishing AG
The registered company address is: Gewerbestrasse 11, 6330 Cham, Switzerland

In memory of David George Ellis (1936–2016)

Preface

When I graduated from high school in 1978, I had no clue about stagflation. As I pursued my dream of racing professional motocross, I did not think of the stagnant economy and high inflation that made it difficult for young people to find good-paying jobs. Often on the road in the years 1979 and 1980, I witnessed the high inflation that contributed to the rising cost of gasoline and high interest rates. It was no fun taking a financial hit when I could only pay the minimum monthly credit card payment. I had assumed all this was normal. It was probably a good thing that I was unaware of how bad the economy was, and how a Keynesian mindset often steered the economy in the wrong direction with fewer employment opportunities. After my motocross career was over by the mid-1980s, I had more time to think about the economy and decisions by leaders who favored politics over economics.

It was only about 10 years ago, however, that I began the process of focusing on economics in my academics. My first book on economic history, published in 2013, was on Reaganomics during the 1980s. Writing about President Reagan's economic policies was exciting, but I realized that I needed to say more about the pre-1980 period. This book, *America's Failing Economy and the Rise of Ronald Reagan*, examines those earlier years and attempts to explain Reagan's window of opportunity to win the White House. The story is about the demise of Keynesianism (1965–1980) as it failed to solve the stagflation that caused many Americans to suffer economic hardship.

I have a passion for reading economic theory and engaging in discussions with anyone who enjoys talking economics, but I find the focus of economic specialists is often too narrow to capture the interest of most students who do not have a background in economics. This is not a book written primarily for economists. Focusing on the big picture, I have avoided technical jargon and attempted to demonstrate that economic history can be very interesting. My approach was to harvest the work of many economists, politicians, and journalists and to see what type of composite would emerge.

Toronto, ON, Canada Eric R. Crouse

Acknowledgments

I have benefited greatly from numerous discussions with Derek Chisholm who teaches economics at Tyndale University College. Given my fascination with the writings of John Maynard Keynes and the Keynesian literature that followed, it was a bonus that Derek's Ph.D. in economics is from the University of Cambridge—the academic home of Keynes. I appreciate his feedback on the early chapters of this book. The comments by the two anonymous readers were also excellent. They prompted me to explain some statements better and to include the research of important books that I had missed. Of course, I am fully responsible for any mistakes in this book.

Palgrave Macmillan has an impressive history of publishing major economics works, and Keynes's majestic *The General Theory of Employment, Interest, and Money* is one of many examples. I am thankful for editor Megan Laddusaw and her assistant Christine Pardue. Their level of professionalism and politeness has been great.

I am also grateful for my wife's proofreading. Ann-Marie is an English high school and journalism teacher who has done an amazing editorial job, year after year, with her school's yearbooks. A book's index requires much work, and I depended heavily on the assistance of my daughter Emily.

This book is in memory of David George Ellis, a wonderful father-in-law and friend who we miss very much.

Contents

Abbreviations

AEI	American Enterprise Institute
AFDC	Aid to Families with Dependent Children
AFL-CIO	American Federation of Labor–Congress for Industrial Organization
AFSCME	American Federation of State, County and Municipal Employees
CBO	Congressional Budget Office
CEA	Council of Economic Advisors
CETA	Comprehensive Employment Training Act
COWPS	Council on Wage and Price Stability
CPI	Consumer Price Index
DOE	Department of Energy
EPCA	Energy Policy and Conservation Act
EPG	Economic Policy Group
FAP	Family Assistance Plan
FCC	Federal Communications Commission
FEA	Federal Energy Administration
Fed	Federal Reserve
FEO	Federal Energy Office
GNP	Gross National Product
HEW	Department of Health, Education, and Welfare
HUD	Department of Housing and Urban Development
JEC	Joint Economic Committee
MIT	Massachusetts Institute of Technology
NEPA	National Environmental Policy Act

NHI	National Health Insurance
NRA	National Recovery Administration
NWRO	National Welfare Rights Organization
OMB	Office of Management and Budget
OPEC	Organization of Petroleum Exporting Countries
PBJI	Program for Better Jobs and Income
SDS	Students for a Democratic Society
UMWA	United Mine Workers of America
URPG	Urban Regional Policy Group
WIN	"Whip Inflation Now"

CHAPTER 1

Introduction

Three weeks before the presidential election of 1980 the polls had President Jimmy Carter and Republican challenger Ronald Reagan dead even in the popular vote poll. Political journalist Elizabeth Drew described the intense buildup for the upcoming televised election debate as "the world heavyweight championship and the Super Bowl combined." Would one of the contenders make a major blunder? On debate night, Carter's eyes were puffy and tired-looking whereas Reagan, 69, appeared "to be in robust health." Success for Reagan hinged on his ability to convince American viewers that he was not an angry, "dangerous" conservative. Under the lights and in front of the cameras, his easygoing manner did the job as did his closing question to the American people concerning the state of the economy: "Are you better off than you were four years ago?"[1]

Carter had genuine concern for those hurt by a floundering economy but were his economic policies the answer? The American people gave their verdict. On November 4, 1980, the United States witnessed the political defeat of Jimmy Carter and the policy defeat of Keynesianism. The Keynesian Revolution had continued uninterrupted for close to four decades in America, struck down when voters responded to the failure of their economic managers to deliver economic growth and price stability.

The election results questioned Keynesian economics that said active government intervention and management of the economy was essential for the economic well-being of society. In the final year of Carter's administration, economists Robert L. Heilbroner, John Kenneth Gailbraith, and

E. R. Crouse, *America's Failing Economy and the Rise of Ronald Reagan*,
https://doi.org/10.1007/978-3-319-70545-3_1

other Keynesians saw higher taxation, comprehensive regulation, and price controls as the correct method to solve America's economic woes. Many had benefited from the economic stewardship of Democratic presidents Harry Truman, John F. Kennedy, and Lyndon B. Johnson, but the economic malaise of Jimmy Carter's administration was another matter. It was a major reason for his political trouncing; he won only 6 states to Ronald Reagan's 44. The weakening of Keynesianism allowed Reagan to reach the White House.

There is much literature on Carter's failure to unite the Democratic Party, disentangle the Iranian hostage crisis (1979–1981), and win the votes of the Religious Right who were generally supportive of free-market thinking—a fact missed by scholars more interested in the social conservative opposition to Carter.[2] Although acknowledging that all these issues were important to Reagan winning the White House, this book focuses on the economic shortcomings of Carter's policies that were decisive in presenting the former actor a window of opportunity.

Politicians, political pundits, journalists, and Main Street Americans all responded in various ways to the record of Keynesian macroeconomic management and the emergence of stagflation—that is, persistent high inflation and high unemployment.[3] For this transformative era, there was a colorful cast of characters, some with economic expertise and many others without economic schooling. If few commentators were aware of the finer points of Keynesian economics, they all recognized "malaise."

I

One only had to look at the post-World War II years to the mid-1960s to find evidence of a vibrant American economy and a sense of optimism at what government could achieve. With noble intentions, politicians devised policies to improve the lives of the poor and the middle class. But something changed during the 1970s—a change that Carter completely missed. Several weeks after his defeat by Reagan, he wrote in his diary that Republicans exaggerated the problems of the economy. As he saw it, "with the exception of interest rates, everything is going surprisingly well."[4] An economic history of the rise and decline of Keynesian ideas explains much about competing visions on the role of the government and the major shift in economic thinking that few envisaged.[5]

The high mark of Keynesianism was during the 1960s. On the issues of inequality and poverty, many had faith in the government—more so than at any other time in history—to find solutions. Before President Lyndon Johnson's "Great Society" programs began to tarnish, there was much confidence in government intervention. Progressive Americans viewed centralized economic planning as the reason for the Soviet Union's transformation from a primitive peasant nation. Basically, a handful of experts could "substitute their judgment for the billions and trillions of decisions that go on in a free market." Keynesianism was not socialism, but both shared the idea of using central planning to "correct" the free-market system.[6]

American intellectuals found European economic ideas appealing. As a better way to protect the public from difficult economic times, Western European countries and elsewhere viewed "government knowledge" superior to "market knowledge." Careful not to completely stifle the market, Western governments sought to modernize and "propel economic growth" while delivering "equity, opportunity, and a decent way of life." Most citizens approved. In 1945, British voters, not wanting a return to the economic hardships of the 1930s, replaced Winston Churchill, their victorious war leader, with social worker Clement Attlee, head of the Labour Party that promised an expansive welfare state.[7]

In the United States, high-ranking officials in government saw that policy drove the budget rather than the budget driving policy; thus, it was more important to get government policies through than make them effective.[8] This was especially true for the 1960s. Government was to intervene in the economy, and it was not only Democratic leaders who acted. Republican President Richard Nixon saw that voluntary price and wage targets were ineffectual, and he believed that the American economy was stronger when government interference was minimal. Yet, to the dissatisfaction of conservatives, he went ahead with wage and price controls in 1971, causing economic problems for the rest of the decade. He also allowed economic regulation to thrive in other sectors. With both Democratic and Republican presidents, America had its own special "brand of regulatory capitalism."[9]

Pursuing the 1976 Democratic nomination for president in a strong field of competitive candidates, former governor of Georgia (1971–1975) Carter, mastered the technicalities of the political process and won the nomination. On the campaign trail against President Gerald Ford, who narrowly defeated Reagan for the Republican nomination in August, Carter promised integrity and openness. The memory of the traumatic Watergate crisis was still fresh for many and Ford's economic record was not great. With his victory over Ford in November, the former naval engineer and self-identified "planner" appeared to have the skills to fix America's most pressing economic problems.

On the issue of economics, Carter did not start on a good footing. As president-elect, he decided it was a good idea to congratulate by phone the American Nobel laureates of 1976, including economist Milton Friedman (1912–2006)—the most influential free-market scholar in America. Friedman's scholarship and mentorship at the University of Chicago, and a *Newsweek* column on economic matters over the years, put him in a special category; he was a scholarly economist able and willing to present insightful analysis in layman's terms for people outside of the field of economics. When Carter told his secretary to call Friedman in December 1976, however, she contacted the wrong Milton Friedman and got the speechwriter with the identical name who had served President Ford. After the mistaken identity episode, Carter finally talked with the correct Friedman; it was their only direct contact ever.[10]

Having faith in Keynesian management of the economy, President Carter and his economic advisors saw no benefit in consulting the free-market Nobel laureate who saw government intervention as more of a problem than a solution. In the summer of 1979, when the White House invited many commentators to Camp David to discuss the malaise with Carter, there were no notable economists with new ideas, and certainly no one with ideas like Friedman's.

Friedman was a formidable critic of Keynesianism and its central idea that free-market economies were inherently unstable, requiring continuous active government intervention. His monetary theory tore down the mainstream consensus that economies required government management to succeed. His grasp of economic theory and history alongside his evidence-based arguments for free-market policies were obvious to anyone paying attention to his *Newsweek* column that began in 1966. With decades of research and university teaching under his belt, the mild-mannered, five-foot Friedman wrote with authority when he targeted the economic shortcomings of Carter's administration. He was a dynamic ball of energy who made people think with his "bewildering array of questions, statements, and relentless logic." He was an "intellectual's intellectual" who went beyond abstractions.

Economist Martin Anderson wrote: "There are many intellectuals who care only for the abstractions they glory in, not the people the abstractions represent. Friedman is driven more by what ideas and policies do to and for people than the theoretical beauty of an argument."[11] With a Jewish immigrant background (both parents were from Europe) and humble origins, his demeanor was not of someone who appeared heartless, only concerned about defending the rich. Friedman's ability to statistically evaluate the evidence on Keynesian policy shed light on government's inability to solve the brutal problem of stagflation. The destructive combination of a stagnant economy (high unemployment) and rising inflation was a heavy burden on the American people during the 1970s.

Other free-market (conservative/libertarian) economists joined in the criticism as the nation struggled with the 1970s' dismal economic conditions.[12] Arguably the most influential American free-market economist after Friedman, at least at the popular level, was Arthur Laffer—a supply-side "showman" known for his Laffer curve, which illustrated the adverse effect of high taxation on productivity and wealth creation. He was of the school that viewed high taxation as a retarding force on economic growth. A graduate of Yale University, Laffer did his graduate studies in economics at Stanford University where he distinguished himself as "one of the brightest students they ever had."

The University of Chicago hired Laffer in 1967 and he worked closely with economics Professor Robert Mundell, a Canadian citizen and reclusive gentleman who many have since acknowledged as "the godfather of modern supply-side economics."[13] Mundell and Laffer teamed up and studied the effects of taxation. In fact, Laffer popularized the work of Mundell, a future Nobel-Prize winner. Building steam in the late 1970s with its emphasis on tax cuts, the "Mundell-Laffer Hypothesis" poked holes in Jimmy Carter's Keynesian attempts to fix the economy.[14]

Even economist Paul A. Samuelson, the Keynesian Nobel-Prize winner who wrote a *Newsweek* column on alternating weeks to Friedman's column showed less enthusiasm for Carter's performance. Under the prevailing Keynesian paradigm, stagflation was supposedly a theoretical impossibility. The Carter years exposed many to the intellectual shortcomings of Keynesian thinking.

II

For analysis of the macroeconomic disappointments of the 1970s, economist Thomas Sowell's identification of two major visions is helpful, each one with a specific framework of assumptions, which dominated the political landscape in the post-World War II period. There were those confident in the human capacity to solve problems with sweeping schemes. Decision making used "the special talents and more advanced views of the few."[15] In America, political economist Alvin H. Hansen of Harvard University became the "leading proponent of Keynesianism," influencing countless students and future high-ranking officials. For three decades after his arrival at Harvard in 1937, Hansen expected the federal government to manage the economy with proper tax and spending decisions.[16] Economist Lester C. Thurow was one of many who demanded government action, arguing in a 1977 *Newsweek* article that the state needed to go further with planning and spending.[17] Both moderate liberals and progressives were confident about such government action.[18]

There was a great deal of faith in government planning and conservatives seldom experienced victories when they presented empirical evidence that pointed to the difference between the noble intentions of liberals and actual outcomes. Sowell argued that the progressive vision was "dangerously close to sealing itself off from any discordant feedback from reality." Supportive of those favoring government planning, much of the media and academia reassured those confident in government effectiveness that they were "morally on a higher plane."[19]

As Sowell saw it, in contrast to the vision of expert management of the economy were those who saw economic "tradeoffs" as the norm, which unfortunately could never satisfy the wishes of all parties. Known as the father of economics, Adam Smith (1723–1790) warned of the doctrinaire who "seems to imagine that he can arrange the different members of a great society with as much ease as the hand arranges the different pieces upon a chess-board."[20] The vision critical of progressivism held that human nature placed restrictions on idealistic schemes. There were people problems, linked to personal choices, unfixable by any amount of government programs and spending. Opponents of progressivism warned of the limitations of any elite group's attempt to "legislate bliss."

Free-market economist Friedrich Hayek wrote: "Compared with the totality of knowledge which is continually utilized in the evolution of a dynamic civilization, the difference between the knowledge that the wisest and that which the most ignorant individual can deliberately employ is comparatively insignificant." Looking back in history one could learn more from "the experiences of the many, rather than the articulated rationality of a talented few." When Hayek received the Nobel Prize in economics in 1974, he drove this message home in his acceptance speech.[21]

For Hayek and others who questioned the less activist position came charges that they lacked compassion. With its government programs, the

Democratic Party saw itself as the party for the poor. Was it not the party of the people contrasted to the Republicans as the party of the rich? Joseph A. Califano Jr., Jimmy Carter's Secretary of Health, Education, and Welfare (HEW) sought "to prove that HEW can be run, that those Great Society programs can work." Demonstrating what government could achieve was vital, Califano wrote to Carter, "because there are still in this nation millions of people whose needs can be met only by Government—and they are the most vulnerable among us."[22] To *Newsweek* readers, conservative journalist George F. Will pointed out that "[t]here is nothing gray about Califano, whose mind is a rainbow of redistributionist plans."[23]

The Keynesian approach of managing the economy to achieve full employment and low inflation appeared to be the only moral option; thus, free-market rivals were at a disadvantage in articulating that they too desired improvement for all citizens. Democrats pointed to the "greed" and "mean-spiritedness" of conservatism. Conservative economists were critical of some of Nixon's policies, but he understood the difficulties they faced with the promotion of free-market ideas: "Conservatives are always at a disadvantage when speaking about economics because their belief that some pain may be necessary now to save the patient later is conventionally interpreted by liberal politicians and commentators as 'heartlessness' or 'callous indifference to human suffering.'"[24]

Conservatives rarely scored points with their arguments that the focus of tax-and-spend politicians was on the next election not the next generation. They lamented that most journalists, society's so-called whistleblowers, seldom questioned whether progressive policies were effective in improving the economy. If there was acknowledgment of a government policy not working, often the solutions were more government spending, smarter management, or some tinkering. Of course, there were some business leaders who hardly helped the conservative cause. There were real people struggling with low-paying jobs and indifferent bosses who seemed to care more about company profits than employee morale. The employers who were uncaring about workers or appeared to be ruthless, often diverted attention from an objective assessment of policy.

It was daunting to win the day against emotion-laden positions that overshadowed empirical evidence marshaled by those critical of Keynesianism. Concerns over "cost or budget limitations were often equated with the voice of right-wing reaction." In the eyes of progressives:

"*Either you want to help people or you don't.*"[25] For example, when Hayek provided analysis that labor union wage increases came at the expense of others, that real wages often rose "much faster when unions were weak," and that it was "a myth" that union efforts caused the standard of the living of the working class to rise as fast as it could, many opponents adopted name-calling tactics rather than addressing the evidence of union activity causing unemployment.[26]

It would take a significant amount of time for challengers of Carter's economic policies to gain ground on the prevailing vision that said Keynesian economics was the only answer to restore equilibrium to an economy subject to boom-and-bust cycles and unemployment. Certainly, the post-World War II economic record of Keynesianism in the United States was impressive. Americans were responsible for the production and consumption of more than one-third of the world's goods and services, despite representing only five percent of the world's population.

III

By the 1970s, all politicians were politically vulnerable given the state of the economy. Both Ford and Carter faced economic difficulties that seemed unsolvable. Carter had his own set of problems, notably his rift with establishment Democrats and dissent from the left flank of the party. Some Democrats accused Carter of being too conservative on economic issues. Carter himself saw three major reasons for his failure to win a second term: a divided Democratic Party with progressives opposing him for supposedly abandoning Democratic principles, the Iran hostage ordeal (1979–1981), and the weak economy at election time.[27] The most progressive of the party scorned Carter's less-than-enthusiastic support for their liberalistic reform ideas.

In addition, the consequences of the Iranian Revolution clearly damaged Carter's image as a competent and strong leader. He showed more interest in redefining America's role in global affairs than domestic economic policy; thus, his weakest record of performance was the economy. Two months before the 1980 election, polling revealed that 61 percent of respondents identified "the high cost of living" as America's most important problem.[28]

Judging Carter's performance as weak, free-market economists saw little evidence of conservatism in his economic policies. Some wrote of "the left-wing administration of Jimmy Carter."[29] Chairman Karl D. Bays of the American Hospital Supply Corporation lamented Carter's attacks on the oil companies: "If he's capable of taking on the oil industry ... any of us could be next."[30] In the eyes of conservative economists and business leaders, his failure to escape Keynesian thinking was good reason to retire Carter from the White House. Pointing to the historical record, they noted that economic growth averaged 3.3 percent from the years 1945 to 1973, significantly higher than the 1.8 percent during the "stagnation decade" of 1973 to 1982.[31] Even Carter's insistence of wanting "to know every detail about everything" did not appear to bring much awareness of the shortcomings of his economic thinking.[32]

In 1980, American voters had two distinct choices. Republican nominee Ronald Reagan, viewed by many in Washington as an outsider, had been an economics major in college, a mid-twentieth-century Hollywood star, and governor of the largest state in the union. "Politicians are notoriously uninterested in economics," but Reagan was different with his passion for economic ideas. He also presented an economic policy distinct from the traditional economic message of the Republican Party: "Political history was being made: a Republican candidate promising growth, not austerity; calling for prosperity, not sacrifice."[33] Did Reagan really mean what he said on the campaign trail? Was America willing to support his economic plan?

America witnessed economic malaise, but, as this book argues, the Keynesian mindset did not die easily in political circles; Carter's supporters were hopeful of a victory over Reagan. In the face of strong media support for government management of the economy and suspicion for any "crackpot" economic theory that pushed for tax reduction amid inflation, acceptance of new free-market ideas came slowly. Even Republicans were slow to abandon the idea that tax cuts overstimulated the economy and caused higher inflation.

Progressives favored Keynesianism, and they knew little about dissenting economists. Writing in the *Nation*, Robert Skole admitted that when an American won the Nobel Prize in economics in 1976, there were journalists who asked: "Who the devil is this Milton Friedman?"[34] Economic ideas associated with the Republican Party were suspect. The Democratic Party did an impressive job of establishing itself as the compassionate party for the poor and middle class, and the shift in public opinion mainly occurred because Americans experienced harder times. Without this reality, the theory or philosophy articulated by free-market voices could only go so far.[35]

In the eyes of free-market economists, the Leviathan of big government rumbled on, only slowing when a significant number of Americans experienced, firsthand, the consequences of a stagnant economy and high inflation. It was this experience that offered an opening for non-Keynesians to state their case more broadly to the American people. From his vast experience, economist Allan Greenspan was certain that "macroeconomic forecasts are far more art than science."[36] It is certain that American politicians could be creative with the views of economists. But in the end, it came down to timing as stagflation hit Americans hard. By the late 1970s, there was so much disillusionment with "big-government liberalism" that in the past seemed to be successful.

There was an economic showdown during the 1970s as colorful as its main participants. After years of back-and-forth defeats and partial victories, free-market proponents finally saw the climate of opinion change enough to see Ronald Reagan—a genuine economic conservative—elected president of the United States. The rise of this "entrepreneur" to the White House is a story of "revolutionary change."[37] Nevertheless, the narrative begins many years earlier with the brilliant British economist named John Maynard Keynes. The 1970s confrontation between conservatism and a progressive vision of the economy had its roots in the economic and political response to the Great Depression. There was a winner. In the post-World War II years up to the Johnson administration, it was not much of a contest—Keynesianism dominated.

Notes

1. Elizabeth Drew, *Portrait of an Election: The 1980 Presidential Campaign* (New York: Simon & Schuster, 1981), 305, 310–312, 319, 322, 325.
2. On the Religious Right and economics, see Eric R. Crouse, *The Cross and Reaganomics: Conservative Christians Defending Ronald Reagan* (Lanham, MD: Lexington Books, 2013). On the important role of cultural issues generating votes for Reagan, see Donald T. Critchlow, *Phyllis Schafly and Grassroots Conservatism: A Woman's Crusade* (Princeton, NJ: Princeton University Press, 2005); and Donald T. Critchlow, *The Conservative Ascendancy: How the Republican Right Rose to Power in Modern America*, Section Edition (Lawrence: University Press of Kansas, 2011).
3. Contrast to microeconomic attention on individuals and businesses, macroeconomics involves the study of the effects of government on the national economy.

4. Jimmy Carter, *White House Diary* (New York: Farrar, Straus and Giroux, 2010), 496–497.
5. A study that explores this occurring beyond the United States is Daniel Yergin and Joseph Stanislaw, *The Commanding Heights: The Battle Between Government and the Marketplace That Is Remaking the Modern World* (New York: Simon & Schuster, 1998).
6. William E. Simon, *A Time for Truth* (New York: Reader's Digest Press, 1978), 26, 31.
7. Yergin and Stanislaw, *The Commanding Heights*, 12, 20.
8. Kenneth W. Thompson, ed., *The Carter Presidency: Fourteen Intimate Perspectives of Jimmy Carter* (Lanham, MD: University of Press of America, Inc., 1990), 32–33.
9. Yergin and Stanislaw, *The Commanding Heights*, 12.
10. Milton Friedman and Rose D. Friedman, *Two Lucky People: Memoirs* (Chicago: University of Chicago Press, 1998), 458–459.
11. Martin Anderson, *Revolution* (New York: Harcourt Brace Jovanovich, 1988), 172–173.
12. I adopt George Nash's definition of the conservative movement as being composed of three major components: libertarians, new conservative traditionalists, and anti-Communists. Consequently, I mostly use the term *conservative* to describe free marketers, but technically *libertarian* would be a more accurate term in some cases, especially for those who refused to identify as a "conservative." See George H. Nash, *The Conservative Intellectual Movement in America Since 1945,* Thirtieth-Anniversary Edition (Wilmington, DE: ISI Books, 2008).
13. Anderson, *Revolution*, 146.
14. Brian Domitrovic, *Econoclasts: The Rebels Who Sparked the Supply-Side Revolution and Restored American Prosperity* (Wilmington, DE: ISI Books, 2009), 11, 15.
15. Thomas Sowell, *The Vision of the Anointed: Self-Congratulation as a Basis for Social Policy* (New York: Basic Books, 1995), ix–x, 3–4, 111–112. Although not adopting Sowell's categories of "anointed" and "benighted," my study appreciates Sowell's point that the dominant intelligentsia appeared reluctant to test competing ideas. At least in the popular press that I used in my research, it is difficult to find any close analysis of free-market ideas by supporters of progressivism. A similar study of visions that is more historical and less polemic is Thomas Sowell, *A Conflict of Visions: Ideological Origins of Political Struggle* (New York: Basic Books, 2007).
16. John E. Miller, "From South Dakota Farm to Harvard Seminar: Alvin H. Hansen, America's Prophet of Keynesianism," *The Historian*, 64, nos. 3–4 (2002): 603–622.
17. *Newsweek*, February 14, 1977, 11.

18. There are many difficulties in defining the terms *liberal* and *progressive*. Sometimes I use them interchangeably, but I usually categorize moderate liberals and progressives under the general banner of liberalism. However, I use the term progressive whenever it is relevant to clarify that a progressive is further to the left than a moderate liberal. For example, in publications, such as the *Nation*, the authors were progressives. I prefer not to use the term "left-wing" (and for that matter, "right-wing") as it complicates the field, notably when one adds socialists, who have had their own battles with liberals, in the mix.
19. Sowell, *The Vision of the Anointed*, 1, 3. Also, Tom Bethel, "The Myth of an Adversary Press," *Harper's*, January 1977, 34. According to Bethel, "[h]aving chosen the only important side—that of big government and all its works—the media can affect an Olympian stance with regard to mere squabbling of factions."
20. Sowell, *The Vision of the Anointed*, 112–113.
21. Ibid., 4, 125, 129. See Hayek's Nobel Memorial Lecture in Friedrich A. Hayek, *New Studies in Philosophy, Politics, Economics and the History of Ideas* (Chicago: University of Chicago Press, 1978), chapter 2 ("The Pretence of Knowledge").
22. Joseph A. Califano Jr., *Governing America: An Insider's Report from the White House and the Cabinet* (New York: Simon & Schuster, 1981), 16, 437.
23. George F. Will, "The Hot Seat," *Newsweek*, March 7, 1977, 96.
24. Richard Nixon, *RN: The Memoirs of Richard Nixon* (New York: Grosset & Dunlap, 1978), 522.
25. Ken Auletta, *The Streets Were Paved with Gold* (New York: Vintage Books, 1980), 216. Italics in original.
26. On Hayek's arguments on labor and employment, see Friedrich A. Hayek, *A Tiger by the Tail: The Keynesian Legacy of Inflation* (San Francisco: Cato Institute, 1979), 63–86.
27. Jimmy Carter, *Keeping Faith: Memoirs of a President* (Fayetteville: University of Arkansas Press, 1995), 576–577. Carter, *White House Diary*, 527–530.
28. See W. Carl Biven, *Jimmy Carter's Economy: Policy in an Age of Limits* (Chapel Hill: The University of North Carolina, 2002), 1–3.
29. For example, Anderson, *Revolution*, xvi. According to Anderson, "American liberalism is but a pale cousin of real socialism, and a very distant relation to the real thing, communism" (8).
30. *Newsweek*, October 24, 1977, 39.
31. Domitrovic, *Econoclasts*, 5.

32. Many high officials in the White House learned of this Carter trait. Shirley Hufstedler, secretary of education in 1979–1981, states: "The fact is that President Carter wanted to know every detail about everything. He knew all the details about all the programs of all the departments…." See Thompson, ed., *The Carter Presidency*, 31.
33. Rowland Evans and Robert Novak, *The Reagan Revolution* (New York: E. P. Dutton, 1981), 9, 83.
34. Robert Skole, "En-Nobeling Milton Friedman," *Nation*, January 22, 1977, 68.
35. Friedman makes this point in his 1982 preface in *Capitalism and Freedom*, xiii.
36. Alan Greenspan, *The Age of Turbulence: Adventures in a New World* (New York: Penguin Press, 2007), 55.
37. Evans and Novak, *The Reagan Revolution*, xiv, 8–9. According to Evans and Novak, Reagan's "whole life was entrepreneurial. His career was deeply affected by the management and organization and financial success of a business enterprise, however personal the ventures" (9).

CHAPTER 2

The Keynesian Revolution, 1936–1965

When 50-year-old economist Alvin H. Hansen arrived at Harvard University from the University of Minnesota in 1937, it was the beginning of a new era of economic thinking. An excellent representative of Keynesianism, he made good use of his subsequent decades at Harvard, sharing his passion for Keynesian ideas to "improve the lot of humanity." He taught hundreds of economics students including future Nobel-Prize winner Paul Samuelson, the author of an economics college textbook loaded with Keynesian ideas that sold millions of copies.[1] Following the teachings of Hansen and Samuelson, young economists recommended planned deficit spending and public debt as the best way to invigorate the American economy to get it out of recessions and depressions. Consequently, these economists received a warm welcome from many Washington politicians.

In politics, the main beneficiary of the rise of Keynesianism was the Democratic Party. From the years 1860 to 1932, the Democrats held the presidency for 16 years, far short of the 56 years for Republicans. From 1933 to 1969, the Democrats held the presidency for 28 years compared to 8 years for Republicans. Before the Great Depression, government spending at the federal, state, and local levels rarely exceeded 12 percent of the national income; however, by the 1970s government spending rose to more than 40 percent of the national income.

As Milton Friedman saw it, there was "a major change in both the public's perception of the role of government and the actual role assigned to

E. R. Crouse, *America's Failing Economy and the Rise of Ronald Reagan*,
https://doi.org/10.1007/978-3-319-70545-3_2

government." These numbers were evidence of the shift "from belief in individual responsibility, laissez-faire, and a decentralized and limited government to belief in social responsibility and a centralized and powerful government."[2] Whether they agreed with Friedman's choice of words, Keynesians viewed this development as positive for America. Having the electorate on their side made it all the easier for politicians to tax and spend.

I

The early history of Keynesianism is about fascinating personalities. Born on the United Kingdom's Isle of Wight, A. C. Pigou (1877–1959) was a bright scholar who became known as the father of modern welfare economics, mainly for his work on the tradeoff between economic growth and equity for workers. The redistribution of money to the poor (via progressive taxation) made sense to him providing the economic well-being of the nation stayed strong.[3] In the years 1908 to 1943, Pigou was chair of Political Economy at the University of Cambridge, a position previously held by Alfred Marshall (1842–1942), one of the most influential economists in history who "helped make economics a field of study in its own right." Pigou taught his students that understanding economics was one way to "see through the bogus economic arguments of the politicians."[4]

Known for his frugality, vanity, and idiosyncratic character, he cut a distinctive figure walking through the Cambridge campus, poorly dressed, with his head down, seemingly unaware of the centuries-old university buildings he passed. In the 1950s, Pigou continued to wear a suit he had purchased before World War I. Polite social etiquette was for others; while in retirement, he showed no enthusiasm to welcome a visit by Milton Friedman who viewed the eccentric Pigou as a "great economist."[5]

As impressive as his Cambridge academic position was, Pigou worked at the same time as John Maynard Keynes (1883–1946), another University of Cambridge graduate in economics and a Pigou rival who gained worldwide fame as the most influential economist of the twentieth century. On Keynes's celebrated work, *The General Theory of Employment, Interest and Money* (1936), in 1951 Pigou wrote: "We frequently read of 'the Keynesian revolution.' Indeed, Keynesianism, or perhaps I should rather say Keynesianism without the tears—for how many Keynesians, or, for that matter, anti-Keynesians either, have seriously studied his own book?"[6] During the Jimmy Carter presidency, economist Edward Meadows of the

University of South Carolina declared "that not one Keynesian economist in a hundred has ever read the *General Theory*."[7]

In Pigou's day, Keynes's "inconsistent use of terms" caused his book to be "barely intelligible" even for professional economists. Few took the time to plow through Keynes's contorted and obscure writing, including run-on sentences loaded with semicolons. Nonetheless, Pigou spoke as one who had professional friction with Keynes; they were two scholars—both homosexuals—who tore apart each other's academic work. An early opponent of Keynesianism, Pigou had reprimanded Keynes for his arrogant statements in *The General Theory*.[8] As it turned out, it did not matter that people did not read Keynes. The basic ideas from his work were enough for those advocating government interventions to smooth jarring boom–bust business cycles.

John Maynard Keynes was born in England to a distinguished family, his father a professor at the University of Cambridge and his mother the mayor of Cambridge. He attended the best schools, completing his education at the University of Cambridge where he was part of a group that embraced bohemian ideas. Historians describe him as a promiscuous man who fit well into the Bloomsbury Group that rejected Victorian conventions.[9] Years later he admitted the group's dismissal of traditional morals and wisdom. As he wrote in his memoirs, "We were, that is to say, in the strict sense of the term, immoralists."[10]

Keynes was, historian Margaret MacMillan writes, a "very clever, rather ugly young man."[11] He was both charming and intimidating. Free-market scholar Friedrich Hayek (1899–1992), who later won a Nobel Prize in economics, crossed swords with Keynes on many occasions, but he recognized his good fortune to experience "the magnetism of the brilliant conversationalist with his wide range of interests and his bewitching voice."[12] Hayek was one of the few who did not allow Keynes to browbeat him, thus earning his respect.

After graduating from Cambridge, the gifted Keynes scored second place on the British Civil Service exam that led to a two-year civil service position in India. Following his return, he taught economics at Cambridge. During World War I, he worked at the British Treasury, a job that caused him emotional pain. In a December 1917 letter to Duncan Grant, one of his lovers, Keynes admitted: "I work for a government I despise for ends I think criminal."[13] His criticism of the British government gained broader attention with the publication of *The Economic Consequences of Peace* (1920), which argued that the Versailles Peace Treaty was too harsh on

Germany. This was one of several books that brought him international fame. There was praise and there was denunciation. Historian Paul Johnson claims it was "one of the most destructive books of the century" for contributing "to the future war Keynes himself was so anxious to avert."[14]

To no one's surprise, his main message won over many Germans. The verdict of the jingoistic press was that the "pro-German" Keynes should be awarded Germany's highest award—the Iron Cross. By June 1920, sales of *The Economic Consequences of Peace* were at more than 100,000 copies worldwide, having been translated into many languages including German.[15] Certainly, Keynes spared no feelings with his attacks on the Versailles politicians he disliked. For example, in his memoirs he penned "a characteristically cruel sketch" of France's minister of finance. Louis-Lucien Klotz was "a short, plump, heavy-moustached Jew, well groomed, well kept, but with an unsteady, roving eye, and his shoulders a little bent in an instinctive deprecation." Keynes claimed that the minister attempted to slow food shipments to starving Germans.[16]

Next was his *A Tract on Monetary Reform* (1923); the book argued that central bank monetary management was the best way forward for domestic macroeconomic prosperity. In the early 1920s, the disastrous effects of inflation were obvious in places—for example, Germany where inflationary taxation was at "a preposterous and suicide point."[17] By the summer of 1923, a German needed to have a million marks to exchange for one U.S. dollar. German children played with worthless bank notes as though they were wooden blocks.

Seven years later, *A Treatise on Money* was Keynes's analysis of the savings–investment relationship as the main reason for cyclical movements in national economies. He claimed that both savings decisions by people and investment decisions by businesses needed to be equalized by the central bank, either by lowering or raising interest rates.[18] Intervention by money experts in the economy was the answer, so said Keynes.

These books and other writings were impressive, but none matched the importance of Keynes's *The General Theory*, which sought to explain the forces behind production, employment, and cyclical movements such as the 1929 to 1933 worldwide depression. This marked the arrival of a new branch of economics called *macroeconomics*. Pointing to the "misleading and disastrous" consequences of classical theory (laissez-faire policy) that had guided macroeconomic thinking since the days of Adam Smith, *The General Theory* opposed the two arguments that said full employment was the normal state of the economy and that high unemployment would eventually correct itself. Because the economy lacked the capacity for self-correction, Keynes argued that it was best to entrust intellectual elites with the task of properly managing the economy.[19]

Years later, Friedrich Hayek lamented his decision not to attack *The General Theory* in 1936. One reason he held back from his analysis is that he believed Keynes might change his mind; Keynes had done so with his *A Treatise on Money*, after Hayek "put a great deal of work into two long articles on it."[20] He recognized Keynes's "supreme mental powers," but he viewed him as "more an artist and politician than a scholar or student." Hayek, who considered Keynes a friend, explained: "If one considers how small a share of his time and energy he gave to economics, his influence on economics and the fact that he will be remembered chiefly as an economist are both miraculous and tragic."[21]

Keynes rejected the principle of government neutrality in the face of economic cycles, and he believed economic theory was a means to improve the lives of others. Yet, *The General Theory* did not push for specific government policy. It was subsequent Keynes promoters, keen for government to take on a greater role in the economy, who used its theoretical foundation for economic action. It was intellectually respectable to argue for government intervention in the economy.[22] Economies could escape recession and depression if government spending was high. If private investment spending faltered, it was the task of the government to borrow money, engage in public investment spending, and run a budget deficit if necessary. The way Keynes envisaged it, once the economy was strong, government was to stop borrowing money, decrease public investment, and repay past loans.[23] Would future politicians see it that way however?

II

As Americans struggled through the Great Depression of the 1930s, politicians felt the pressure to do something to alleviate the high unemployment and other disturbing economic realities. In his short visit to America in 1931, Keynes received a warm welcome from academics and politicians seeking new ideas. Two years later, Keynes sent President Franklin D. Roosevelt (1933–1945) a copy of his pamphlet, *The Means to Prosperity*. He also addressed the president in an open letter published late in December 1933 in *The New York Times*. The first sentence revealed much: "You have made yourself the Trustee for those in every country who seek to mend the evils of our condition by a reasoned experiment within the framework of the existing social system." For Keynes, the alternative to Roosevelt's "social reform" was for "orthodoxy and revolution to fight it out."

Even though he was critical of some of Roosevelt's policies, he sought to reassure the president: "You remain for me the ruler whose general outlook and attitude to the tasks of government are the most sympathetic in the world. You are the only one who sees the necessity of a profound change of methods and is attempting it without intolerance, tyranny or destruction." According to Keynes, by making adaptations and enlargements to the New Deal, Roosevelt could put America on the road to economic recovery with full employment, and give "comfort to men's minds through restoration of their faith in the wisdom and the power of Government!"[24]

In the 10 months prior to Keynes's letter, Roosevelt had established far-ranging policies that brought about a level of government intervention never witnessed in American economic history. Indeed, decades later, Keynesian economist John Kenneth Galbraith argued that the business and financial sector welcomed Roosevelt as "an angel of rescue."[25] Roosevelt's wife Eleanor viewed Inauguration Day in early March 1933 as "very, very solemn and a little terrifying."[26] Pledging "direct, vigorous action" in his oath of office, President Roosevelt pointed to the "incompetence" of business leaders. He reassured the American people that the only thing they had "to fear is fear itself," declaring his faith thus: "This great Nation will endure as it has endured, will revive and will prosper."[27]

In his first 100 days, Roosevelt ushered in important legislation including the Federal Emergency Relief Act, the Agricultural Adjustment Act, the Tennessee Valley Authority, and the National Industrial Recovery Act. When Roosevelt's assistant, Raymond Moley, warned him in 1933 that he was "taking an enormous step away from the philosophy of equalitarianism and laissez faire," the president replied: "If that philosophy hadn't proved to be bankrupt, Herbert Hoover would be sitting here right now."[28]

Launched with much fanfare, Roosevelt's boldest action was the creation of the National Recovery Administration (NRA) led by General Hugh Johnson. Displays of the NRA Blue Eagle Insignia were everywhere—at workplaces, in stores, and on billboards. The promotional parade on New York's Fifth Avenue was impressive, but the NRA's attempt to setup a corporatist combine to plan output and prices had a short life.

In 1935, the Supreme Court declared it unconstitutional. Director Johnson's journey was "from a reformist hellcat to a sobbing alcoholic."[29]

Before Roosevelt's New Deal it was common to see federal budgets with peacetime surpluses. A shift took place, symbolized by Roosevelt's redefinition of "freedom" in the sense that government could guarantee economic security and prosperity. It became passé to define political freedom as freedom from the state. For conservatives, this reversal of thinking meant that the government was "man's tenderhearted protector and provider" rather than a potential enemy of freedom. The government had "both the moral obligation and the competence to 'run' the macroeconomy and guarantee its citizens economic security."[30] In 1938, newspaper columnist Walter Lippmann wrote: "The predominant teachings of this age are that there are no limits to man's capacity to govern others and that, therefore, no limitations ought to be imposed on government."[31] After the New Deal, federal budgets ran in the red nearly every year.

Other numbers cast doubt on the belief that government intervention solved the economic miseries of the Great Depression. The New Deal was more a political success than an economic success.[32] Conservative scholars maintain that Roosevelt's New Deal, built on the government intervention of President Herbert Hoover in the years 1929 to 1933, prolonged the years of high unemployment and a weak economy. With Roosevelt in the White House, unemployment remained above 14 percent for the rest of the decade. If the New Deal was the answer, how does one explain the 1937 to 1938 recession and unemployment rising to 17.4 percent (the 1931 level)?[33]

Yet perceptions and a likable president mattered more than dry statistics. Roosevelt gave Americans hope when many of them faced heartbreaking, daily hardships. Most of Roosevelt's policies remained popular, and he easily won the elections in 1936 and 1940. The sending of millions of soldiers into battle in World War II and massive war production ended unemployment, not Roosevelt's interventionist policies. Nonetheless, Americans stayed true to their war president. At age 62 and in poor health, he won again in 1944. The government's extensive role in the war convinced many Americans that centralized government was efficient.[34] American soil was fertile for a Keynesian Revolution in subsequent decades.

In the immediate years after World War II, it became gospel that government planners had directed the U.S. economy to successfully ensure industrial superiority and Allied victory. Winning the day for Keynesianism were economists such as Alvin H. Hansen. The South Dakota farm boy, known for his geniality, energy, and ability to translate difficult economic ideas into laymen's terms, became "the point man" for the triumph of Keynesianism in college and government circles.[35] In Harvard classrooms, in testimonies before Washington politicians, and in public statements reaching general audiences, he earned the praise of becoming "a great teacher not only of students of economics but of a whole generation of thinking laymen."

Near the end of his life, Hansen received the following tribute from Milton Friedman: "As you know, I have often disagreed with you on substance. But I have always admired your shining intellectual integrity, your concern solely with the truth and ... your extraordinary capacity for clarity and forthrightness in exposition."[36] Hansen's popularization of Keynesian ideas made it difficult for those who wanted to slow the growth and spending of government. Even Friedman had embraced much of Keynesian thinking during World War II when he worked for the government. Years later, he admitted: "I had completely forgotten how thoroughly Keynesian I then was. I was apparently cured, or some would say corrupted, shortly after the end of the war."[37]

Early opponents to Keynesianism were few. One dissenting voice was Friedrich Hayek who witnessed how hyperinflation had destroyed the Austrian and German economies after World War I. He was a student at the University of Vienna when it barely functioned because of a shortage of coal, light, and food.[38] He feared that Keynesian economics and inflation went hand in hand. After his years challenging Keynes's work of the 1930s, he became a favorite of conservative Americans. Most of his reputation was the result of his opposition to government planning, especially by socialist politicians. Visits to the United States and an eventual teaching post at the University of Chicago brought his work to the attention of Americans concerned about government's increasing intervention in the business world.

Rejected for publication in America by three publishers before the book's acceptance by the University of Chicago Press, *The Road to Serfdom* (1944) warned of the dangers of state control of the economy. Although the University of Chicago expected modest sales at best, within a month a second and third printing were necessary to meet the demand. When *The Reader's Digest* offered a 20-page condensed version in April 1945, sales climbed higher, and Hayek attracted large crowds at speaking engagements on his American book tour. It is a controversial book: "I was at first a bit puzzled and even alarmed when I found that a book written in no party spirit and not meant to support any popular philosophy should have been so exclusively welcomed by one party and so thoroughly excoriated by the other."[39] The criticism of progressives was unmistakable with political scientist Herbert Finer claiming Hayek's book constituted "the most sinister offensive against democracy to emerge from a democratic country for many decades."[40]

Overall, Hayek was not much of a threat to those favoring economic planning.[41] Enrolled in the School of Commerce, Accounts and Finance at New York University, Alan Greenspan, future chairman of the Federal Reserve Board, witnessed how economic students were on a mission to echo the wisdom of Keynes. Many saw Keynesianism as offering a more superior path than either socialism or the classical economics of the free marketers. Memories of the Great Depression lingered. Future New York University economics professor Robert Kavesh, one of Greenspan's classmates, explained years later of the rarity "to find anyone who was not strongly influenced by the Democratic Party and John Maynard Keynes and his idea about the very strong role that government could and should play in dominating economic affairs."[42]

Greenspan acknowledged the magnitude of Keynesianism, but he was the rare young American economist who was not an ardent Keynesian. One of his closest intellectual friends, years later, was Ayn Rand, the Russian émigré who wrote influential novels championing laissez-faire capitalism. If conservatives found her secular, rationalist praise for capitalism problematic, her work became a favorite among libertarians not troubled with her attacks on Christianity. It was not ideology, however, behind Greenspan's modest attention to Keynesianism; his focus was on the technical challenges of economic thinking rather than policy.[43] In those early days, he was more passionate about classical music and playing clarinet in an orchestra, letting others take on the mission to improve society by way of macroeconomic policies.

Unpredictably, it was a 24-year-old with a recent B.A. degree in English literature who stood out for publicly challenging Keynesian and socialist theorizing. William F. Buckley Jr. (1925–2008) became an influential American public intellectual of the twentieth century. A devout Catholic, he wrote *God and Man at Yale* (1951) soon after graduating from Yale University. His book rocked academia and Yale administrators with the message for alumni to stop financially supporting the university until it ceased to undermine Christianity and free-market ideas.[44] Buckley's challenge was heresy to the old-line Yale families who defended the university's elite liberalism.[45]

The findings in *God and Man at Yale* indicated that Yale University's economic faculty was roughly 80 percent in favor of some type of economic collectivism. He acknowledged that most economic professors at Yale did not teach "the overthrow of capitalism, violently or otherwise"; however, they did follow another approach envisaged by Karl Marx—that is, "a slow increase of state power, through extended social services, taxation, and regulation, to a point where a smooth transition could be effected from an individualist to a collectivist society." If there was any confusion on where Buckley stood concerning Keynesianism, he wrote of the "slavish disciples of the late Lord Keynes" who "do not so much as acknowledge the existence of economists who violently dispute Keynes's conclusions."[46]

Yale's economics students read the introductory work of Keynesian Paul A. Samuelson who wrote: "'Cradle-to-grave' security has great popularity; if the private economy cannot supply it naturally, people will insist upon getting it artificially from governments."[47] With a strong background in mathematics, Samuelson received his Ph.D. in economics from Harvard University. The Massachusetts Institute of Technology (MIT) offered him a teaching position, and he became full professor at age 32. His authorship of a best-selling introductory textbook earned him fame and a small fortune. Beyond his scholarship on Keynesian macroeconomics, consumer choice, and international trade, Samuelson promoted expansionary macroeconomic policies in Washington, DC.[48] Describing his life philosophy, he wrote: "Mine is a simple ideology that favors the underdog and (other things equal) abhors inequality."[49]

Other required reading at Yale promoted central macroeconomic management without any tribute to the free enterprise system that, conservatives argued, raised America's standard of living to number one in the world. One textbook taught that "most Americans insist on" wealth redistribution by heavy taxation on higher income groups. Taxation during World War II was as high as 94 percent, which Ronald Reagan experienced firsthand clearing only six cents for every dollar he earned. Even when the war ended, it remained acceptable to have high taxation during peacetime.[50]

Buckley noted that in Theodore Morgan's *Income and Employment* (1947) college students learned that going into business for one's self "is not a basic freedom."[51] There was little praise for private businesses' creating employment; more sensible was government exercising its power to ensure full employment. These economists looked to the teachings of Keynes for their blueprint of government planned full employment. With war spending over, many Americans worried that jobs would be scarce.

In 1946, Congress passed the Employment Act that promoted "conditions under which there will be afforded useful employment, for those able, willing, and seeking to work."

Fortunately, postwar prosperity absorbed most war workers and veterans seeking employment. There was much faith in Keynesianism and some, such as Samuelson, rejected arguments that it would cause a high national debt. The belief that internal debt would be passed on to future generations was "unmistakably false." The overall argument was that there was no limit to government spending.[52]

Buckley warned of a troubling claim by Keynesians: "All the society's ills—the economic, the social, the ethical—can be ameliorated by Bigger and Bigger Government." Too many of these economists did "not consider private property or private enterprise essential to democracy or even to freedom."[53] For Buckley, the ideological position of Wilfrid E. Binkley, who wrote *A Grammar of American Politics—The National Government* (1949), was instructive: "It is of importance whether a Coolidge or a Roosevelt occupies the White House.... One man may be obsessed with an obstinate faith in an outmoded economic or social ideology while another is a crusader for the good life by increasing the social services of the government."[54] There was strong optimism for the notion of government creating the good life for all citizens. Besides, who could oppose this goal? No one wanted people to be without the necessities of life.

Buckley's *God and Man at Yale* created a stir; its dire warning pointed to how entrenched the policies of government intervention had become (although America escaped the state ownership policies of post-World War II Britain and France). Nonetheless, Americans paid little attention; few saw the word "liberal" in a negative light—*liberal* was "forward-looking." As late as 1960, Charles Frankel in *The New York Times Magazine* wrote that Herbert Hoover, Dwight Eisenhower, and Richard Nixon "had kind words to say about 'liberalism' and ... would bridle if he were called 'anti liberal.'"[55]

With the war-torn economies of Europe and Japan many years from recovery, it was a golden age for American production and employment. Without much international industrial competition, America experienced impressive postwar prosperity and the necessary revenue, liberal politicians believed, for increased government spending. Critics, such as Buckley, remained mostly on the periphery.

III

The first Republican president since Herbert Hoover did not reverse the enthusiasm for Keynesian thinking. Yes, President Dwight Eisenhower (1953–1961) did appoint business executives, including the president of General Motors, to his cabinet, and he stated his opposition to "artificial and arbitrary governmental controls."[56] He also declared his government's "determination to reduce the federal budget."[57] In 1957, Treasury Secretary George Humphrey argued that government spending during recession was a bad idea: "I don't think you can spend yourself rich."[58] But then again, Eisenhower made no serious assault on welfare programs, and conservatives declared he did not go far enough to reduce budgets. The issue that mystified Eisenhower and others was the power of regulatory agencies—created in the New Deal years to regulate markets and prevent monopolies. No one had a clear idea how to deal with these agencies.[59]

Economic activity in Eisenhower's last two years was modest and unemployment was relatively high, only falling below five percent for one month.[60] Given that there were recessions during the winter of 1953–1954, in 1957–1958, and in 1960, the notion of "Eisenhower prosperity" was off the mark. In fact, economic growth for the Eisenhower years was only 2.4 percent, about half of the rate of growth during the Truman years. The 1948 tax cut and the government's commitment to eliminate the debt resulted in better economic times than what took place during the Eisenhower years.[61]

The government continued to grow and most Republican leaders were unable or unwilling to alter the dominance of Keynesianism, seen as essential to keeping employment numbers healthy. The overall role of the government continued to grow and Keynesians pointed to a rising standard of living. Keynesian John Kenneth Galbraith described America's "affluent society."[62] By the early 1960s, America witnessed a transition on the issues of social welfare and employment. Economist Alvin Hansen wrote in 1961: "The progress we shall make in the decades ahead toward a truly high standard of living will depend above all else upon the degree to which we choose to employ the vast powers of a democratic government.... More and more the trend toward a 'service' society will be paralleled by the growth of the welfare state."[63]

The following year, President John F. Kennedy (1961–1963) presented his welfare message to Congress; it was to change the federal government's role in assisting Americans. Roosevelt's New Deal was the government using emergency and temporary measures to get Americans back on the right track such as financial assistance to a widow with small children in the short term. Kennedy's understanding of the role of government represented a major departure: government was to provide long-term assistance for Americans, including people disadvantaged by an unjust system. It became acceptable for the government to disseminate money to employable and healthy adults "year after year."[64]

The role of government also was to ensure full employment, and Keynesians believed that demand rarely equaled supply; thus, government was to "lift demand to the level of supply" and ensure "that what is supplied is bought." Without the injection of government spending, the volatile investment expenditures of businesses would cause workers to lose their jobs.[65] Many legislators embraced the narrative that government spending caused people's incomes to rise, triggering more consumer spending, which in turn increased the demand for goods and services.

In 1965, Washington policymakers following Keynes's ideas were able "to lift the nation through the fifth, and best, consecutive year of the most sizable, prolonged and widely distributed prosperity in history." Even businessmen were receptive. No longer viewing deficit spending as immoral, they supported government intervention to minimize recession or inflation. Optimism abounded; a *Time* article noted that if America has "economic problems, they are the problems of high employment, high growth and high hopes."[66]

One important tool for Keynesians during the 1960s and beyond was the Phillips curve, named after economist A. W. Phillips; it demonstrated a long-term inverse relationship between unemployment and inflation (as one rose, the other declined). Since the Kennedy administration, policymakers used the curve to guide the government's objective of full employment, defined as approximately four percent unemployment. Because of labor market frictions (going from one job to another took time) zero unemployment was an unrealistic marker. Using the Phillips curve, Keynesian policymakers argued that an unemployment rate of four percent in the United States would only mean an inflation rate of about three percent, seen as a reasonable tradeoff.[67]

Macroeconomic management of the economy looked promising. Besides, many legislators saw no advantage in exercising financial restraint. Political leaders gained power by promising to pay and solve the economic problems that concerned vocal groups, who wanted more government programs to meet their needs.[68] The normalization of greater government intervention and the welfare state opened the door for others to press for more radical changes.

Radicalism, birthed in the 1950s, came in many shapes with distinct agendas. With the rise of the so-called New Left, there was criticism of those "pragmatic liberals" who were unwilling to go the distance for genuine reform. If members of the New Left were reluctant to embrace revolutionary Marxism, they at least were enthusiastic about the ideas of American intellectuals such as C. Wright Mills, a sociologist at Columbia University.

In *The Power Elite* (1956), Mills pointed to the shortcomings of establishment thinking that corrupted liberalism. An impoverished postwar liberalism saw no liberals defending "any left or even any militantly liberal position." In this climate, there was no negative stereotype "widely formed of the corporate rich and the political outsider; and if one or two should crop up in popular imagery, they are soon vanquished by the 'forward-looking,' energetic, clean-cut American boy as executive." Mills lamented that "two or three hundred giant corporations" dominated the economy.[69]

In the early 1960s, one important college radical wrote his sociology master's thesis on Mills. University of Michigan graduate student and Irish-Catholic Tom Hayden was a leader of Students for a Democratic Society (SDS), the leading organization of the New Left. According to Hayden, there was much wrong with America. Half of the early SDS elite were from broken homes and so it filled a void for young radicals desiring "to find a community of peers to take seriously and be taken seriously by."[70] Hayden spearheaded its manifesto, called the Port Huron Statement, written in 1962 in a rundown union building in Port Huron, Michigan.

In five days, delegates, many experiencing sleepless nights because of intense excitement and "pure exaltation," put together a 50-page document that identified "their intellectual and political home." Nevertheless, there were notable tensions. When 17-year-old Jim Hawley, an activist in the Communist Party orbit, crashed the gathering, a few opposed his presence while most voted that he stay as an observer. His seating symbolized a significant trajectory of Left activism.[71] America, the Left argued, could do better than Keynesianism.

The Port Huron Statement was a rambling document covering a wide range of political causes. There was a sense of urgency to find "revolutionary leadership" to correct modern problems, many mired in traditional thinking. A significant component of the statement was on the economy:

the power of the wealthiest one percent, the scandal of 35 million in poverty, the shortsightedness of consumerism and materialism, the lost jobs and social dislocation caused by automation, and the evil of "Big Business." The American economy was the envy of the world, but the radical students demanded more: "We take for granted the existence and desirability of the New Deal reforms, and we look with anger at the legacies, the unfinished reforms, of our liberal ancestors."[72] It was time for political action.

Responding to an earlier draft of the statement, one of Hayden's friends advised caution. Well-known socialist and Irish-Catholic Michael Harrington wanted Hayden's draft to be more critical of the Soviet Union; it appeared "to imply the United States was the prime source of evil in the Cold War."[73] In his mid-30s, Harrington was someone worth listening to. His book, *The Other America* (1962), received widespread attention among liberals. Born in 1928 and educated at Holy Cross College, Yale University Law School, and the University of Chicago (M.A. in English Literature), Harrington worked as an editor for the *Catholic Worker* in the early 1950s and later joined the Young People's Socialist League, the youth affiliate of the American Socialist Party.

In *The Other America*, Harrington argued that there were as many as 50 million poor Americans who were "becoming increasingly invisible." As he saw it, the welfare state "helped the poor least of all."[74] It favored not the desperate, but those who were "capable of helping themselves."[75] In affluent America, it was little consolation that the poor were better off than the poor in Italy, India, Russia, or an earlier America. His standard of comparison was how much better the poor "could be if only we were stirred."[76] Harrington discussed various categories of the classic poor, including a subculture of poverty composed of "intellectuals, bohemians, [and] beats" who were graduate students and artistic others who rejected standard social conventions and the working world. This subculture lived "in the midst of physical deprivation."[77]

One major problem for the poor was housing, but the building of low-cost projects fell short of the demand. An estimate to cure the problem of slums was a $125 billion investment that was "not beyond the bounds of possibility."[78] There was hope in the labor movement, but the best approach to fight poverty was federal government planning, using "knowledge in a rational and systematic way."[79] Washington had money and location for coordination and national planning.[80] Harrington, Hayden, and a growing number of young leftists desired deliberate centralized economic planning instead of modest macroeconomic management.

IV

Harrington influenced the New Left and many others into the 1970s.[81] With his book there was less consideration that independent choice played a role in people not having employment. Few denied Harrington's concern for the poor, yet his assessment of the poor as victims had a destructive legacy, according to conservatives. When he argued that economic expansion was not helpful to the poorest poor and that the poor's self-destructive behavior had little relevance, he gave poverty activists a false understanding of economic inequality. Guided by such thinking, academia, the press, and the judiciary told the poor their condition was due more to a defective economic order than issues of personal responsibility and self-control.[82]

Some radicals found themselves on another path. Former Marxist economist Thomas Sowell was one who had experienced an ideological transformation and his publications during the 1970s were part of the shift to free-market ideas offering new solutions to economic malaise. Born in 1930 in North Carolina, Sowell never met his father who died before the newborn entered the world. Having four other children, his mother was unable to care for the new baby. Aunt Molly "Mama" raised Thomas, who learned later in life that he had brothers and sisters. There were many years of living in poverty. One of "the most amazing things" in his childhood was learning that hot water could come from an indoor faucet.

Mama and Thomas moved to New York City before he turned nine and Harlem was an education for the young Sowell. One day a white kid asked him why he did not act "like the colored people" in the movies. Sowell answered: "Well, they get paid to act that way—and I don't." How did Sowell act? Apparently not foolishly, except for the school pranks. Teachers discovered his high intelligence. Pity the teacher who received Sowell's answer to a question—in Latin. Then, there was the teacher who gave him a 93 on a term report, even though he never scored less than 95 on any test. Confronted by a stubborn Sowell, the "long-suffering man" changed the mark to 96.[83]

Nonetheless, stubbornness is good and bad, and at age 16 Sowell quit high school. His first full-time job was as a Western Union messenger. He lived alone, experiencing periods of unemployment and often down to his last dollar as he juggled work with night school. His appetite for reading was enormous and he bought an old set of encyclopedias for $1.17 and under the entry on Karl Marx were "ideas I was to be attracted to for the next decade."[84] After serving two years in the Marine Corps, Sowell entered Howard University followed by Harvard University. He graduated from Harvard magna cum laude, writing an impressive honors thesis on Karl Marx.

Next, he earned his Master's degree in economics at Columbia University—in nine months, the minimum time allowed—writing his thesis on Marx's business cycle theory. Still a Marxist, Sowell got his Ph.D. at the University of Chicago, where he took classes from professors such as Milton Friedman. It was not his academic education that pushed him to question whether government intervention was beneficial. After working as an intern at the U.S. Department of Labor in 1960, Sowell began rethinking the idea of government as a "benevolent force in the economy and society."[85]

Sowell focused his research on how the free market presented opportunities for all Americans. There was economic progress for all ethnic groups, an important observation given that many people in the world continued to "live at an economic level not much above that of their ancestors." The greatest improvement in the United States was Jews who rose from nineteenth-century poverty to earning more than any other ethnic group by the 1970s. Much of this was because of their attitude toward self-improvement: "Jews seized upon free schools, libraries, and settlement houses in America with a tenacity and determination unexcelled and seldom approached by others."[86]

Equally important to Sowell's empirical research on economic growth was his analysis of American politics driven by either a constrained or unconstrained vision. Philosopher and economist Adam Smith was representative of the constrained vision; it recognizes human nature as unchangeable and attempts "to determine how the moral and social benefits desired could be produced in the most efficient way, within that constraint."[87] The constrained vision favors tradeoffs rather than the "perfectible" solutions implicit in the unconstrained vision.

Echoing the themes of philosopher William Godwin, modern progressives in America believed in the unconstrained possibilities of humans and were confident of solving social problems institutionally. This vision saw the promise of government in improving the economy: "[P]overty or other sources of dissatisfaction could only be a result of evil intentions or blindness to solutions readily achievable by changing existing institutions."[88] Sowell's *A Conflict of Visions* offers helpful insights on government action; however, his critical evaluations of government in the 1960s, when he began his academic teaching, had yet to be heard beyond a small circle of people.

By the 1960s, there were only two schools of economics offering any worthwhile challenge to Keynesianism and each upheld the constrained vision that was suspicious of central planning. The Austrian School of economics led by Friedrich Hayek and Ludwig von Mises (1881–1973) made its mark as part of a growing conservative movement composed of classical liberals (libertarians), traditionalists, and anti-Communists.[89] Libertarian in their thinking, the Austrian economists were especially anti-government.[90] In addition to Hayek's *The Road to Serfdom*, Mises's *Human Action* (1949) was a compelling book on the problems of planned economies. The Austrians rejected the vision of progressives and trusted the market to allocate society's limited resources in an efficient manner.[91]

For the Austrian School, the entrepreneur was key to wealth creation, someone alert to new opportunities for innovative goods and production and willing to take a chance when there was no guarantee of success. Those who exercised poor judgment in the market were responsible for their actions; this accountability encouraged people to conduct business as intelligently as possible.[92] The Austrians distrusted economic and governmental "experts" and complicated algebraic equations or formulas that sought to manipulate economic conditions to realize market equilibrium. They knew an economy was too complex to plan and control, even by the best and brightest Keynesians who thought otherwise. For one, consumers "are constantly learning, changing tastes, and demanding new products to meet new wants."[93]

During the 1950s and 1960s, Austrian School arguments trickled down in popular form in libertarian and conservative magazines such as the *Freeman*, which was influential among conservatives despite its small readership. Economist Henry Hazlitt did much to explain Austrian economics on a popular level. In short, well-written articles, he spoke with authority and clarity when he responded to a wide range of attacks on free enterprise. In Hazlitt's eyes, the free market was the "most 'human' of all systems" because of its ability to provide a wealth of goods and services for everyone. With simple language, he exposed what he saw were the problems with too much government intervention. The imposition of a progressive income tax, minimum wage laws, coercive unionism, and flawed welfare policies all represented a "sabotaged" capitalism.[94]

The Chicago School of economics, which made major contributions on monetary theory, likewise presented important critiques of Keynesian thinking.[95] In addition to reaffirming classical theory, monetarists focused on the role of money in causing both inflation and cyclical disturbances. They saw the Keynesian preoccupation with fiscal policy as misguided.[96] The key spokesman was Milton Friedman whose parents came from the small town of Beregszasz located in Austro-Hungary. Both emigrated to the United States in the 1890s and met and married later in Brooklyn, New York. His father was self-employed as a petty trader and his mother's working experience began as a seamstress in a "sweatshop." Contrary to the bad reputation of sweatshops, she never spoke negatively of her seamstress work.

Friedman entered Rutgers University at age 16 and worked part time to pay for his tuition. Before he went to the University of Chicago for graduate studies, he did a stint of door-to-door encyclopedia sales.[97] A good scholarship led him to Columbia University where he completed his Ph.D. Friedman had established ties with the Austrian School through his participation in the Mount Pélerin Society, an organization named after Mount Pélerin in Switzerland where prominent free-market economists held a conference in 1947. Subsequent yearly conferences earned the Mount Pélerin Society the title of the "international 'who's who'" of non-statist scholars.[98]

Friedman feared the government was serving "as a parent charged with the duty of coercing some to aid others." He lamented the popular belief that individuals faced uncontrollable forces, and, thus, the government's role went beyond acting as an umpire; government was to intervene by way of the growing number of "benevolent" public servants. It seemed that older notions of individual responsibility, laissez-faire, and smaller government were of the past and out of step with a progressive vision. The modern welfare state was the government taking the leading role and responsibility in making society better rather than the individual.[99]

Friedman's book, *Capitalism and Freedom* published in 1962, represented a "daring and iconoclastic assault" on the failures of conventional "liberal wisdom."[100] He was one of the first economists to make a strong case that the severe unemployment of the Great Depression was a result of "government mismanagement" rather than systematic problems with capitalism.[101] One lesson he learned from history was how the concentrated power of statist planners wrought havoc. As he saw it, "the country is the collection of individuals who compose it, not something over and above them."[102] To ensure freedom, he wanted government power limited and dispersed.

Friedman observed that many arguments against the free market hinted of "a lack of belief in freedom itself." Egalitarians arguing for justice in economic policies inevitably would chose equality over freedom, whereas Friedman understood that at some point "equality comes sharply into conflict with freedom."[103] The ideas expressed in *Capitalism and Freedom* found an audience and the publisher sold hundreds of thousands of copies. Nonetheless, his vision was at odds with much of the mainstream press; *The New York Times*, *Chicago Tribune*, *Newsweek*, and other major national publications failed to review the book.[104]

The following year Milton Friedman and Anna J. Schwartz published the pathbreaking *A Monetary History of the United States, 1867–1960* that, according to economist Mark Skousen, "did more than any other work to dispel the conventional wisdom that unfettered capitalism was responsible for" the irregular up and down of production and jobs—that is, the business cycle. The statistical evidence compiled by Friedman and Schwartz was prodigious and challenged many nonbelievers to seriously reconsider the role of monetary policy in cyclical movements of economic activity.[105]

Keynesians faced a valiant opponent who possessed learning and wit. Friedman's election as the president of the American Economic Association in 1967 was evidence of his international reputation as a scholar. If press accounts are an accurate indicator, many liberals ignored free-market economists. But then again, he and other Chicago School economists had one significant advantage over the Austrian School. Suspicious of "quantitative economics," Mises and the Austrians favored "a gigantic philosophy of human action which opposed interventionism on principle." More relevant to academia, the Chicago School welcomed the empirical data of economic scholarship used to demonstrate how "government programs actually malfunctioned in practice."[106]

While the Austrian and Chicago Economic Schools continued their criticisms of Keynesianism, there was a future Nobel Prize-winning economist setting the foundation of another school of economics that became a major player years later. In the early 1960s, Robert Mundell presented interesting work on taxation, charting new territory that earned him many academic awards in the future.[107] Mundell seemed an unlikely scholar to shake up American economic thinking. A Canadian who lived his early years near Kingston, Ontario, before moving with his family to British Columbia, he studied economics at the University of British Columbia while working an assortment of jobs. The next stop for him was the University of Washington in Seattle and finally MIT on a scholarship.

He entered MIT with "zero" knowledge of calculus, but he was a quick learner and earned the reputation as an expert in composing graphs in economics.

A fellowship at the London School of Economics introduced Mundell to key economic luminaries. After completing his Ph.D. in 1956, he taught at several universities as he worked on an economic policy favoring monetary tightness and lower taxes. Tight money caused interest rates to rise, which attracted foreign capital, and lower taxes encouraged greater production and employment. The idea of foreign capital flow threw a wrench in the Keynesian notion of national economic management.[108] Still, Mundell's work was just economic theory, only exciting to a few academics. It would be a number of years before challenges to Keynesianism began to take political expression and reach the attention of others outside the field of economic scholarship.

The Keynesianism that economics professors, such as Harvard's Alvin Hansen, taught was the language many politicians embraced. It encouraged the government to stimulate the economy and, thus, promise opportunity for the American people. The free-market theory of the Austrian and Chicago Schools remained completely outside the circle of most Washington politicians. There were too few challengers, even if several were future Nobel Prize winners, to make a significant impact on how politicians interpreted Keynesian ideas. The Keynesian Revolution persisted, virtually unaffected by challenges from radicals and free-market scholars during the 1960s. Most Americans enjoyed unprecedented affluence and confidence for the future.

There was little for them to complain about; Keynesian micromanagement of the economy seemed successful. Simply put, deficit spending remained an attractive option for stimulating the American economy out of recession, and the Democratic Party benefited greatly. Lyndon Johnson was ready to take the Keynesian Revolution one extra step to make society great. In addition, Richard Nixon surprised many with economic policies much in line with Keynesian thinking.

Notes

1. John E. Miller, "From South Dakota Farm to Harvard Seminar: Alvin H. Hansen, America's Prophet of Keynesianism," *Historian*, 64, nos. 3–4 (2002): 604, 608, 614, 620.
2. Milton Friedman and Rose Friedman, *Free to Choose: A Personal Statement* (Orlando, FL: Harcourt, 1990), 91–92.

3. Steven Pressman, *Fifty Major Economists*, Third Edition (New York: Routledge, 2014), 137.
4. Pressman, *Fifty Major Economists*, 86, 134.
5. Ibid., 134–135. Milton Friedman and Rose D. Friedman, *Two Lucky People: Memoirs* (Chicago: University of Chicago Press, 1998), 53.
6. A. C. Pigou, *Keynes's General Theory: A Retrospective View* (London: Macmillan & Co. Ltd., 1951), 1.
7. Edward Meadows, "The Decadence of Economic Theory," *National Review*, January 6, 1978, 23.
8. Nicholas Wapshott, *Keynes Hayek: The Clash That Defined Modern Economics* (New York: W. W. Norton & Company, 2011), 172–173.
9. Pressman, *Fifty Major Economists*, 140. On his homosexuality, see Paul Johnson, *Modern Times: The World from the Twenties to the Nineties*, Revised Edition (New York: HarperPerennial, 2001), 29–30, 167. Wapshott, *Keynes Hayek*, 5–6. Margaret MacMillan, *Paris 1919: Six Months That Changed the World* (New York: Random House, 2003), 478. W. Carl Biven, *Who Killed John Maynard Keynes? Conflicts in the Evolution of Economic Policy* (Homewood, IL: Dow Jones-Irwin, 1989), 11–12. At age 42, Keynes married Russian dancer Lydia Lopokova.
10. John Maynard Keynes, *Two Memoirs* (London: Rupert Hart-Davis, 1949), 98.
11. MacMillan, *Paris 1919*, 181.
12. Friedrich A. Hayek, *A Tiger by the Tail: The Keynesian Legacy of Inflation* (San Francisco: Cato Institute, 1979), 97–98.
13. Quoted in Johnson, *Modern Times*, 30.
14. Ibid., 30. In *Paris 1919*, Margaret MacMillan also disagrees with Keynes. She writes: "When historians look, as they have increasingly been doing, at the other details, the picture of Germany crushed by a vindictive peace cannot be sustained" (481).
15. Wapshott, *Keynes Hayek*, 13–14.
16. Quoted in MacMillan, *Paris 1919*, 190.
17. John Maynard Keynes, *A Tract on Monetary Reform* (LaVerge, TN: BN Publishing, 2008), 60.
18. See Wapshott, *Keynes Hayek*, 54–56. Pressman, *Fifty Major Economists*, 141–142.
19. Pressman, *Fifty Major Economists*, 142. John Maynard Keynes, *The General Theory of Employment, Interest, and Money* (New York: Harcourt, 1964), 3. Biven, *Who Killed John Maynard Keynes?*, 15.
20. Hayek, *A Tiger by the Tail*, 98.
21. Ibid., 102.
22. Keynes writes, the book's "main purpose is to deal with difficult questions of theory, and only in the second place with the application of this

theory to practice." See Keynes, *The General Theory of Employment, Interest, and Money*, v. Biven, *Who Killed John Maynard Keynes?*, 36.

23. Pressman, *Fifty Major Economists*, 145.
24. Keynes's Letter to Roosevelt: la.utexas.edu/users/hcleaver/368/368KeynesOpenLetFDRtable.pdf (accessed April 5, 2016).
25. John Kenneth Galbraith, *A Life in Our Times: Memoirs* (Boston: Houghton Mifflin, 1981), 40.
26. Daniel Yergin and Joseph Stanislaw, *The Commanding Heights: The Battle Between Government and the Marketplace That Is Remaking the Modern World* (New York: Simon & Schuster, 1998), 51.
27. Franklin D. Roosevelt: "Inaugural Address," March 4, 1933. Online by Gerhard Peters and John T. Woolley, The American Presidency Project, http://www.presidency.ucsb.edu/ws/?pid=14473 (accessed August 18, 2017).
28. Yergin and Stanislaw, *The Commanding Heights*, 51.
29. Ibid., 52.
30. William E. Simon, *A Time for Truth* (New York: Reader's Digest Press, 1978), 113, 116.
31. Walter Lippmann, *The Good Society* (New York: Little, Brown and Company, 1937), 40.
32. Herbert Stein, *Presidential Economics: The Making of Economic Policy from Roosevelt to Clinton*, Third Revised Edition (Washington, DC: American Enterprise Institute for Public Policy Research, 1994), 63.
33. Although with less fanfare, President Hoover likewise saw government action as the solution. A participant and supporter of Roosevelt's New Deal, Rex Tugwell wrote: "I once made a list of New Deal ventures begun during Hoover's years as secretary of commerce and then as president… The New Deal owed much to what he had begun." See Amity Shlaes, *The Forgotten Man: A New History of the Great Depression* (New York: HarperCollins, 2007), 149. According to Jude Wanniski, Hoover's signing of the Smoot-Hawley Tariff Act of 1930 and bringing in higher income and business taxes were serious errors of government intervention that spelled economic disaster. See Jude Wanniski, *The Way the World Works*, Fourth Edition (Washington, DC: Regnery Publishing, Inc., 1998), 139–152. For a concise introduction to this argument, see Jim Powell, *FDR's Folly: How Roosevelt and His New Deal Prolonged the Great Depression* (New York: Three Rivers Press, 2003), vii-xvi. Henry Aaron was one Democratic scholar who acknowledged that "Rooseveltian economic policy did little to stimulate the economy." See Henry J. Aaron, *Politics and the Professors: The Great Society in Perspective* (Washington, DC: The Brookings Institution, 1978), 147.

34. Friedman, *Free to Choose*, 5, 94. The Friedmans wrote: "As to the war, it is one thing for government to exercise great control temporarily for a single overriding purpose shared by almost all citizens and for which almost all citizens are willing to make heavy sacrifices; it is a very different thing for government to control the economy permanently to promote a vaguely defined 'public interest' shaped by the enormously varied and diverse objectives of its citizens" (94–95).
35. Miller, "From South Dakota Farm to Harvard Seminar," 604, 608, 614, 620.
36. Ibid., 611, 613, 619.
37. Friedman, *Two Lucky People*, 113.
38. Pressman, *Fifty Major Economists*, 165. Sylvia Nasar, *Grand Pursuit: The Story of Economic Genius* (New York: Simon & Schuster, 2011), 275.
39. Bruce Caldwell, ed., *The Collected Works of F. A. Hayek, Volume II—The Road to Serfdom Text and Documents: The Definitive Edition* (Chicago: University of Chicago Press, 2007), 18–20.
40. Ibid., 21. Finer's statement was the first sentence of his *Road to Reaction* (1945) book.
41. Interestingly, Keynes told Hayek in a private letter that it was "a grand book." Yet he did question Hayek's judgment on drawing a line with his argument: "[Y]ou give us no guidance whatever as to where to draw it." Quoted in Caldwell, ed., *The Collected Works of F. A. Hayek, Volume II*, 24.
42. Alan Greenspan, *The Age of Turbulence: Adventures in a New World* (New York: The Penguin Press, 2007), 30.
43. Ibid., 29–30, 40, 52–53.
44. William F. Buckley Jr., *God and Man at Yale* (Washington, DC: Regnery Publishing, Inc., 2002), xi.
45. Austin W. Bramwell, in Buckley, *God and Man at Yale*, xii.
46. Ibid., lxi, 42, 58.
47. Ibid., 46.
48. Pressman, *Fifty Major Economists*, 225–226, 228.
49. Paul A. Samuelson, "My Life Philosophy: Policy Credos and Working Ways," in *Eminent Economists: Their Life Philosophies*, ed. Michael Szenberg (Cambridge: Cambridge University Press, 2001), 236.
50. Buckley, *God and Man at Yale*, 52, 54.
51. Ibid., 57.
52. Ibid., 62–67.
53. Ibid., 71, 74.
54. Ibid., 90.
55. Quoted in Charles Murray, *Losing Ground: American Social Policy, 1950–1980* (New York: Basic Books, 1994), 22.

56. Dwight D. Eisenhower, *The White House Years: Mandate for Change, 1953–1956* (Garden City, NY: Doubleday & Company, Inc., 1963), 124.
57. Ibid., 296.
58. Since 1957, many conservatives have used this quote or a similar version.
59. Yergin and Stanislaw, *The Commanding Heights*, 58.
60. Milton Friedman and Anna Jacobson Schwartz, *A Monetary History of the United States*, 1867–1960 (Princeton: NJ: Princeton University Press, 1963), 601. The authors wrote that this particular economic expansion was "the shortest expansion during the postwar period."
61. Brian Domitrovic, *Econoclasts: The Rebels Who Sparked the Supply-Side Revolution and Restored American Prosperity* (Wilmington, DE: ISI Books, 2009), 65.
62. For his critique of this affluence, see John Kenneth Galbraith, *The Affluent Society* (New York: The New American Library, 1958).
63. Quoted in Aaron, *Politics and Politicians*, 149.
64. Murray, *Losing Ground*, 18, 20, 22–23.
65. Domitrovic, *Econoclasts*, 66.
66. "U.S. Business in 1965," *Time*, December 31, 1965, 48–49, 53.
67. Biven, *Who Killed John Maynard Keynes*, 42–47.
68. Simon, *A Time for Truth*, 97–99.
69. C. Wright Mills, *The Power Elite* (New York: Oxford University Press, 1956), 7, 334, 341–342.
70. Todd Gitlin, *The Sixties: Years of Hope, Days of Rage* (New York: Bantam Books, 1989), 107.
71. Ibid., 111–113.
72. "Original draft of the Port Huron Statement," *Resistance and Revolution: The Anti-Vietnam War Movement at the University of Michigan, 1965–1972*, http://michiganintheworld.history.lsa.umich.edu/antivietnamwar/items/show/128 (accessed August 18, 2017).
73. Gitlin, *The Sixties*, 111–113.
74. Michael Harrington, *The Other America: Poverty in the United States* (Baltimore: Penguin Books, 1963), 9, 14, 16.
75. Ibid., 158.
76. Ibid., 24.
77. Ibid., 83.
78. Ibid., 137, 145, 151.
79. Ibid., 62, 164, 166.
80. Ibid., 167.
81. Myron Magnet, *The Dream and the Nightmare: The Sixties' Legacy to the Underclass* (San Francisco: Encounter Books, 1993), 121–23.
82. Ibid., 1, 125.

83. Thomas Sowell, *A Personal Odyssey* (New York: The Free Press, 2000), 1, 5, 26, 37, 40–41.
84. Ibid., 59–60.
85. Thomas Sowell, *A Man of Letters* (New York: Encounter Books, 2007), 5.
86. Thomas Sowell, *Ethnic America: A History* (New York: Basic Books, 1981), 275, 280.
87. Thomas Sowell, *A Conflict of Visions: Ideological Origins of Political Struggle* (New York: Basic Books, 2007), 12–13.
88. Ibid., 18, 23.
89. On the conservative movement, see George H. Nash, *The Conservative Intellectual Movement in America Since 1945*, Thirtieth-Anniversary Edition (Wilmington, DE: ISI Books, 2008), xx.
90. Henry Hazlitt, "Understanding 'Austrian' Economics," *Freeman* 31, no. 2 (1981): 73.
91. Mises's *Socialism* first appeared in 1922 (English translation in 1936) and *Human Action* in 1940 (English translation in 1949). Hayek wrote that for "those of us who experienced its first impact, *Socialism* will always be his decisive contribution." See Ludwig von Mises, *Socialism: An Economic and Sociological Analysis*, trans. J. Kahane (Indianapolis, IN: Liberty Fund, 1981), xxii.
92. Jack High, "The Case for Austrian Economics," *The Intercollegiate Review*, 20, no. 2 (1984): 39.
93. Charles McDaniel, *God & Money: The Moral Challenge of Capitalism* (Lanham, MD: Rowman & Littlefield, 2007), 10. Craig M. Gay, *With Liberty and Justice for Whom? The Recent Evangelical Debate over Capitalism* (Grand Rapids, MI: William B. Eerdmans Publishing, 1991), 65n2. Nash, *The Conservative Intellectual Movement in America Since 1945*, 452. Hazlitt, "Understanding 'Austrian' Economics," 67, 71, 75–77.
94. See Henry Hazlitt, "Why Anticapitalism Grows," *Freeman* 33, no. 7 (1983): 409–412.
95. For a concise comparison of the Austrian and Chicago Schools, see Mark Skousen, *Vienna & Chicago: Friends or Foes?—A Tale of Two Schools of Free-Market Economics* (Washington, DC: Regnery Publishing, Inc., 2005), 3–8.
96. Biven, *Who Killed John Maynard Keynes?*, 56.
97. Friedman, *Two Lucky People*, 19–20, 28.
98. Nash, *The Conservative Intellectual Movement in America Since 1945*, 33–35. Friedman attended the first conference but had spotty attendance until later in his career.
99. His best articulation of these ideas came later in Friedman, *Free to Choose*, 5, 70.

100. Nash, *The Conservative Intellectual Movement in America Since 1945*, 447.
101. Milton Friedman, *Capitalism and Freedom*, 40th Anniversary Edition (Chicago: University of Chicago Press, 2002), 38.
102. Ibid., 1–2.
103. Ibid., 3, 5, 195.
104. Ibid., xi.
105. Skousen, *Vienna & Chicago*, 11.
106. Nash, *The Conservative Intellectual Movement in America Since 1945*, 452.
107. Domitrovic, *Econoclasts*, 10. The emergence of supply-side economics in the 1970s owed much to Mundell's formidable intellect.
108. Ibid., 63–65, 67–68, 74, 89. Mundell's work tested in academic circles became a key component of supply-side economics.

CHAPTER 3

Johnson's Great Society to Nixon's Gamble

Two symbolic economic events took place less than six years apart. The first was a feature article on economist John Maynard Keynes and Keynesianism by the *Time* magazine issue of December 31, 1965. In addition to Keynes's photograph on the cover, there was a lengthy and positive assessment of his impact on the United States. Keynes died in 1946, but his "central theme" continued to dominate American political thinking—it was the proper role of the government to intervene in the economy for capitalism to work at the highest level of efficiency. As *Time* explained, economic management in Washington was the new orthodoxy, and there were ample Keynesian economic experts teaching at American universities and advising politicians how government promoted growth and stability.[1] There was no shortage of momentum in society for government to take a larger role in managing or fine-tuning the economy to obtain full employment. Major federal domestic programs increased from 40 to more than 400 in the 1961 to 1969 period, causing one commentator to argue that the "domestic side of the federal government had gotten so big that it was literally impossible to grasp it, intellectually, in its entirety."[2]

The second notable event occurred on an August weekend in 1971 when 16 people from the Richard Nixon administration gathered at Camp David to discuss the economy. Economist Herbert Stein called it "one of the most exciting and dramatic events in the history of economic policy." Sworn to secrecy and cut off from all communication, the Nixon team planned the unveiling of the New Economic Policy, apparently unaware

E. R. Crouse, *America's Failing Economy and the Rise of Ronald Reagan*,
https://doi.org/10.1007/978-3-319-70545-3_3

that the name was identical to Lenin's economic plan of 1921. Preempting the popular *Bonanza* television show Sunday evening, August 15, Nixon informed viewers that the government closed the gold window and instituted price controls that froze prices and wages for up to 90 days. After the announcement, Stein's son told him: "Ideologically you should fall on your sword but existentially it's great."

During the Nixon years, the extent of government intervention in the economy was conspicuous.[3] Political journalists Rowland Evans and Robert Novak wrote that Nixon "decided to cure the problem of too much government with more government."[4] On the economy, the Lyndon Johnson administration changed the American political landscape significantly, and when Republican Richard Nixon became president, Keynesianism continued to loom large.

I

Lyndon Johnson was born in 1908 near the town of Stonewall, Texas. His schoolteacher mother pushed him to excel in school. He could read at age four and he graduated from high school at 16. After high school, he ran away from home, eluding the police and his father who wanted him arrested as a runaway. He ended up in California where he remained for almost a year working as a clerk at his cousin's law office. Johnson's later claim of holding poorly paid jobs over a period of two years was pure mythmaking as was his claim that he hitchhiked the 1500 miles back to Texas. When he returned, his parents pressured him to begin college, which he did at 19. They wanted him to read books and broaden his education at college, but he was reluctant to read books, a reluctance that continued throughout his adult life.

Unlike many of his peers in federal politics, Johnson's college education was quite modest—a degree from the Southwest Texas State Teacher's College where the academic standards were lower than at the University of Texas. Historian Robert A. Caro writes of Johnson's insecurities and that he feared not being "somebody at college."[5] In the early 1930s, he took a job as the secretary of Texas congressman Richard Kleberg. In 1937, he entered the House of Representatives and 12 years later became a senator. Another 12 years later, he entered the White House as vice president in the Kennedy Administration. On the tragic day of Kennedy's assassination in November 1963, Johnson became president, the first president from the South since the Civil War.

The Keynesian revolution allowed Johnson to be somebody; there was money for his administration to do something big for the American people. Johnson was legendary for his ability to persuade allies and outmaneuver adversaries and few matched his "prodigious energy." He drove his staff mercilessly, often to the point of complete exhaustion, and they learned of his irritation when they fell short of his demands. Johnson loved to eat, and his irritability was due in part to doctors putting him on a strict diet to control his weight.[6]

The legacies of Johnson include his Great Society of domestic programs. It was not radical enough for the emerging New Left, but it was a step in the right direction. A man who worked with Johnson day and night for three-and-half years, Joseph A. Califano Jr. wrote: "What Lyndon Johnson was about during his presidency was social and economic revolution, nothing less."[7] Confident in the abilities of government to remedy the economic and social problems of the day, Johnson favored a type of corporatism of government working with business to bring prosperity.[8] His Great Society offered major new social programs targeting healthcare, welfare, urban development, and education, to name only a few. Enacted by Congress in 1965, Medicare and Medicaid provided health care for older and poor Americans. In his first State of the Union address on January 8, 1964, Johnson declared: "Let this session of Congress be known as the session which did more for civil rights than the last hundred sessions combined; as the session which declared an all-out war on human poverty; as the session which finally recognized the health needs of all our older citizens; as the session which helped to build more homes, more schools, more libraries, and more hospitals than any single session of Congress in the history of our Republic."[9] With no fear of rising deficit spending, money was not a problem for Democrats.

The hubris of Charles Schultze, Johnson's budget director, was standard fare. He was positive that the government could prevent any major dips in the economy.[10] With economists confident of lasting prosperity, Washington policymakers could afford to attack poverty with government programs designed by the best and brightest. The previous year, Swedish economist Gunnar Myrdal told a Georgetown University audience that the United States needed "a Marshall Plan to eradicate poverty in the nation." Public spending, not private enterprise, was the way forward to a prosperous nation and the eradication of destitution.[11]

An "unconditional war on poverty in America" made good economic sense to Johnson; the return of a $1000 investment on an unemployed youth would be "forty thousand dollars in his lifetime."[12] Johnson respected Keynesian stalwart John Kenneth Galbraith who favored a new and independent agency to fight poverty. In a memo to the president, Galbraith advised: "Do not bury the program in the departments. Put it in the Executive offices, where people will know what you are doing, where it can have a new staff and a fresh man as director."[13] Johnson agreed and an independent agency that reported directly to Johnson handled the program. He wanted a "strong man" to lead and the director he chose was Sargent Shriver, John Kennedy's Director of the Peace Corps.

After meeting with "experts" from inside and outside the government, Shriver took their ideas on eliminating poverty and set up the office of the program in the old Federal Court of Claims. Perhaps a bad omen, the building was in disrepair and the poverty program moved to a bygone morgue in the basement of an abandoned emergency hospital. Shriver's people worked, Johnson wrote in his memoirs, "with a fervor and created a ferment unknown since the days of the New Deal."[14] Johnson approved the program on March 16, 1964, and sent it to Congress as the Economic Opportunity Act.

Aggressively promoting the bill in an election year was the next important step, but one obstacle was the Republicans and Southern Democrats who opposed progressive legislation. Masterfully, Johnson and the Democrats pitched the War on Poverty as a nonpartisan effort and the morally right thing to do for poor people. After visiting "the scarred mountains of Appalachia," he had plenty of anecdotes about the American poor. One was Tom Fletcher who lived in a tar-papered shack with his wife and eight children—the two oldest forced out of school by poverty. The government was there to help the Tom Fletchers of America keep their children in school.[15]

In Washington, Johnson's speeches presented a simple and powerful message: "People are just not going to stand and see their children starve and be driven out of school and be eaten up with disease in the twentieth century." The Johnson government would not accept poverty. The people "will forego stealing and they will forego fighting, and they will forego doing a lot of violent things and improper things as long as they possibly can, but they are going to eat, and they are going to learn, and they are going to grow. The quicker you find it out, the better."[16] Government investment in "human capital"—in the form of education and training—paid dividends;

a working class with greater opportunities "to produce and earn" meant a stronger nation.[17]

Passed in the Senate by a vote of 61 to 34 and by the House by 226 to 185, the poverty bill illustrated the strength of progressive thinking. On August 20, Johnson signed the Economic Opportunity Act and declared: "for the first time in all the history of the human race, a great nation is able to make and is willing to make a commitment to eradicate poverty among its people."[18] Accepted was the idea that the American economy had unused potential; economic growth was more than sufficient to absorb the cost of politician promises. The only challenge was deciding how to spend the growing national income.[19]

II

John Kenneth Galbraith's *The Affluent Society* (1957) and Michael Harrington's *The Other America* (1962) opened Joseph Califano's eyes to the social injustice of a wealthy America. Califano was born in Brooklyn, New York. After high school, he attended the College of the Holy Cross where he wrote his senior thesis on F. Scott Fitzgerald, even though he graduated as a philosophy major as was the case for all Holy Cross graduates at the time. His Jesuit education prepared him for Harvard Law School where he was sixth academically out of 456 students in his second year. This remarkable performance earned him a spot on the *Harvard Law Review*. His mother was a devout Catholic who worried that the materialistic atheism of Harvard would have a bad influence on her son. She was also clear that it was World War II and not Roosevelt's New Deal that had turned the economy around. She read and then sent him a copy of William F. Buckley's *God and Man at Yale*, warning of the rampant secularism of Ivy League education.[20] If Califano read the book, he showed no signs of adopting Buckley's economic ideas.

As a young man, he enjoyed reading the most liberal paper in the city, the *New York Post*. He visited Catholic social activist Dorothy Day, drinking her "awful tea" and hearing her argue for a "purified socialism."[21] Her ideology was too radical for him, but he had great faith in what experts working in government could achieve for society. The New Deal fascinated him, especially the role idealistic, bright young men could play in government. President John F. Kennedy (1961–1963) wanted to attract "the best talent" to government and Califano was confident of his intellectual abilities to be one of those elites shaping America. Turning down a job offer to teach law at the University of Wisconsin, he was anxious to be a part of Kennedy's "New Frontier" and "have some impact on society."[22]

Califano began as a special assistant for Department of Defense General Counsel Cyrus Vance, arriving at the Pentagon in April 1961 when the building had no security check. Califano had an embarrassing start because Vance forgot to tell his staff about him, so the young lawyer spent hours waiting in a "nondescript burgundy chair" typical for high-level government offices.[23] Did Califano make a mistake? With his first shaky day in the bureaucratic behemoth of the Pentagon behind him, he became a proud "whiz kid"—the label attached to the bright young men working for Secretary of Defense Robert McNamara.

Califano's importance increased during the Johnson administration while he worked as the special assistant to McNamara. He was a tough lawyer who played hard as a troubleshooter, but he had higher moral standards than many in his political circle. He refused the request by White House aide Bill Moyers to lie to the media about the Democratic Party not reimbursing the Pentagon for Johnson's political trips on Air Force One during the 1964 campaign.[24]

Domestic policy became Califano's passion. As he wrote in his memoirs: "Didn't Harvard Law School expect its graduates, especially its *Law Review* editors, to run the country, as so many had during the New Deal?"[25] Johnson recruited Califano to help push through the "revolutionary goals" of his "Great Society" program. Seeing it as a moral mandate, Califano embraced the idea of redistribution of wealth.[26] Even as a practicing Catholic, he was "comfortable" with Johnson being the first president to push government involvement in the "business of family planning at home and abroad." What mattered was that the government's family policy meant less poverty.[27] As Califano saw it, Johnson's domestic programs "saved" America. The Harvard man had great faith in the role of government to legislate social justice:

There was no child we could not feed; no adult we could not put to work; no disease we could not cure; no toy, food, or appliance we could not make safer; no air or water we could not clean. …[S]eeing hundreds of bills I worked on enacted into law, I believed I could do anything I put my mind to next.[28]

Although conservatives questioned the affordability of the Great Society programs, the progrowth tax cut of 1964—initially proposed by President Kennedy in late 1962—gave taxpayers and businesses more after-tax income to spend on goods and services, thereby boosting the economy and giving the Johnson administration breathing room. Unfortunately, it did not last. By late 1965, there were signs of inflation because of increased government expenditures on domestic and military programs. With living costs rising in 1965, workers demanded higher wages. The remedy for Johnson was for "immediate government action" of more taxation "to cool an overheated economy."[29] He disagreed with those who saw reduced government spending as the best strategy to hold inflation to an acceptable level.

Given that most Americans opposed higher taxes, Johnson had no choice but to proceed carefully. In his State of the Union address of January 12, 1966, he called for automobile and telephone excise taxes and faster collection of tax payments from citizens and corporations. The added $6 billion in federal revenues from these measures was welcome news for Johnson, but less welcoming was the vigorous opposition of business leaders to these additional taxes. On March 30, not one of approximately 150 businessmen invited to a White House dinner supported Johnson's plan for a tax increase.[30]

Despite this resistance, Johnson pressed for a six percent surcharge to take effect by July 1967. When July came with evidence of higher inflation than expected, he argued for a surcharge as high as 10 percent. To bolster his argument, Johnson pointed to racial injustice and deadly riots in American cities as proof for the need of additional taxation. Riots caused the death of 26 in Newark and 43 in Detroit. On August 2, in the final draft of tax legislation, with the consultation of Wilbur D. Mills, chairman of the House Ways and Means Committee, the White House wrote:

For we cannot turn our backs on the great programs that have been begun, with such promise, in the last 3-1/2 years.... Nevertheless, we must move with determination to assure that those for whom these programs were begun are not robbed by the inflation that would accompany an unacceptable deficit.[31]

Repeatedly Johnson pushed for the tax bill, but had difficulty explaining that it was a 10 percent tax on a tax and not a 10 percent increase of the income tax rate. He maintained that the tax surcharge "was the most urgent issue facing the country" next to peace in Vietnam and the world. When he told Americans on March 31, 1968, that he would not run for another term as president, he also declared: "The passage of a tax bill now, together with expenditure control that the Congress may desire and dictate, is absolutely necessary to protect this nation's security, to continue our prosperity, and to meet the needs of our people...."[32]

Aware that impassioned pleas were not enough to convince everyone, Johnson conceded that a $6 billion cut in spending might be a necessary compromise in order to reach the number of votes needed for Congress to pass the bill. When the bill went to the House, Johnson's staff predicted winning big or "not at all." It was a good prediction: 268 voted yes, 150 no. With the Senate's approval, Johnson signed the 10 percent surcharge into law on June 28.[33] Johnson got his tax bill and deficit spending continued to finance the Great Society, but inflation remained a major concern. Businesses and workers paid little attention to the government's voluntary "guideposts" for wage and price controls.

Johnson's dependence on the media to send his economic message directly to the American people did not stop him from calling reporters "puppets" who "simply respond to the pull of the most powerful strings"; he said there was "no such thing as an objective news story."[34] Still, a media sympathetic to progressive policies is only helpful to a point. When it became obvious that the economy was in trouble, no amount of positive spin could hide inflation and joblessness. Some policy failures were too visible to ignore. For example, housing subsidies was a government program with a dismal record in New York City and cities coast to coast. In 1965, the Johnson administration created the Department of Housing and Urban Development which grew to almost 20,000 employees and dispersed billions of dollars for housing programs. Earning a reputation as hotbeds of crime, public housing projects failed one after another. Commenting on housing conditions in a low-income area of Los Angeles, one man concluded that public housing was "the worst thing that ever happened to Watts."[35]

As expected, conservatives delivered harsh assessments of Johnson's administration. With dramatic language, William Simon wrote of the shattering deficits, inflation, and the transfer of "torrential sums of nonexistent cash to the pockets of the 'poor,' whose numbers and needs multiplied under the attentive supervision of the new 'poverty professional.'" Johnson's "prosperity without parallel" in American history was mostly "a vast speculative and inflationary bubble, blown up by devalued money and by ravenous borrowing from the capital markets and fed by a war without end, from which victory had been barred."[36] Helping the poor was a noble aim; however, were programs effective in assisting and strengthening families and were they fiscally responsible when the national economy was at risk of inflation? Friedrich Hayek pointed to "oversimplified Keynesianism" as the cause of much of the inflation of the postwar years.[37]

In some circles, the shine on Keynesianism and the Phillips curve diminished when unemployment and inflation failed to act like a playground seesaw, one going up while the other went down. Keynesians argued that higher unemployment meant less upward pressure on wages and prices, and lower unemployment (more jobs) meant an increase in wages and prices as a result of the tighter labor market. The Keynesian approach to fighting inflation was for the government to decrease the amount of money. To stimulate employment, Keynesians desired that the government do the opposite and increase the amount of money. Keynesian policymakers were at a loss.[38] How could the government intervene and put money in the pockets of consumers to fight stagnation while decreasing the amount of money in consumers' pockets to fight inflation? This quandary became more obvious during the 1970s.

III

Radicals spoke loudly at college campuses across the nation and their protests throughout the 1960s and into the 1970s covered the Vietnam War, racism, feminism, and capitalism. Often those protesting led privileged lives. Conservatives pointed out that the wealth created by capitalism gave radical protesters better schools and opportunities denied to most of the world, much of which was under socialist control in one form or another. Still, those desiring changes found mentors to show them the way.

One influential activist was Saul D. Alinsky, author of *Rules for Radicals: A Practical Primer for Realistic Radicals* (1971). Born in 1909 in Chicago, Alinsky did graduate work at the University of Chicago in criminology. During the Great Depression, he prepared the poor to fight oppression and his organizational skills and tactics of protest earned him international recognition. A future Democratic star attracted to his work in Chicago was college student Hillary Rodham who met Alinsky while she was a student at Wellesley College. She chose him as the subject of her senior thesis; he offered her a job after she completed college, but she went to Yale Law School instead. In her memoirs, *Living History* (2003), the former First Lady wrote that she "agreed with some of Alinsky's ideas." The idea of changing the system was appealing: "His prescription for social change required grassroots organizing that taught people to help themselves by confronting government and corporations to obtain the resources and power to improve their lives."[39]

At the beginning of *Rules for Radicals*, Alinsky acknowledged "the first radical known to man who rebelled against the establishment and did it so effectively that he at least won his own kingdom—Lucifer." Speaking highly of Satan was a unique approach to introduce a book. For progressives reading Alinsky, establishment capitalism was a good target. He wrote that today's generation "[has] rejected their materialistic backgrounds, the goal of a well-paid job, suburban home, automobile," and other status symbols representing success as understood by their parents. An important step for the community organizer was to agitate and "rub raw the resentments of the people of the community; fan the latent hostilities of many of the people to the point of overt expression."[40]

Alinsky listed 13 rules of power tactics for the "Have-Nots" to take power from the "Haves."[41] He claimed there was much raw material to work with given that most Americans felt "helpless in the huge corporate economy."[42] By disguising their power, keeping the pressure on, and causing confusion and fear, an organizer could provoke "an irrational anger" from corporate leaders. When Alinsky visited Rochester, New York, he mocked its largest company, photographic giant Eastman Kodak.

The company had no labor union, and he told a reporter: "[A]as far as I know the only thing Eastman Kodak had done on the race issue in America has been to introduce color film."[43] It was time for corporations to "forget their nonsense about 'private sectors.'" Every "corporation is public as well as private; public in that we are Americans and concerned about our national welfare." The survival of corporations would only happen if they acted on a concern for poverty and discrimination. Otherwise, it would "be the people against Madison Avenue."[44]

Others adopted diverse strategies to oppose free-market capitalism. There were those who fought the idea of economic growth, or what John Kenneth Galbraith called "the cult of production."[45] Ezra J. Mishan, a progressive economist teaching at the London School of Economics, warned that a consequence of "growthmania" was less social welfare. Another criticism of economic growth was the loss of community. Peter Laslett suggested in his book, *The World We Have Lost* (1965), that those living in the preindustrial age were happier and more intimate in the "circle of loved, familiar faces."

The bestselling book *Small Is Beautiful* (1973) by British economist E. F. Schumacher looked to the future with its motto "the maximum of well-being with the minimum of consumption."[46] Connected to the issue of consumption was population. At the bidding of the environmentalist

Sierra Club, Paul Ehrlich wrote *The Population Bomb* (1968), an alarming book about the overpopulation of the world. As an entomologist, Ehrlich had better scientific success with parasitic mites and butterflies, but he attracted attention with his promotion of policies that limited growth. He appeared many times on Johnny Carson's *Tonight Show*. Aurelio Peccei's *The Limit of Growth* (1972) was another book that influenced progressives and the position that economic growth was not the answer to America's problems.[47]

As greater government intervention in the economy became the norm, others took additional steps down the road of progressivism. The radical voices of the 1960s and early 1970s made their mark among college students, intellectuals, and various activists. In a technical sense, most were not Keynesians. However, they wanted radical economic solutions out of step with much of America. The system in place since World War II worked fine. The less radical path of Keynesianism won the day with ordinary Americans and in mainstream political circles. In fact, the Keynesian push for bigger government seemed reasonable compared to the idealistic demands of radicals.

IV

Richard Nixon was born in 1913 in the house his father Francis built in the small town of Yorba Linda, located about 30 miles from Los Angeles. Leaving behind employment in the oil fields, his father borrowed money for a service station when he expected the few automobiles on the road to multiply, replacing the horse-drawn buggy. Francis added a general store where the whole family worked and entrepreneurial life became a key component of Richard's childhood. When he was old enough, he traveled early in the morning to a market in Los Angeles to purchase fruits and vegetables for his family's business. After high school, Nixon studied at Whittier College where he learned in class that history was "more than a chronicle of past events—that it could be a tool of analysis and criticism." His academic study and participation on the college debate team convinced him of the wisdom of free trade over protectionism.[48] Next stop was Duke University Law School where he graduated near the top of his class. Returning to the West, Nixon passed the Californian bar and began working at Whittier's oldest law firm.

In late 1941, Nixon took a government job in Washington with the Office of Price Administration. An eight-month stint in the tire-rationing division gave him lasting impressions on government bureaucracy. His supervisor told him he could have a promotion if he built a small staff to assist with his work. When Nixon replied, "But I don't need a staff," the supervisor declared: "Then you won't get a promotion." He met dedicated and competent government workers, but there were others obsessed with power and took "delight in kicking people around, particularly those in the private sector."[49] Eager to be closer to the action, Nixon applied for and received a commission as a naval officer, spending the remaining years of the war in the United States and in the South Pacific.

At age 33, politics beckoned. Nixon won a seat in the House of Representatives representing the Twelfth District of California in 1946. Four years later he rose to the Senate and from 1953 to 1961 he served as vice president in the Dwight Eisenhower administration. A run for the presidency in 1960 resulted in a loss to Democrat John F. Kennedy by a slim margin of 119,000 votes out of approximately the 69 million cast. Another loss came when he ran for governor of California in 1962, defeated by Pat Brown (who lost to Ronald Reagan in 1966). Although it appeared he had left politics for good, he returned to win a close presidential victory over Democrat Hubert Humphrey in 1968.

Soon after he entered the White House, Nixon sought "to get rid of the costly failures of the Great Society."[50] His highest domestic priority was to reform the expensive and inefficient welfare system, yet he later declared: "I am now a Keynesian in economics."[51] It was significant that Nixon was the first president in the twentieth century to have the opposing political party controlling both the House and the Senate, and that he selected John Connally, a Democrat, as his Secretary of the Treasury in December 1970.

The picture one gets from reading Nixon's memoirs—his position on price controls, job creation, and productivity, for example—is a president with an economic vision much in line with conservative economists. His opposition to price and wage controls was because they interfered with the free market and built a bureaucracy with dictatorial regulatory power. Comparing government and private success in creating jobs, there was no mistake where he stood: "government enterprise" was the most costly and inefficient way to create jobs. American history revealed that the private enterprise system, despite its faults, "has waged the most successful war on poverty in the history of civilized man." Private enterprise generated change and progress whereas government discouraged change and inhibited progress.

Nixon looked to the Soviet Union as proof that America understood wealth creation: Soviet leaders have "found it necessary to turn to *our* way to increase production." But he noted a troubling trend in the United States: "At a time when the Communists are by necessity providing increased incentives for more efficient producers, the United States seems to be slowly but surely turning *their* way by discouraging incentives."[52]

Who was the real Richard Nixon in the White House? Do his 1978 memoirs clarify or confuse his economic record? Despite the statements that were appealing to conservatives, Nixon was a complex man and calculating politician who set aside principles and made bad economic decisions if such an action won him more time in the White House. In his memoirs, he pretty much, with skill, acknowledged this fact: "It is unfortunate that the *politics* of economics has come to dictate action more than the *economics* of economics. Not surprisingly, when prudence clashes with political reality, the latter sometimes triumphs." Although admitting that this oversimplification sounded too cynical, he added: "I can personally attest to how even someone with strong economic ideas can be affected by the sting of criticism and the clamor of those who want a different policy."[53]

It was clear that the momentum of Keynesianism and the welfare state was strong when Nixon entered the White House. Some advisors cautioned him to proceed slowly, not to respond with policies too conservative. In the Oval Office pacing back and forth and often waving his arms to drive home his points, Daniel Patrick Moynihan, Nixon's Democratic advisor, who was the assistant secretary of labor in the Kennedy and Johnson administrations, warned Nixon of the Great Society activists ready and willing to defend liberal programs. There were many defenders Moynihan listed: "the professional welfarists, the urban planners, the day-careers, the social workers, the public housers."

Nonetheless, Nixon had no patience to wait a year to fix a welfare system that gave families financial incentives to break up. It was public record that most families collecting welfare had absent fathers and that a large majority of welfare births were out of wedlock. Referring to the problems that Great Society programs generated, Nixon wrote: "if you could prove that your income was below a certain level you could qualify for any number of free or subsidized goods and services. I felt that this kind of approach encouraged a feeling of dependence and discouraged the kind of self-reliance that is needed to get people on their feet."[54]

The Nixon administration's answer was the Family Assistance Plan (FAP), announced on August 8, 1969. The FAP was unique in that federal financial assistance would go to both the unemployed poor and the working poor with the proviso that each person collecting benefits "accept work or training for work if suitable jobs were available within a reasonable distance." Nixon understood the risks of "making thirteen million more people eligible for federal help than were currently eligible in an effort to reward work and not punish the poor for holding jobs." The calculated cost of the program for the first year was $4 billion, yet the gamble was worth it if people became certain that jobs offered more money than staying on welfare. A job's paycheck would bring stability and provide incentive to strive for better paying jobs.[55]

Opposition to FAP from conservatives was no surprise. Many saw the "megadole" as a scheme better-suited for progressive thinkers. Yet liberals were also unhappy with FAP, arguing the payments were too small and the work requirements too repressive. The National Welfare Rights Organization (NWRO) held hearings where welfare recipients demanded: "You'd better give me something better than I'm getting on welfare." Senator George McGovern introduced a NWRO plan that, Nixon wrote, "would have put about half of America on welfare."[56] Even though FAP did pass the House on April 16, 1970, it languished in the Senate Finance Committee, eventually dying in 1972. All that survived were sections of the FAP guaranteeing income for older and disabled people.

Bouncing back from this failure, Nixon had short-term political success in 1971 with price controls and detaching the dollar from the gold standard.[57] The "discomfort index" or "misery index"—measured as the sum of the unemployment rate and the inflation rate—had been growing since the late 1960s.[58] There was also the issue of the gold standard that allowed foreign treasuries and central banks to convert their U.S. dollars into gold for the price of $35 per ounce of gold. The United States spent more on imports than what it earned from exports and, consequently, foreign nations accumulated large quantities of dollars that surpassed America's supply of gold. A potential problem was the United States running out of gold.

Nixon ended gold convertibility and allowed the dollar to depreciate even though this might have signaled that the government was not serious about inflation. Any decline of the value of the dollar meant a rise in the dollar price of imports. To counteract the optics of less concern for inflation, the Nixon government packaged the plan with "a mandatory comprehensive freeze on prices and wages." The New Economic Policy announced on August 15 received the praise of the public delighted that Nixon outmaneuvered international speculators and acted at home "against landlords, grocers and other scoundrels."[59] Free-marketers wanting to keep the gold standard objected, but the greatest opposition from conservatives concerned Nixon's wage and price controls.

Alan Greenspan found it shocking that something anathema to free-market economists was brought to the table by a Republican president. Greenspan began public life in 1967 when Columbia University finance professor Martin Anderson asked him for assistance developing policy and writing speeches for Richard Nixon's presidential campaign. After meeting him, Greenspan marveled at Nixon's intelligence—his thoughtful questions and articulation of ideas "in perfectly turned sentences and paragraphs." Still, another side of Nixon disturbed him. Greenspan and senior staff met at a beach resort on Long Island, where Nixon went on a profanity-laced tirade about the Democrats. The effect on Greenspan was significant and after Nixon's successful election he decided not to join the team when asked by the White House staff.[60]

The White House consulted Greenspan about price and wage controls, but his position was that central planning the economy would fail—"the market will always undermine any attempt at control."[61] In contrast to Greenspan's opposition to price controls, most businesses welcomed the policy even though economists warned of difficulties ahead—a prediction that came true when the policy fell apart. Although Nixon knew it was a harmful idea from the beginning, his eye was on the short term, notably the 1972 election. Conservatives were unhappy, but Keynesians, such as Paul Samuelson, wanted a continuation of wage controls.[62]

Campaigning for the 1972 election, Nixon identified the policies of his opponent Democrat George S. McGovern as draft-dodging "amnesty, pot, abortion, confiscation of wealth (unless it is theirs), massive increases in welfare, unilateral disarmament, reduction of their defenses, and surrender in Vietnam."[63] Economist John Kenneth Galbraith campaigned for McGovern, his "closest friend in politics," in the primaries and throughout the fall; he saw McGovern as a man of "stubborn honesty of liberal purpose."[64] Although Galbraith was a member of the jet set who wintered in Gstaad, Switzerland, and squired Jacqueline Kennedy around, his socialism explains his support for McGovern.[65] The Democrats' choice of McGovern was good for Republicans, and they looked forward to the showdown.

Nixon assessed the situation when he told his staff that "the Eastern Establishment media finally has a candidate who almost totally shares their views."[66] The president believed that the press sought to soften McGovern's progressive views during the campaign, giving him a better chance to win the White House. If this was indeed the case, however, it failed.[67] Americans went to the polls on November 5 and gave Nixon a massive victory over McGovern; the 60.7 percent to 37.5 percent margin was a remarkable achievement for him and the Republican Party and a blow for McGovern and the Democratic Party. Nevertheless, the Democrats still controlled Congress. Nixon's victory came with the news of Republicans losing one Senate seat to the Democrats and gaining only 12 House seats.

V

The landslide unnerved some in the media. One powerful news editor declared to Nixon speechwriter William Safire: "There's got to be a bloodletting." By early 1973 there increasing attention was paid to the Watergate issue. In addition to their dislike of Nixon, journalists feared extralegal "plumber" or Watergate-type business that might target them personally under the direction of Nixon's inner circle. With growing revelations of government misuse of power, concerns about what the FBI or the IRS could do to any targeted individual were real. This was hardly new territory for the White House given that Franklin D. Roosevelt used the FBI, IRS, and the Department of Justice to harass business and press opponents, and the IRS hassled conservative radio and television stations during the Kennedy administration.[68] It was inappropriate action for either a Democratic or a Republican president.

There was plenty of bad behavior to go around. In the eyes of Safire, neither Nixon nor the media acted honorably: "He [Nixon] had contempt for them, as elitist, antidemocratic, lordly, arrogant lookers-down-their-noses at the elected representatives of the folks, and he did everything he could get away with to destroy them—becoming, along the way, elitist, lordly, and dangerously arrogant."[69] In the months that followed, the showdown was between an elected politician and an unelected media. As an adversary, the media stood to win in the long run.

Further corruption accelerated opposition to Nixon. In late 1973, Vice President Spiro Agnew resigned after confronted with evidence that he accepted bribes while in office as governor of Maryland and as vice president. Confirmation of Gerald Ford for as a replacement vice president went well. The Senate vote in November was 92 to 3 in support and the House vote in December was 387 to 35. Chief Justice Warren Burger, a distinguished-looking man who looked the part of someone straight from central casting in Hollywood, had Ford repeat the oath of office. After the ceremony, the new Vice President of the United States rode to the White House to receive Nixon's congratulation: "It's good to have a teammate at last."[70] With the well-liked Ford replacing Agnew who Democrats detested, however, Nixon's opponents had more incentive to pursue impeachment.

On the front pages every day, Watergate continued to drain the life out of the presidency, so Ford thought it wise to keep his distance from the tawdry spectacle. On the advice of Maggie Hunter of *The New York Times*, Ford read George E. Reedy's *The Twilight of the Presidency*. A press secretary for Lyndon Johnson, Reedy wrote how a faulty structure of the presidency isolated a president from the pulse of the nation. At the White House, directly under the president, "is a mass of intrigue, posturing, strutting, cringing and pious 'commitment' to irrelevant windbaggery—that all too frequently successful collection of the untalented, the unpassionate and the insincere seeking to convince the public that it is brilliant, compassionate, and dedicated." Taking the analysis to heart, Ford made sure everyone on his staff got the message. He had no patience for "little tin gods."[71]

While there was political angst in Washington, the American people faced new challenges as the adverse effects of Nixon's wage and price controls hit home. Although price controls for the oil industry initially did result in lower gas prices for consumers, the long term saw crippling shortages and higher gas prices. With the government intervening to keep prices lower, what was the incentive for American oil companies to invest in oil production? The Yom Kippur War in October 1973 compounded the problem. Israel defeated its Arab attackers, but Nixon's replenishing of Israel's weapon supplies angered Middle East oil producers, leading to a spike in oil prices to punish the United States. Even though the United States had an inflation problem before the Organization of Petroleum Exporting Countries (OPEC) raised the price of oil, many pundits blamed inflation on the "oil shock." It was a "convenient catchall explanation" for those confused about the failing economy.[72]

OPEC deserved some blame and so did Nixon. To better understand the higher price of oil one had to revisit 1971, more than two years before the Yom Kippur War. The American dollar was the world's foremost currency and Middle Eastern oil producers sold their oil for American dollars. When Nixon dropped the gold standard in August 1971, OPEC worried about a sinking dollar. The answer for its members was to demand more dollars for their oil to offset the currency devaluation. At a September 1971 meeting in Beirut, OPEC adopted the following: "Member Countries shall take necessary action and/or shall establish negotiations, individually or in groups, with the oil companies with a view to adopting ways and means to offset any adverse effects ... from the international monetary developments as of 15th August 1971."[73] As Robert L. Bartley explained: "The real shock was that the dollar was depreciating against oil, against gold, against foreign currencies and against nearly everything else." It appeared that only Arab sheiks and a small number of "gold bugs" understood the full impact of Nixon's decision on the gold standard.[74]

Every time Americans went to the gas pumps they experienced first-hand the seriousness of the energy crunch. Chosen as Nixon's energy czar to tackle the oil embargo, William E. Simon gained widespread unpopularity and received numerous death threats. Until the Arabs lifted the embargo, he rarely slept more than four hours a day, working hard to ease the worst effects. One night he got an earful from his wife. Having dined on a couple of apples, he was hungry and "bone tired." When he went home at midnight, he only wanted to flatten himself with "a strong scotch." At the door, his "normally loving" wife sprang at him, telling him she had to wear dark glasses and avoid her customary gas station so she would not to be recognized. She shouted, "Do you know how long I waited in line?"[75]

Simon, however, was a free marketer who believed that the roots of the energy crisis began with the previous years' mistaken policies, such as the 1970 National Environmental Policy Act (NEPA), which added years before drilling operations for energy resources could start. It was not a conservative Nixon who signed this act; he signed as a "political pragmatist" looking ahead to the 1970 midterm elections and his reelection campaign in 1972.[76] The NEPA and other restrictive policies were the domain of a large bureaucracy that Simon disliked: "The bureaucrat's standard of efficacy is obedience to the rules and respect for the vested interests of the hierarchy, however unyielding of a solution; response to external reality is often irrelevant." As for Congress, he marveled at "the extraordinary irresponsibility of that collection of economic planners."

First the government paralyzed the operations of oil companies and then offered them tax exemptions and subsidies "'to stimulate incentive'—an incentive which the government itself had done its utmost to destroy."[77] On the claim of oil "monopolies" and "obscene profits," Simon pointed out that this was nonsense given that there were 8000 different oil and gas producers. Exxon was the largest single producer, but its production was less than 10 percent. One study showed the pretax profit for the oil industry to be 8.2 percent compared to 19.1 percent for the television industry that approved the "greed" rhetoric directed at conservatives by liberal congressmen.[78]

Meeting face to face with politicians was quite an experience. When Simon discussed allocation of fuel to farmers before the House Committee on Agriculture, he found the hearing room to be a "madhouse." With his "startling high, shrill voice," Chairman W. R. "Bob" Poage continued a barrage of "incessant squeaking." Other congressmen talked to each other with their microphones still open, thus drowning out Simon's testimony that government interventionism was not necessarily the answer. Peanuts were a heavily subsidized product and at this agricultural meeting, as was the case for all agricultural meetings, participants each had a bag of Planter's peanuts before them. As the congressmen nosily ripped open their bags and chomped on the peanuts, Simon never heard a question: "I merely replied to what I guessed they were asking."[79]

With America beginning its worst economic downturn since the Great Depression, there was panic.[80] Still, the Nixon government had a good eye for talented economists. The White House made another attempt to recruit Alan Greenspan—this time as the chairman of the Council of Economic Advisors (CEA), a small but important consulting firm that provided economic advice for the president of the United States. Only two other posts are higher for an economist in Washington: Secretary of the Treasury and chairman of the Federal Reserve Board. Because Greenspan disagreed with Nixon's wage and price controls, he said "no" to the CEA offer even though it was a job he would have normally accepted in "a heartbeat." Former energy czar and then Treasury secretary, William E. Simon, refused to take no for an answer; he got Greenspan to agree to talk to Al Haig, Nixon's chief of staff.

The White House flew Greenspan by military jet to Key Biscayne, Florida, where Haig reassured him that the administration wanted to move away from wage and price controls. This meeting and the persuasive tactics of esteemed economist Arthur Burns at another meeting in New York City convinced Greenspan to take the job.[81] William Safire declared that when Nixon was in a tight corner he tended "to adopt the economic suggestions of his Democratic opponents, and with a vengeance."[82]

But this side of Nixon would not be an issue for the conservative Greenspan. His Senate confirmation hearing on August 8, 1974, was the same day Nixon made his TV announcement of resignation.

From Lyndon Johnson to Richard Nixon, Keynesian thinking thrived; economic management in Washington was the accepted orthodoxy. Nixon spoke of his preference for conservative economics and his economic team saw themselves as conservatives very different from their Democratic predecessors. Economist Herbert Stein thought otherwise—"the differences between them [was] … not great."[83] As a recent study argues, "the New Deal seemed intact for much of the country" during the Nixon administration.[84] During the Nixon years, the federal deficit grew, government regulation mushroomed, and inflation increased. The year 1973 was a watershed; the new trend for American workers was a decline in real after-tax wages.[85]

Nixon's Keynesian gamble brought him victory in the 1972 election, but the standard fare for the months that followed was economic anxiety. Overall, "the great paradox of the Nixon administration, and by its own standard the great sin, was the price and wage controls."[86] It was now President Gerald R. Ford's time to tackle a failing economy that was obvious to a growing number of Americans.

Notes

1. "U.S. Business in 1965," *Time*, December 31, 1965, 48–53.
2. Martin Anderson, *Welfare: The Political Economy of Welfare Reform in the United* States (Stanford, CA: Hoover Institution, 1978), 7.
3. Herbert Stein, *Presidential Economics: The Making of Economic Policy from Roosevelt to Clinton*, Third Revised Edition (Washington, DC: American Enterprise Institute for Public Policy Research, 1994), 176–179.
4. Rowland Evans and Robert Novak, *The Reagan Revolution* (New York: E. P. Dutton, 1981), 15.
5. Robert A. Caro, *The Years of Lyndon Johnson: The Path to Power* (New York: Alfred A. Knopf, 1982), 120, 124–125, 129.
6. Joseph A. Califano Jr., *The Triumph & Tragedy of Lyndon Johnson: The White House Years* (New York: Simon & Schuster, 1991), 10, 93, 98.
7. Ibid., 9, 12.
8. Randall B. Woods, *LBJ: Architect of American Ambition* (New York: Free Press, 2006), 447.
9. Quoted in Fred I. Greenstein, *Presidential Difference: Leadership Style from FDR to George W. Bush*, Second Edition (Princeton, NJ: Princeton University Press, 2004), 75.

10. Charles Murray, *Losing Ground: American Social Policy, 1950–1980* (New York: Basic Books, 1994), 25.
11. Gunnar Myrdal, "The War on Poverty," *New Republic*, February 8, 1964, 15.
12. Lyndon Baines Johnson, *The Vantage Point: Perspectives of the Presidency 1963–1969* (New York: Holt, Rinehart and Winston, 1971), 75.
13. Quoted in Johnson, *The Vantage Point*, 76.
14. Ibid., 76–77.
15. Ibid., 79.
16. Ibid., 80.
17. Stein, *Presidential Economics*, 96.
18. Johnson, *The Vantage Point*, 81.
19. Stein, *Presidential Economics*, 99.
20. Joseph A. Califano Jr., *Inside: A Public and Private Life* (New York: PublicAffairs, 2004), 39, 48, 50, 63.
21. Ibid., 70–71, 81.
22. Ibid., 75, 83–84.
23. Ibid., 86–87.
24. Ibid., 88, 146.
25. Ibid., 152.
26. Ibid., 154, 159.
27. Beyond domestic policy, Johnson insisted that India adopt a family planning program before the United States delivered food to ease its famine. See Califano, *Inside*, 172–174.
28. Ibid., 181, 186. His devotion to government service came at a personal cost of a failed marriage (176–178, 184).
29. Johnson, *The Vantage Point*, 440.
30. Ibid., 444.
31. Quoted in Johnson, *The Vantage Point*, 446.
32. Ibid., 450–452.
33. Ibid., 454, 460.
34. Woods, *LBJ*, 447.
35. Milton Friedman and Rose Friedman, *Free to Choose: A Personal Statement* (Orlando, FL: Harcourt, 1990), 109–110.
36. William E. Simon, *A Time for Truth* (New York: Reader's Digest Press, 1978), 118–119.
37. Friedrich A. Hayek, *A Tiger by the Tail: The Keynesian Legacy of Inflation* (San Francisco: Cato Institute, 1979), 101.
38. Alan Greenspan, *The Age of Turbulence: Adventures in a New World* (New York: The Penguin Press, 2007), 60.
39. Hillarly Rodman Clinton, *Living History* (London: Headline, 2003), 38.
40. Saul Alinsky, *Rules for Radicals: A Practical Primer for Realistic Radicals* (New York: Vintage Books, 1989), xiv, 116.

41. Ibid., 126–130.
42. Ibid., 178.
43. Ibid., 136–138.
44. Ibid., 195–196.
45. Robert M. Collins, *More: The Politics of Economic Growth in Postwar America* (New York: Oxford University Press, 2000), 132.
46. Ibid., 133–134.
47. Gregory L. Schneider, *The Conservative Century: From Reaction to Revolution* (Lanham, MD: Rowman & Littlefield, 2009), 140. Another historian writes "that within the space of a single decade, the central governing challenge of liberalism changed from allocating abundance to rationing scarcity." See Steven F. Hayward, *The Age of Reagan: The Conservative Counterrevolution, 1980–1989* (New York: Crown Forum, 2009), 80.
48. Richard Nixon, *RN: The Memoirs of Richard Nixon* (New York: Grosset & Dunlap, 1978), 15, 17.
49. Ibid., 26.
50. Ibid., 424.
51. Bruce J. Schulman, *The Seventies: The Great Shift in American Culture, Society, and Politics* (Boston: Da Capo Press, 2001), 25.
52. Nixon, *RN*, 516, 522. Italics in original.
53. Ibid., 522. Italics in original.
54. Ibid., 424–426.
55. Ibid., 426.
56. Ibid., 427.
57. Ibid., 519.
58. Jimmy Carter introduced the "misery index" in 1976 as a tactic to attack President Gerald Ford. See Ronald Reagan, *Ronald Reagan: An American Life* (New York: Pocket Books, 1990), 220.
59. Stein, *Presidential Economics*, 162–167, 176–180.
60. Greenspan, *The Age of Turbulence*, 59.
61. Ibid., 61–62.
62. Peter N. Carroll, *It Seemed Like Nothing Happened: The Tragedy and Promise of America in the 1970s* (New York: Holt, Rinehart and Winston, 1982), 129.
63. Quoted in William Safire, *Before the Fall: An Inside View of the Pre-Watergate White House* (Boston: Da Capo Press, 1975), 360.
64. John Kenneth Galbraith, *A Life in Our Times: Memoirs* (Boston: Houghton Mifflin, 1981), 523.
65. Stein, *Presidential Economics*, 98.
66. Safire, *Before the Fall*, 360.

67. Typical of the "left wing," according to Nixon, the progressive journalists "are willing to use any means whatever to get their man nominated, even if it means covering up his real views…." William Safire disagreed, claiming that the press did McGovern no favors. See Safire, *Before the Fall*, 360–361.
68. Safire, *Before the Fall*, 364.
69. Ibid., 364–365.
70. Gerald R. Ford, *A Time to Heal* (New York: Berkley Books, 1980), 108–109.
71. Ibid., 116.
72. Brian Domitrovic, *Econoclasts: The Rebels Who Sparked the Supply-Side Revolution and Restored American Prosperity* (Wilmington, DE: ISI Books, 2009), 103–104.
73. Quoted in Robert L. Bartley, *The Seven Fat Years: And How to Do It Again* (New York: The Free Press, 1992), 31.
74. Ibid., 32. OPEC, however, did move slowly. The world price for oil was about 1/12 of an ounce of gold per barrel in 1969 and 1/16 of an ounce of gold in 1972. The OPEC correction in 1974 put the price back to almost 1/12 of an ounce of gold.
75. Simon, *A Time for Truth*, 54.
76. Meg Jacobs, *Panic at the Pump: The Energy Crisis and the Transformation of American Politics in the 1970s* (New York: Hill and Wang, 2017), 27.
77. Simon, *A Time for Truth*, 53–56, 66–67.
78. Ibid., 70–71.
79. Ibid., 56–57.
80. Robert M. Collins, *Transforming America: Politics and Culture in the Reagan Years* (New York: Columbia University Press, 2007), 8.
81. Greenspan, *The Age of Turbulence*, 63–64.
82. Quoted in Jacobs, *Panic at the Pump*, 104.
83. Stein, *Presidential Economics*, 206.
84. Jacobs, *Panic at the Pump*, 7. Jacobs states that "Richard Nixon himself was not a New Dealer, but he lived and governed in this world."
85. Godfrey Hodgson, *The World Turned Right Side Up: A History of the Conservative Ascendancy in America* (New York: Houghton Mifflin, 1996), 191. Helpful is Hodgson's chapter, "The Strange Death of John Maynard Keynes," 186–215.
86. Stein, *Presidential Economics*, 207.

CHAPTER 4

Ford's Economy

On May 13, 1975, New York City Mayor Abe Beame met with President Gerald Ford at the White House to request federal support. America's largest city was nearly bankrupt. When Ford suggested that the mayor consider raising subway fares and ending free tuition at community colleges, Beame became furious, stating that free tuition at the City College of New York was a lasting tradition.[1] Ford's opposition to a federal bailout to save the city prompted New York Representative Bella Abzug to declare he had "branded New York as diseased, and now he wants to pull the plug." The president's speech at the National Press Club on October 29 continued the theme of financial illness: "This sickness is brought on by years and years of higher spending, higher deficits, and so on. It is a progressive disease, and there is no painless cure."

Letting the "contagion spread" spelled grave times for the nation; there would be a day of reckoning if spending continued to outpace available money. When that day arrived, "who will bail out the United States of America?" The ball was in the court of New Yorkers critical of the White House's position and their response was surly. A headline of the New York *Daily News* drove home the point: "Ford to City: Drop Dead."[2] In less than a month, Ford announced a stunning reversal of policy, agreeing to give the State of New York a line of credit. It was nobler politics.[3] The response of Ford to the New York crisis sheds light on his economic thinking and the persistence of Keynesian thinking in politics.

E. R. Crouse, *America's Failing Economy and the Rise of Ronald Reagan*,
https://doi.org/10.1007/978-3-319-70545-3_4

Any politician favoring conservative economic policy faced the critical eye of the pro- Keynesian media. Nonetheless, the story goes beyond the press. It may have been reasonable to expect New York City politicians to address their problematic fiscal policies and not require taxpayers residing in other states to bail them out, but many Americans became accustomed to and had considerable faith in greater government intervention to address economic problems. Even many businessmen proclaiming their devotion to free enterprise were not immune, running to the government at times of crisis looking for bailouts, handouts, loans, and protection from competitors. Socialist ideas were too radical to gain any meaningful support in the United States, but Keynesianism was another matter.

As an economic model, it stayed strong even during the Gerald Ford years. The growth of government prompted some conservatives to introduce a new "holiday" celebrating the day when Americans had worked enough to stop paying taxes. Given that more than 40 percent of their incomes went to federal, state, and local taxes, Americans would have to wait until the month of May to see "Personal Independence Day" and be free of paying taxes.[4] Even if this tax-day scheme scored political points for conservatives, economists and others who challenged Keynesian and progressive policies made little headway in political circles.

I

No one predicted Gerald Ford's elevation to the White House. He was born in Omaha, Nebraska, in 1913 and christened Leslie L. King Jr. Fighting often, his parents divorced in 1915 prompting his mother to move to Grand Rapids, Michigan, where she married Gerald Rudolf Ford. Leslie became Gerald R. Ford Jr.[5] After high school, he attended The University of Michigan, majoring in economics and political science. After his B.A. degree, he studied law at Yale University and then entered the navy, reaching the rank of lieutenant commander during World War II. In 1948, his run for Congress was successful; for the next 25 years he served in the House of Representatives.

When Nixon resigned in 1974 and Ford became president, Americans simply wanted their nation to move on to better times. Considered a mushy, moderate lightweight by conservative opponents, Ford sought to get America's economic house in order. What victories he enjoyed were modest because of the economic challenges of the time brought on by previous government policies that looked good in the short term, but less so in the long term.

When Ford became president on August 9, 1974, America faced the major economic challenges of soaring inflation, increasing unemployment numbers, and a jittery stock market.[6] The national output dropped, and unemployment was the highest since World War II.[7] Even worse was the inflation rate, the highest since 1919.[8] *The New York Times* report on the economy was grim: "the worst inflation in the country's peacetime history, the highest interest rates in the century, the consequent severe slump in housing, sinking and utterly demoralized securities markets, a stagnant economy with large-scale unemployment in prospect and a worsening international trade and payments position."[9] The problem of inflation did not go away, and General Motors reported that their 1975 model year cars would have an average price increase of 9.5 percent, sure to trigger rising prices in other industries. Nixon's policies deserved blame, but he had advised Ford not to repeat his mistake of 1971 and impose wage and price controls. Ford identified another reason for the weak economy: the legacy of misguided policies of the New Frontier and Great Society. The new president accepted Senator Mike Mansfield's idea to organize a domestic summit meeting to tackle the problem of inflation.[10]

Taking the traditional Republican outlook, Ford believed that an economic cure would not occur without pain. Since the 1930s, the Democratic Party focused on stimulating the economy to increase employment, and the Keynesian rewards were good. Democrats controlled Congress in 38 of the previous 42 years and for most of those years, inflation had not been a problem. When inflation rose in the late 1960s, Democrats did not view it as the most important problem, as was the case for Republicans. By reducing inflation, Republicans expected greater confidence for businesses to grow and the hiring of new employees. In his first address to Congress, on October 8, Ford identified inflation "as public enemy number one."[11] Two months earlier, Ford phoned General Motors Chairman Dick Gerstenberg, requesting GM exercise restraint on automobile pricing. Not expecting GM's cooperation, Ford won a psychological victory when the company agreed to a modest rollback of one percent (an average of $54 per vehicle) on automobile prices for 1975.[12]

Most of Ford's policies were economically sound in the context of Republican economic orthodoxy: keep federal spending under control;

balance the budget; and focus on long-term, stable growth. He had learned much about federal budgets during the years he served on the House Appropriations Committee. Nevertheless, Ford was not immune to strange notions about how to deal with inflation. A White House staff member hatched the idea of combating inflation with a campaign and a symbol that would encourage volunteer action. Ford speechwriter Robert Hartmann thought the marketing idea was a great one.[13] The plan horrified Alan Greenspan, chairman of the Council of Economic Advisors.

In a meeting in the Roosevelt Room of the White House, he learned of the campaign, "Whip Inflation Now" (WIN), and called it an example of "unbelievable stupidity" that included a national voluntary price freeze and numerous task forces meetings across the nation to discuss inflation. It was "surreal" for Greenspan, the only economist present. Did the Ford people actually think that small-business owners and their suppliers would voluntarily forgo price increases?[14] William Simon wrote: "Every time the 'WIN' issue came up we at the Economic Policy Board would hide our heads in embarrassment. I still have a box of old 'WIN' buttons at home which I look at any time I develop partisan delusions."[15] Of course, the Whip Inflation Now campaign failed. The Ford administration lacked interest in anti-Keynesian economic solutions voiced by free-market economists—specifically the Mont Pélerin Society members who had recently met in Brussels.[16]

By November 1974, Greenspan told Ford of the real possibility of a serious economic recession in the following year. An ordinary recession is a part of the business cycle when production exceeds demand, causing businesses to cut production. More serious are the catastrophic recessions when demand collapses. Basically, "consumers stop spending and business stop investing." Because the forecast models were inadequate, no one could say with certainty how bad the recession would get. If Congress acted with increased government spending, there was a greater risk of sustaining even higher inflation and serious long-term problems. Greenspan was thankful to see that Ford did not panic with reckless government spending, but instead approved a mild, restrained response to the economic slide.[17] When Greenspan testified before politicians, he would joke that it might be a "good idea" to wear a bulletproof vest and armor. Using apocalyptic rhetoric, Democratic and union leaders demanded decisive action. George Meany, president of the AFL-CIO declared: "America is far beyond the point where the situation can correct itself. Massive government action is needed."[18]

In early 1975, Ford acknowledged that the economy was in a severe recession, but as bad as the numbers were, there was a reprieve because the economy showed improvement later in the year. A problem for Ford was that many Americans did not perceive there was improvement. Economists and the public have different perceptions of business cycles. Whereas economists plot the numbers from statistical analysis to see whether the economy is expanding or contracting, the public is mostly unaware of the antiseptic data that points to economic recovery. American families instead experience firsthand the distressing and lasting cost of unemployment. Those who resume employment likely will have significant debts to pay.

Economists' rhetoric of forward momentum did not always compute in the minds of Main Street Americans. In other words, a recession, over in a statistical sense, was not necessarily comforting news for many ordinary people. Moreover, the economic growth after March 1975 was too weak to provide enough jobs for the growing population and entrance of new and young workers into the workforce. Unless a population stays the same, there must be significant job growth to prevent a rise in the unemployment rate.[19]

Always critical of the confident vision of central planners, William Simon argued that the economic crisis exploded the idea that "a small number of intellectuals" could effectively run the economy.[20] Of the 15-year period before 1975, 14 were deficit years. With this new trend, the federal government increasingly usurped capital funds needed for private investment.[21] Less private investment jeopardized job creation. Government also undermined its own goals when there was intense competition among various government departments for scarce resources.

At the state and local levels, for example, the amount of money needed for welfare programs hurt other services. One controversial program was Aid to Families with Dependent Children (AFDC), which provided benefits for the nonworking poor. Its budget in 1965 was $1.8 billion and rose 10 years later to $9.3 billion. Despite the rising costs and concerns over sustainability, various government bureaucrats and academics planned "for a guaranteed income for the non-working poor to serve as the touchstone of welfare policy."[22]

In May 1975, the unemployment rate reached 9.2 percent; however, in the summer months the economy began to recover, and gross domestic product (GNP) growth was good in the fall, apparently justifying Ford's restrained approach. Nevertheless, a sore point for conservatives was when Ford failed in late 1975to heed the advice of his top economists Simon,

Greenspan, and William Seidman. Even though he knew it was bad economics, he signed the Energy Policy and Conservation Act, thus extending price controls on domestically produced crude oil for another 40 months. It was, Milton Friedman argued, another example of politics overriding economics.[23]

There were other examples of economic inconsistency with Republican leaders governing in a Keynesian era. When Ford proposed a $394.2 billion budget for fiscal year 1977, *Newsweek* described it as "draconian." Friedman thought the budget was a step in the right direction, but there were disturbing numbers that he shared in his February 9, 1976 *Newsweek* article. The budget amount was roughly 25 percent of the total income of the country and 5.5 percent higher spending than the 1976 fiscal year. The spending target for health, education, and welfare was $190 billion, almost twice the amount of the total military budget. Friedman was blunt: "The appetite for income transfer and other social programs is insatiable. The more they fail to achieve their announced objectives, the greater the pressure to expand them in order to redeem unrealistic promises." Nonetheless, there was the reality that most Americans opposed higher taxes. Friedman saw only one solution—the spending "trend will be reversed if and only if the public makes it unmistakably clear that voting for ever larger budgets is a sure prescription for being retired from elective office."[24]

Certainly, the cost of welfare programs escalated. Since the Johnson administration, welfare reform was a pressing issue. Although welfare reform planners sought simplification, Johnson and Nixon found the task of improving the welfare system far more difficult than they initially realized. Nixon considered welfare reform, but the plan recommended by Daniel P. Moynihan, the liberal Democrat directing Nixon's Urban Affairs Council, did not hold up under the scrutiny of congressional committees. Attired in a cream-colored suit and wearing a red bow tie, Moynihan was a charming Irish rogue unable to sell his plan.

Ford encountered welfare bureaucrats who proposed a costly welfare reform package that would add more than 20 million people to the welfare system. He rejected it.[25] Still, there was no welfare reform and government spending on social welfare programs continued to climb, increasing from $77 billion to $286 billion in the years from 1965 to 1975. There was recognition of the generosity of the American people, but then again, did the government assist poor people in a way that was helpful to them and the nation.

II

The economic viability of government programs and the higher taxes to pay for them did not appear to be major concerns for many politicians in the mid-1970s. This attitude was noticeably prevalent in specific geographical regions and the consequences included industrial decline and the migration of citizens to regions where greater employment opportunities existed. The northeastern states where population growth slowed, lost congressional seats, electoral votes, and political power.[26] Weighed down by high living costs, an aging physical infrastructure, and a shrinking tax base, the Northeast faced major difficulties as it came up short in competing with other regions. New York state and New York City were particularly in trouble.[27]

In 1965, New York City Mayor Robert Wagner, a Republican, declared: "I do not propose to permit our fiscal problems to set the limits of our commitments to meet the essential needs of the people of the city."[28] Another Republican, who did not run as a Republican candidate when he sought the New York City mayoralty later the same year, took an opposing position. William F. Buckley Jr. saw the impossibility of getting the Republican nomination in New York if one ran as a traditional Republican. As a mayoral candidate, Buckley represented the New York Conservative Party, founded three years earlier. His assessment of the city was blunt: "New York City is in dire financial condition as a result of mismanagement, extravagance, and political cowardice." Unless the city lived within its income, bankruptcy was unavoidable, he said.[29]

Neither this position nor his humor won him much praise. When people questioned his relationship with the Bronx Democratic boss Charles Buckley, he clarified that there was no political or biological relationship, and all confusion would disappear if Charles, not running for political office at the time, did the proper thing and changed his last name. To his Republican opponent (John V. Lindsay) who criticized him as a candidate from Connecticut, Buckley stated at a press conference: "I don't know why he is so hostile to Connecticut. Perhaps he went there to be educated and, for manifest reasons, is displeased with the results." Buckley knew that Lindsay had attended Yale University.

Buckley's insults of *The New York Times* in front of a television crew also illustrated the uniqueness of his political approach. Asked what he would do first if New York City voters elected him mayor, he replied: "Hang a net outside the window of the [*New York Times*] editor."[30]

Keynesians need not have worried; John V. Lindsay won the election with Buckley receiving only 13 percent of the vote.

In subsequent years, New York City politicians interpreted "essential needs" broadly and created a vast City University system, rewarded government employees with generous wages and pensions, and subsidized middle-income housing. According to urban journalist Ken Auletta, this "ideological commitment to the redistribution of wealth" was costly.[31] The annual debt of New York City almost tripled between the years of 1961 and 1975.[32] The high spending practices of New York City since the 1960s was no secret; however, in the Great Society climate where promise-borrow-spend was acceptable, there were few people raising an alarm.[33] The city imposed the highest taxes in the nation and borrowed heavily to pay the bills. But it was not enough.

The Census Bureau showed that most major cities employed about 30 workers per 1000 inhabitants. New York City employed approximately 50 workers per 1000 and paid them far more than the private sector. Most citizens subsidized the wages of city workers. One harmful consequence was the steady exodus of industry and skilled workers who were upset with the city's excessive tax rate.[34] Using the latest figures available in November 1975, Milton Friedman calculated government (federal and state) spending per person living in New York City was much higher than any other American city. Big spender San Francisco spent approximately 30 percent less per person, and Chicago spent less than 50 percent per person than New York. As Friedman wrote: "New York's lavish spending reflects the most welfare-state-oriented electorate in the U.S."

The city's financial crisis was no surprise to Friedman who considered default as a viable option. New York City had an "exaggerated sense of self-importance." Its total financial assets were about one percent of the nation's total assets and the overall effect of default by the city would be small with "no chance that it could cause a serious financial panic." The best option, according to Friedman, was for "New York City to tighten its belt and create a large enough current-account surplus to pay off its debt without default. But that is a pipe dream."[35] Symbolic of its economic mess was the city's wildcat strike in the summer of 1975 that resulted in streets littered with tens of thousands of tons of garbage (equal to the area and height of the two World Trade Centers). The city became "Stink City."[36]

There was intense pressure from Democrats, notably Mayor Abraham D. Beame and Governor Hugh Carey, for the federal government to bail out New York City, already approaching bankruptcy. Ford adopted a cautious approach, stating his opposition to providing federal funds "on an open-spigot basis."[37] At a Washington press conference, he explained: "I do not think it is a healthy thing for the federal government to bail out a city, and I mean any city that has handled its fiscal affairs as irresponsibly over a long period of time as New York City has." His reasons for vetoing federal bailout legislation were twofold. First, New York City officials would not confront "the city's massive network of pressure groups as long as any other alternate [was] … available." Second, a federal bailout would set "a terrible precedent for the rest of the nation."[38] Ford's stand throughout 1975 generated resolute language from Democrats and the media. Democrat Edward L. Koch declared "Mongol hordes" surrounded the city, "and I look out the window and the faces aren't those of barbarians; they are those of the White House."[39]

What the White House saw as fiscal responsibility others saw as inhumanity. Faced with the reality of the city's economic chaos, socialist Irving Howe wrote in *The New York Times*: "Our true sin, in the eyes of Philistine skinflints and neoconservative ideologues, has been the decency—if not sufficient, still impressive—with which New York has treated its poor…."[40] Not to be undone, the New York press offered colorful headlines and sharp criticism. One "villain" was William Simon for his testimony to the Senate Banking Committee.

Ignoring most of his remarks, journalists focused on one statement: the terms for any federal assistance for New York City should be "so punitive, that no other city will be tempted to turn down the same road." For this, the *New York Post* headline was "Simon on U.S. Aid: Make City Suffer," a headline that stunned him. As a representative of the entire nation, Simon sought to discourage other states and municipalities from making poor economic choices; he wanted to improve the situation rather than seek to punish the city.[41]

The apparent economic illiteracy of many journalists also frustrated Simon. Outnumbered by liberals at a dinner party, he and his wife faced the criticism of other guests at the home of Washington columnist Joseph Alsop. One critic was Sydney Gruson, the executive vice president of *The New York Times*, who found Simon's economic position concerning New York City troubling. Gruson demanded to know why he had never heard Simon's explanation on the White House's approach to the economic state of New York City. Pointing out the bias of *Times* reporters, Simon answered: "I've been explaining it for months before Congress and in speeches all over the country. If you don't know my side of the story, ask your own staff for an explanation."[42] A New Yorker himself, Simon had Ford in his corner; the president appreciated his intelligence, fiscal responsibility, and "desire to work with others."[43]

Others entered the debate. Completing his second term as governor of California in January 1975, Ronald Reagan was making about 10 speeches a month, earning him an average $5000 per speech. Both his radio commentaries on more than 200 radio stations and his column in 174 newspapers kept him in the public eye.[44] Critical of the doomsday rhetoric of New York's Governor Hugh Carey, Reagan had news for Carey: "To large numbers of Americans across this new decentralized nation, New York symbolizes what's wrong: too-powerful union leaders and news media, timid elected officials, wild spending, mismanagement, dirty streets, pornography and a general decline in civility." He knew from experience that people in "Ohio or Texas (or almost anywhere else outside of New York)" erupted with "wild applause" when told the federal government should not bail out New York. Nonetheless, the problem went deeper. The growing federal government, demanding more money from taxpayers, promoted the myth that "federal dollars were free dollars."[45]

In November 1975, Theodore White linked American Keynesian politics to socialism: "Together the welfare population and the city employees dominate our electoral politics. As in a giant soviet, they elect their bosses and paymaster…."[46] To no one's surprise, William R. Buckley Jr. voiced a similar message: "We have conducted a noble experiment in local socialism and income distribution, one clear result of which has been to redistribute much of our tax base and many jobs out of the city."[47] For conservatives, one glaring problem for New York City was the policy of rent control that appeared to be beneficial. Rent control had become law throughout America in November 1943 and after the war some cities decided it was a good program to continue.

It became obvious to those paying attention that rent control caused chronic housing shortages (not as much new apartment construction) and adversely affected the tax base.[48] New York City politicians, however, saw the issue as political dynamite; thus, there was little opposition. Statistical evidence indicated that there was an exodus of people and jobs out of the city, but conservatives found it difficult to convince others of the wisdom for a different strategy that could benefit both businesses and workers. What looked like fiscal responsibility to them was heartlessness to Democrats.

If the Republican Party wanted to position itself for a good run at the presidential election of 1976, it had to proceed carefully without giving the impression that it was a probusiness party with little compassion for working people. In December 1975, Ford signed legislation into law giving \$2.3 billion loans per year to the city through mid-1978. The city could not repay many of its noteholders; it defaulted, even if most of the press failed to understand this.[49] Governor Carey promised that the city would "never need a bailout again," and city politicians had their bag of tricks—for example, charging the salaries of teachers to the next year's budget to prove they could keep the city running. Conservatives remained skeptical that there was the political will for New York officials to change their way of running the city.[50]

III

When National Basketball Association star Bill Walton signed a \$2 million contract in 1973 to play for the Portland Trail Blazers, he responded in bewilderment saying he "couldn't spend that much in a lifetime." He was clear about his politics and economic thinking: "I'll tell you one thing. I won't invest in the United Fruit Co. I don't believe in capitalism.... I believe wealth should be spread around."[51] In the past, Walton's statement would categorize him a radical. Progressives believed that the poor were victims of a flawed economic order and the answer to social injustice was wealth distribution carried out by government legislation. By the 1970s, many Americans were accepting of the progressive idea of wealth distribution when not pitched by genuine socialists.

If opinions were to change on economic policy, a greater number of free-market economists was necessary to articulate a conservative vision that was not callous to the needs of the poor. One of the more astute economic commentators of the 1970s was Irving Kristol, a former Trotskyist whose ideological journey led to liberalism and, finally, "neoconservatism." As a nonobservant Jew, he learned to appreciate the certainty of Christian theologians "that the human condition placed inherent limitations on human possibility."[52] By the early 1970s he lost faith in liberal social and economic policies and in the years that followed, he wrote insightful articles on economics and politics for the *Wall Street Journal*.

Kristol's September 11, 1975, article, "On Conservatism and Capitalism," pointed to the lack of candor in properly identifying socialists: "I find it striking that the media, and members of the business community too, should consistently refer to John Kenneth Galbraith as a 'liberal' when he has actually taken the pains to write a book explaining why he is a socialist." Another example Kristol cited was Michael Harrington, head of a socialist party, often introduced as "a leading liberal spokesman." Those who sought to increase "the scope of governmental authority indefinitely" became more acceptable than conservatives and their outdated idea of "liberty" and defense of capitalism.[53] John Maynard Keynes was no socialist, but the Keynesian Revolution saw the redefining of liberalism that put conservatism on the defensive. Liberalism's faith in government intervention in the economy promised an optimistic egalitarianism more attractive than what defenders of free-market capitalists offered.

Statist policies under the brand of liberalism seemed reasonable. One significant consequence of Keynesian policies was the Republican Party's loss of the African American vote. Social programs at all levels of government and the promise of government spending creating jobs assured overwhelming black support for the Democratic Party. Thomas Sowell was a rarity among black intellectuals for his opposition to Keynesian ideas. His personal misfortune taught him lessons distinct from the black activists and intellectuals who aligned with the Democratic Party: "[E]ven my misfortunes were in some ways fortunate, for they taught me things that would be hard to understand otherwise, and they presented reality from an angle not given to those, among intellectuals especially, whose careers have followed a more straight-line path in familiar grooves."[54]

Sowell examined other government programs, finding it difficult "to believe they were a net benefit to society."[55] No more a socialist, Sowell had collected ample data contradicting the claims and policies informed by Keynesian ideas. When Representative Augustus Hawkins, a black liberal Democrat, contacted Sowell in 1972 to get his view on the issue of "full employment," Hawkins was not happy with the conclusions of Sowell's research.[56]

One of Sowell's professors in graduate school was Milton Friedman, whose reputation grew as he went beyond challenging Keynesianism in academic circles and took up the challenge at the popular level with his *Newsweek* articles throughout the 1970s. His writing was logical and devoid of any insensitive rhetoric arguing the superiority of capitalism. His expertise allowed him to articulate his message from different angles, clarifying confusing theory for the general public. In March 1975, he wrote that the Federal Reserve (Fed) and the government were incapable of learning from past mistakes. The policy that brought high inflation from 1971 to 1974 was a replay of the inflationary periods of 1963 to 1966 and 1967 to 1968. When the Fed slowed the money supply in 1974, "it did so too late and [went] too far." As was the case during the 1960s, it deepened economic recession.[57]

Friedman lamented the deepening recession and the sorry excuses of the Fed: "Whenever things go well, the Fed is delighted to claim credit. Whenever they go badly, forces outside its control are responsible." The best hope for the Fed was to stay focused on the quantity of money without trying to control interest rates. Attempts to "control monetary growth by the highly indirect method of controlling a particular interest rate—the Federal-funds rate"—were foolish. Friedman preferred that the Fed make weekly calculations on how large an addition to reserves was necessary for the desired monetary growth.[58] By combining economic analysis and history, Friedman won over Americans who otherwise were wary of free marketers.

Friedman criticized the bad economic policies of both Democrats and Republicans. He thought Ford was on the right path with his proposal to cut taxes but was the president offering serious cuts? In October 1975, Friedman acknowledged Ford's proposal to cut taxes and government spending to the amount of $28 billion. On closer inspection, however, the $17 billion was not new cuts; this amount of proposed cuts simply replaced "the rebates and temporary tax cuts enacted earlier this year." Moreover, inflation and the automatic tax increases it caused basically wiped out both the so-called $17 billion tax cut and the remaining $11 billion tax cut.[59]

If free-market scholars were less than optimistic about Ford, they had less faith in government bureaucracy. Friedman found no enthusiasm for welfare programs because what appeared humanitarian and noble often fell short of stated objectives. A major problem he identified was the issue of who did the spending. The best case for responsible spending was if it was done by those using their own money. In this category, people shopping for themselves at a supermarket have incentive to economize and spend their money wisely. The second category is when a consumer is spending their own money on someone outside their family. In this case, the incentive to economize also is compelling, but there is less motivation to get full value. If one wanted a recipient to get the fullest value, they would simply give the recipient cash. A third category is the spending of someone else's money on yourself. With company expense accounts, the employee has no solid motivation to purchase a thrifty lunch. The least responsible spending category is when someone spends someone else's money on a third party.

Crucial in the operation of the welfare state are the bureaucrats who "spend someone else's money on someone else." Even with the best intentions of spending the money wisely, the typical result is wastefulness.[60] If this analysis represented common sense, it still generated spirited responses by those resistant to any cut to the government bureaucracy.

Friedman's defense of Hillsdale College, in December 1975, provided a specific example of the injurious effect of bureaucracy. The Department of Health, Education, and Welfare (HEW) pressured colleges to embrace affirmative-action programs to eliminate discrimination of students based on sex or race. The objective was honorable, but Friedman argued that the results were problematic: overburdening paperwork, misplaced and impractical hiring criteria, and often "substitution of reverse discrimination for no discrimination." Because most colleges and universities received federal funds, HEW had the legal justification to enforce federal hiring practices. Yet, Hillsdale was unique. To protect its independence, it did not accept any federal funds. Not willing to accept defeat, HEW bureaucrats claimed Hillsdale was subject to HEW control because some students received federal grants from veterans and other programs. For Friedman, this case was a sad testimony of the "climate of opinion favorable to big government."[61]

Other free marketers began to make their voices heard and joined Friedman's efforts to shine a light on questionable government policies. It was during the Ford administration that "supply-side" economists began to consolidate as a group; in less than five years they offered a convincing critique of Keynesian government. In 1974, early supply-side thinkers met at the Michael 1 restaurant located in Manhattan near the American Stock Exchange building. Gathering with academic economists Robert Mundell and Arthur B. Laffer were Robert L. Bartley and Jude Wanniski of the *Wall Street Journal*. Future Nobel Prize winner Mundell spoke in a low slur and added enough wry remarks to make his speech difficult to understand. Three years earlier he had won the Guggenheim—"the top fellowship in American academe." At the same time, his article, "The Dollar and the Policy Mix: 1971" published by Princeton, articulated all the important components of supply-side theory; however, his analysis remained unread by those who might have benefited as they struggled with the problem of stagflation. Laffer had known Mundell since their days teaching at the University of Chicago.[62]

Born into a wealthy family, Laffer grew up in Ohio. After graduate studies, he worked briefly under George Shultz at the Office of Management and Budget (OMB) and held teaching positions at Stanford and the University of Chicago before moving to the University of Southern California.[63] He identified his economics with nineteenth-century economist Léon Walras, the Frenchman who wrote on how a market economy reached general equilibrium.

Laffer did not earn the respect of Keynesian Paul Samuelson who delivered a lecture in 1971 at the University of Chicago titled "Why They Are Laughing at Laffer." Awarded the Nobel Prize for economics the year before, Samuelson was a genuine Keynesian giant who many years earlier had staked out the supposed superiority of Keynesian management: "By the proper choice of monetary and fiscal policy we as the artists, mixing the colors of our palette, can have the capital formation and rate of current consumption that we desire."[64] Samuelson guarded Keynesian turf from threats of academics not sharing his confidence that the best and brightest could be masters of the economy.

Samuelson mocked one of Laffer's economic forecasts given when working at the OMB. The issue of whether Samuelson made a good or bad argument mattered less to some than his intellectual bullying of a young scholar. One of his students wrote of Samuelson's impressive mind and his distinctive appearance: "Samuelson's brilliant mind and knack for razor sharp analysis was hidden behind a homely face. His small, pointed ears gave him an extraterrestrial look, a look enhanced by his short, slender body. He was small, and he was mean."[65] Protecting one's vision of how politics and the economy mixed was serious business.

Both mavericks, Laffer and Mundell apparently cared little about criticism from Keynesians. Mundell even was unafraid to take on Milton Friedman, the founder of monetarism, at University of Chicago workshops. A former Mundell student recalled that "Friedman obviously admired the sheer creativity of Mundell but would not let him get by; sparks would fly." They were gladiator events, but there would be a functional alliance between supply-siders (Mundell) and monetarists (Friedman) in the future. Both blamed the government for stagflation. For supply-siders, the government was at fault for the crisis for two main reasons: (1) the excessive printing of money caused inflation and (2) the raising of tax rates discouraged business investment and job creation.[66]

An eager learner of supply-side economics while at Michael 1 was veteran journalist Jude Wanniski who had an insatiable appetite for understanding economics. Wanniski grew up in Brooklyn in the late 1930s and 1940s and studied at UCLA. He was "dark and swarthy" and failed "to crack the social circuit of the high Washington reporters." Nonetheless, the *Wall Street Journal* recognized talent and his inquisitive mind and gifted writing, which landed him a job with the editorial page. Wanniski developed a close friendship with Laffer and Mundell and the three occasionally met in Manhattan to discuss economics. It was Wanniski's December 1974 article, "It's Time to Cut Taxes," that introduced *Wall Street Journal* readers to supply-side economics.

By coincidence, December was also the time of the "single most famous incident in the history of supply-side economics." The facts remain murky, but Wanniski and Laffer met at Washington's Two Continents restaurant with Richard Cheney, who worked for Ford's chief of staff Donald H. Rumsfeld, to discuss supply-side ideas. To illustrate for Cheney how tax cuts might generate more rather than less revenue, Laffer drew a graph of tax rate percentages (vertical axis) and revenues (horizontal axis). What became known as the Laffer curve suggested that as tax rates increased, people lost the incentive to earn a higher income. Consequently, high tax rates meant less revenue for government.[67]

In 1976, *Wall Street Journal* editor Robert Bartley became a booster of supply-side ideas.[68] Born in the Midwest on Columbus Day, Bartley was a small man who wore thick glasses and unpretentious clothes and was suspicious of Ivy Leaguers whose ambition appeared to narrow them intellectually. His father was a professor of veterinary science, but Robert's academic direction was a bachelor's degree in journalism and a master's degree in political science. In 1972, Bartley became editor of the *Wall Street Journal* editorial page, a good place to promote supply-side thinking and marginal tax cuts. Viewed by others as deeply patriotic, Bartley fought ideas suggesting that the United States was better off to limit its economic aspirations.[69]

Supply-side thinking offered optimism; cutting taxes was the right path to economic growth. It was the good fortune of supply-side politicians that Bartley was a superb writer with their best interests at heart. Nevertheless, supply-side theory was radical and found no significant political support until the Carter years. The free-market theory having influence in the Ford administration was the Republican standard fare of fiscal responsibility and balanced budgets.

IV

The economic news in the last year of Ford's government was not promising. There was evidence of economic recovery in the first half of 1976, but indicators for the third quarter pointed to a slowdown. Unfortunately for Ford, the growth rate slowed to less than two percent by summer. Alan Greenspan argued that "this was not a cause for concern," except that the Democrats again demanded an economic stimulus.[70]

Conservatives pointed to the problem of high taxes, a story that would receive national media attention in 1978. For example, auditors, hired to assess the tax situation of the Dallas-based conglomerate Michigan General Corporation, discovered that the company paid a total tax rate of 86 percent (i.e., federal plus taxes for sales, real estate, withholding, franchise, payroll, excise, etc.) in 1976. Investors provided 100 percent of the capital, but only received 14 percent of the earnings. The chairman of the board reported that the "multiple government bureaucracies had absorbed the rest like some vengeful sponge hurled at us from outer space by our worst enemies."[71] This story was one of many similar cases of overburdening taxation. Regardless of who Americans blamed most, what mattered was their perception of a struggling economy.

In 1975, Milton Friedman had predicted that the economy would be better when Americans went to the polls to decide whether Ford deserved an electoral win.[72] Friedman was correct since the economy during the summer of 1976 was technically in recovery mode, even though most voters did not sense that this was the case. Economic recovery was less obvious when the unemployment rate reached 7.8 percent as the election approached.[73] His analysis of the economy less than three months before the presidential election painted a bleak picture. One revealing indicator was the bond market.

Bondholders discovered the important difference of the "nominal" and "real" interest rate. When there was high inflation, an interest rate of 10 percent was, in truth, low. In fact, if goods and services rose 10 percent a year, the 10 percent "nominal" interest rate became a zero percent "real" rate. As Friedman explained to *Newsweek* readers in August, those who purchased bonds lost money. A government bond giving five percent interest per year was a poor deal when the bond purchaser cashed in the bond during high inflation. In this case, the purchaser of government savings bonds paid "for the privilege of lending to the government."[74]

A lesson in numbers was also important on the topic of government spending on unemployment insurance. To *Newsweek* readers, Friedman pointed to the billions of dollars spent on unemployment insurance payments and asked: Was the large amount spent because of high unemployment or was the high unemployment a consequence of the government spending this amount? More to the point, what was the cause and what was the effect? In exploring this issue, Friedman cited the example of unemployment in Massachusetts; it was 7.5 percent in October 1974, 11.1 percent in October 1975, and back down to 7.1 percent in October 1976. The drastic swing in these unemployment figures was interesting given that the actual employment numbers "changed hardly at all."

The explanation for the change was the government's extension of unemployment benefits that took effect in January 1975. The extension of benefits "brought 100,000 people out of the woodwork and on to the unemployment rolls—not because they had lost their jobs, but because the state and the Federal government were offering a good deal." This explained the rise of unemployment to 11.1 percent in October 1975, but why the decrease one year later. To counteract what occurred in 1975, the Massachusetts government "tightened up the state's unemployment-compensation program—making it impossible for people who quit their jobs voluntarily to collect benefits." Once again there was a major shift; the unemployment number plunged. This change was "not because our economy was booming, but because the benefits were no longer available."[75]

Friedman noted that the availability of unemployment benefits had the same effect on the national level. Comparing national data for the years 1961–1962 and 1975–1976, he demonstrated the problem when people simply focused on unemployment percentages. For 1961–1962, the unemployment number was in the four percent range (never reaching five percent), whereas for 1975–1976 the unemployment number stayed above five percent. Based on this comparison, the early 1960s looked stronger for jobs than the mid-1970s. Still, the percentage of people working in 1961–1962 was lower (closer to 61 percent) than for the years 1975–1976 (in the 63–64 percent range). These set of employment percentages indicated that the job situation was stronger during the Ford years than the Kennedy years. But why the higher unemployment numbers for the Ford years?

As Friedman explained, the calculation of the percentage of people employed depended on the answer of a sample survey question: "Has [member of the household] been looking for work during the past four weeks?" The availability of unemployment benefits influenced this number.

Typically, people were eligible for unemployment benefits providing they stated their availability to work. For this reason, they had "a strong incentive to go through the motions of looking for work." Consequently, with unemployment benefits greater during the Ford years, there was a higher percentage of people looking for work (and thus, a higher unemployment number). Included in this category were "people who might otherwise not be in the labor market" but now had incentive to seek employment to qualify for benefits. If unemployment benefits were not available, there was less incentive for jobless people "to look for work or say they are looking for work."

On the issue of employment policy, Friedman pointed to the intellectual inconsistency of those who favored a generous unemployment insurance system but complained about "the high recorded rate of unemployment."[76] As for Ford's quest to win another term in office, the perception of high unemployment, in part a consequence of Keynesian policies, did him no favors.

A more clear-cut problem for all Americans during the Ford administration concerned energy. Nixon's wage and price controls in 1971 came when gasoline prices were high and heating oil prices were low, which meant it was more profitable for the oil industry to refine gasoline rather than heating oil. Ford understood that lifting the controls would alleviate the shortage of heating oil and had he acted, the economic and political picture of 1976 would have been different. He did not act before the congressional elections of 1974 nor did he lift controls later. To the dismay of conservative economists, Ford agreed with the White House advisors who pressed him to sign an Omnibus Energy bill passed in November 1975.

Winning Ford's confidence on economic and energy policy was Frank Zarb, head of the Federal Energy Administration, rather than the free market advice of William Simon who demanded a veto.[77] Ford's signing of the bill on December 27 represented one more loss to Keynesian thinking. The *Wall Street Journal* declared that the signing was "the clearest blunder of his administration."[78] In 1976, the rising price of energy was not something the American people could forget. It was not necessary for them to know the specifics of Ford's economic decisions to appreciate a cheerless economy. Even if they did not blame Ford directly, they still were angry when they experienced high prices at the gas pumps, paid more taxes, and witnessed the costs of rising inflation.

Liberalism lost big in the 1972 election, but the judgment that it "was fatally wounded" is not accurate.[79] Keynesianism continued to look better to voters than anything offered by Republicans. In fact, Ford wavered too much for conservatives to have much faith in his economic decisions. One good idea came too late. Ford honored his promise to "take the shackles off American businessmen" by promoting deregulation; however, unfortunately for the Republican Party it took years before Congress deregulated railroads, trucking, and airlines.[80] Others simply believed that the Ford government, driven by political necessity, made a mess of the economy.

The Keynesian mindset still ruled the day and many Americans looked to greater government intervention to solve economic problems. The economists who challenged Keynesian and progressive policies made little progress in political circles. Ford's mediocre economic record left him vulnerable to challenges within the Republican Party and from whoever the Democrats chose as their candidate for the 1976 presidential election.

Notes

1. John Robert Greene, *The Presidency of Gerald R. Ford* (Lawrence: University Press of Kansas, 1995), 91–92.
2. Gerald R. Ford, *A Time to Heal* (New York: Berkley Books, 1980), 305, 310.
3. Following another twist, one historian suggests that the goal of Ford's political policymaking was to earn the gratitude of New York Senator James Buckley and, thus, gain his support for the 1976 presidential election. See Greene, *The Presidency of Gerald R. Ford*, 95.
4. Milton Friedman and Rose Friedman, *Free to Choose: A Personal Statement* (Orlando, FL: Harcourt, 1990), 65. "A New Holiday," *Newsweek*, August 5, 1974, 56.
5. Ford, *A Time to Heal*, 41–42.
6. Ibid., 122.
7. Robert M. Collins, *Transforming America: Politics and Culture in the Reagan Years* (New York: Columbia University Press, 2007), 8. W. Carl Biven, *Jimmy Carter's Economy: Policy in an Age of Limits* (Chapel Hill: The University of North Carolina Press, 2002), 28.
8. Herbert Stein, *Presidential Economics: The Making of Economic Policy from Roosevelt to Clinton*, Third Revised Edition (Washington, DC: American Enterprise Institute for Public Policy Research, 1994), 209.
9. Quoted in Ford, *A Time to Heal*, 147.
10. Ibid., 28, 131.
11. Ibid., 190.

12. Ibid., 132, 148.
13. Ibid., 189.
14. Alan Greenspan, *The Age of Turbulence: Adventures in a New World* (New York: The Penguin Press, 2007), 66.
15. William E. Simon, *A Time for Truth* (New York: Reader's Digest Press, 1978), 105.
16. John Chamberlain, "Economic 'Gospel' Available to Ford," *Evening Independent* (St. Petersburg, FL), September 27, 1974, 20A.
17. Greenspan, *The Age of Turbulence*, 67–68.
18. Quoted in Greenspan, *The Age of Turbulence*, 70–71.
19. Biven, *Jimmy Carter's Economy*, 28–29.
20. Simon, *A Time for Truth*, 120.
21. Ibid., 91. According to Simon, "[a]pproximately 70% of the long-term capital funds available in private money markets was being borrowed by the federal government and 80% by governments at all levels" (95).
22. Jeff Bloodworth, "'The Program for Better Jobs and Income': Welfare Reform, Liberalism, and the Failed Presidency of Jimmy Carter," *International Social Science Review*, 82, nos. 3–4 (2006): 138.
23. Milton Friedman, "The Politics of Economics," *Newsweek*, October 16, 1978, 92.
24. Milton Friedman, "Ford's Budget," *Newsweek*, February 9, 1976, 64.
25. Martin Anderson, *Welfare: The Political Economy of Welfare Reform in the United* States (Stanford, CA: Hoover Institution, 1978), 134.
26. Bruce J. Schulman, *The Seventies: The Great Shift in American Culture, Society, and Politics* (Boston: Da Capo Press, 2001), 106–14.
27. Ken Auletta, *The Streets Were Paved with Gold* (New York: Random House, 1979), 138.
28. Friedman, *Free to Choose*, 101.
29. Greene, *The Presidency of Gerald R. Ford*, 90.
30. William F. Buckley Jr., *Miles Gone By: A Literary Autobiography* (Washington, DC: Regnery Publishing, Inc., 2004), 518, 521–22, 531–32, 542.
31. Auletta quoted in Friedman, *Free to Choose*, 101.
32. Auletta, *The Streets Were Paved with Gold*, 32.
33. Simon, *A Time for Truth*, 130.
34. Ibid., 135–136, 141–142.
35. Milton Friedman, "New York City," *Newsweek*, November 17, 1975, 90.
36. "New York City Is 'Stink City,'" *Daily Item* (Sumter, SC), July 2, 1975, 16B.
37. Ford, *A Time to Heal*, 305.
38. Ibid., 308–309. Also, see Mike Waters, "Senate Panel Votes New York $4 Billion Loan Guarantees," *Kentucky New Era* (Hopkinsville, KY), October 30, 1975, 1.

39. Quoted in Ford, *A Time to Heal*, 305.
40. Quoted in Simon, *A Time for Truth*, 134.
41. *Evening News* (Newburgh, NY), October 25, 1975, 7A.
42. Simon, *A Time for Truth*, 171.
43. Ford, *A Time to Heal*, 128.
44. Lou Cannon, *Governor Reagan: His Rise to Power* (New York: PublicAffairs, 2003), 399.
45. Simon, *A Time for Truth*, 143. Rick Perlstein, *The Invisible Bridge, The Fall of Nixon and the Rise of Reagan* (New York: Simon & Schuster, 2015), 516. "The Governor's Appeal," *Hour* (Norwalk, CT), October 25, 1975, 4.
46. Quoted in Simon, *A Time for Truth*, 143.
47. Ibid.
48. Thomas Sowell, *Basic Economics: A Common Sense Guide to the Economy*, Fifth Edition (New York: Basic Books, 2015), 41–47.
49. Simon, *A Time for Truth*, 167, 169.
50. Auletta, *The Streets Were Paved with Gold*, 91, 100.
51. "Bill Walton Identifies with Radicals," *Blade* (Toledo), March 15, 1975, 19.
52. Irving Kristol, *Neoconservatism: The Autobiography of an Idea* (Chicago: Elephant Paperbacks, 1999), 4–5.
53. Ibid., 230–231.
54. Thomas Sowell, *A Personal Obyssey* (New York: The Free Press, 2000), xi.
55. Sowell, *A Personal Odyssey*, 132.
56. Thomas Sowell, *A Man of Letters* (New York: Encounter Books, 2007), 92–93.
57. Milton Friedman, "What Is the Federal Reserve Doing?," *Newsweek*, March 10, 1975, 63.
58. Ibid.
59. Milton Friedman, "Tax Rhetoric," *Newsweek*, October 27, 1975, 90.
60. Friedman, *Free to Choose*, 116–117.
61. Milton Friedman, "Bureaucracy Scorned," *Newsweek*, December 29, 1975, 47.
62. Brian Domitrovic, *Econoclasts: The Rebels Who Sparked the Supply-Side Revolution and Restored American Prosperity* (Wilmington, DE: ISI Books, 2009), 9–10, 92, 96–97.
63. Martin Anderson, *Revolution* (New York: Harcourt Brace Jovanovich, 1988), 147.
64. Quoted in Perlstein, *The Invisible Bridge*, 310.
65. Anderson, *Revolution*, 148. Also, see Domitrovic, *Econoclasts*, 11.
66. Domitrovic, *Econoclasts*, 10, 88. Many key supply-siders also pointed to the importance of a gold standard as a way to discourage inflation.

67. Ibid., 106–107, 109–112
68. Bruce R. Bartlett, *Reaganomics: Supply Side Economics in Action* (Westport, CT: Arlington House Publishers, 1981), 127.
69. Domitrovic, *Econoclasts*, 115–118, 124.
70. Greenspan, *The Age of Turbulence*, 75.
71. Ira G. Corn, "Personal and Economic Freedom: Yesterday, Today, and Tomorrow," *Imprimis*, 9, no. 1 (1980): 5.
72. Milton Friedman, "The Economy and the 1976 Elections," *Newsweek*, February 17, 1975, 80.
73. Biven, *Jimmy Carter's Economy*, 28–29.
74. Milton Friedman, "Interest Rates and Inflation," *Newsweek*, August 23, 1976, 23.
75. Milton Friedman, "Behind the Unemployment Numbers," *Newsweek*, February 7, 1977, 63.
76. Ibid.
77. Greene, *The Presidency of Gerald R. Ford*, 72, 78.
78. Quoted in Meg Jacobs, *Panic at the Pump: The Energy Crisis and the Transformation of American Politics in the 1970s* (New York: Hill and Wang, 2017), 152.
79. On the "fatally wounded" liberalism, see Maurice Isserman and Michael Kazin, *America Divided: The Civil War of the 1960s* (New York: Oxford University Press, 2000), 287.
80. Greenspan, *The Age of Turbulence*, 71–73.

CHAPTER 5

The Presidential Campaign of 1976

Politicians are ambitious, and Governor Jimmy Carter of Georgia was exceptionally ambitious. In 1972, Tip O'Neill, future speaker of the House, heard about this southern governor wanting to be president, someone eager to travel anywhere across the country to speak for the Democratic Party. In the next two years, Governor Carter did speak for candidates, including those in areas where a Democrat's victory was virtually impossible. He met thousands of Democratic activists and earned the gratitude of many local candidates who appreciated a governor speaking for them, thus elevating their stature in the community.[1]

Carter began campaigning in Iowa as early as 1975, a strategy that turned Iowa into an important campaign stop for future candidates. He rented a large ballroom at a hotel in Des Moines where he set out soft drinks, crackers, and cheese and waited for people to attend his reception. A total of four people showed up. With his assistant Jody Powell, he left the hotel and strolled the city streets seeking voters. With their visits to more than 120 Iowa centers, they were fortunate if 20 people gathered for one of their meetings.[2]

Among his inner circle, few had national experience "or indeed much political experience at all." Carter had a long way to go, but the bicentennial of the Republic was a year of surprises. Conservative Ronald Reagan thought he could defeat President Gerald Ford for the Republican nomination, and Carter was confident of rising to the top of the Democratic

E. R. Crouse, *America's Failing Economy and the Rise of Ronald Reagan*,
https://doi.org/10.1007/978-3-319-70545-3_5

leadership. As the political process unfolded, the state of the economy played a significant role on how Americans voted in November. The timing was good for the winner.

I

President Ford experienced his share of rough patches in 1975, his first full year in the White House. Many Americans remained critical of his pardon of Richard Nixon and the North Vietnamese takeover of South Vietnam was a sad legacy he could not escape. Conservatives bristled over his selection of liberal Republican Nelson Rockefeller for his vice president, and they lamented Betty Ford's endorsement of abortion and her flippant attitude on the topics of marijuana use and premarital affairs—all discussed by Ford's wife on national television.[3]

As for the economy, there were signs of improvement, but the economic bounce was not strong enough to erase the perception of many Americans that there was no improvement. When Ronald Reagan, former governor of California, decided to make a serious run for the Republican nomination few initially expected he had much of a chance. Reagan's convincing showing in the later primaries demonstrated he might reach his goal.

Born in 1911 in Tampico, Illinois, Reagan moved around with his family before spending most of his childhood in Dixon, Illinois. He was an avid reader and as a young boy, he checked out an average of two books every week at his local library. In high school, he was president of the senior class and president of the school drama club. He majored in economics at Eureka College, a Disciples of Christ institution located in rural Illinois.[4] As an economics student, Reagan learned Say's Law, named after Jean Baptiste Say (1767–1832) whom future supply-siders looked to for guidance.[5]

Reagan moved to California where he experienced success as a film actor until the early 1950s. After his marriage to film star Jane Wyman ended in divorce, he married actor Nancy Davis. His next job was host of *General Electric Theatre*, traveling throughout the country acting as a motivational speaker and corporate ambassador of the General Electric Company. On the road, he discovered "the native conservatism of working America."[6]

A New Deal Democrat who switched to the Republican Party in the early 1960s, Reagan campaigned for Republican presidential nominee

Barry Goldwater in 1964. Two years later, he ran for governor of California against incumbent Governor Pat Brown, "a classic tax-and-spend Democrat" and formidable opponent.[7] Surprising many, Reagan won by a margin of 58 percent to 42 percent, and again four years later, notable achievements for a conservative politician.

On many issues, he set a distinct tone, including his response to California's surplus revenues: "Give it back to the taxpayers." The Democratic legislature, however, rejected this proposal with one state senator declaring, ironically: "I consider this an unnecessary expenditure of public funds."[8] Reagan failed to reach his goal of a tax limitation amendment to the California constitution, but his efforts did help launch a national movement for lower taxes.[9]

With Gerald Ford only president for several weeks, Reagan sent him a telegram reminding him of the 1972 election mandate of no new taxes and reducing the size of the federal government.[10] Neither knew each other well. Yet, in contrast to Democrats, Ford understood that Reagan was someone to take seriously and gave him the "choice of virtually any position" in the cabinet—an offer Reagan rejected to complete his second term as governor.[11] There was something better ahead. He had a sense of destiny and one of his most striking characteristics was his sunny optimism: "I was raised to believe that God has a plan for everyone and that seemingly random twists of fate are all a part of His plan. My mother—a small woman with auburn hair and a sense of optimism that ran as deep as the cosmos—told me that everything in life happened for a purpose."[12] In 1975, he left office with high approval ratings.[13]

Reagan combined his optimism with an economic message built on free-market principles. Although missed by many people at the time, his understanding of economics was quite sophisticated, a fact uncovered by historians analyzing his handwritten speeches of the 1970s.[14] During the mid-1970s, many Americans heard him on the radio sharing his economic vision of smaller government and fewer regulations. For example, in early 1975 he presented radio listeners with one of his essays underscoring the serious problem of inflation, linked to burdensome regulations.

Reagan noted that the required paperwork for American companies with less than 500 employees ate up more than 100 million "man hours a year" and added approximately $50 billion to the cost of doing business. There were so many federal agencies, bureaus, and commissions with virtually no one knowing the exact number. The essay went on to say that the

Federal registry listing regulations had more pages than a set of *Encyclopedia Brittanica*. Entrepreneurs targeted for regulatory infraction by a government body did not have their day in court; each agency had regulatory power of "judge, jury, [and] executioner." One case Reagan described was that of a small California businessman who was ordered to install separate washrooms for men and women. This made no sense because he only had one employee—his wife.

In others he mentioned, an Illinois baker found the government forms too complicated and too time-consuming to fill out. A Connecticut chemical researcher discovered that he had to fill out 37 different reports for 12 federal agencies. Reagan shared that the situation was even worse for larger corporations. Inflation was a problem because the government spent more money than it received and too much money was chasing too few goods and services. He felt that lifting burdensome regulations would result in more production (goods and services) causing inflation to slow down.[15]

With the encouragement of various Republican leaders, Reagan decided to run for the Republican nomination in 1976. Declaring that the GOP would not nominate him, *National Review* publisher William Rusher wanted him to run under a third political party.[16] Reagan thought otherwise. Ford's pardoning of Nixon for his role in the Watergate fiasco and his wobbly position on some conservative principles made him vulnerable. Reagan, however, pledged to follow the Eleventh Commandment and not attack Ford personally.

Representing a rising conservative and anti-Washington movement, he was ready to present voters with a powerful message of opposition to Democrats and big government. Summarized years later in his autobiography, Reagan's` campaign theme was straightforward: "It was time to scale back the size of the federal government, reduce taxes and government intrusion in our lives, balance the budget, and return to the people the freedoms usurped from them by the bureaucrats."[17]

Reagan received good press from free-market economists in the face of criticism from those pointing to the doubling of spending during Reagan's eight-year tenure as governor. In early 1976, Milton Friedman gave *Newsweek* readers an economic comparison of Reagan's record as governor of California and the record of New York governors. In 1966, the year before Reagan became governor, government spending per capita was 16 percent higher in California than per capita spending in New York. In the last year of Reagan's governorship, per capita spending in California was 19 percent lower than New York.

Although spending did indeed double in California during the Reagan years, it almost tripled in New York. A comparison of debt numbers also favored Reagan. In 1966, New York debt per capita was 12 percent higher than California, but in 1974 the New York number astoundingly was 147 percent higher than California's. Put another way, the California debt increased 50 percent during the Reagan years while the New York debt increased 300 percent. The numbers for welfare spending also showed a dramatic rise in New York compared to California. As Friedman pointed out, Reagan's record as governor was "highly relevant in judging his qualifications for the Presidency."[18]

Reagan sought to convince Americans of his accomplishments as governor, particularly the reduction of waste and welfare abuse. His solution was for the state and local governments to take direct control over various federal programs and have "the taxing power to pay for them."[19] Reagan effectively outlined the problems of high inflation, high unemployment, and high federal taxes. He said that even more problematic for Americans was "… the belief that government, particularly the federal government, has the answer to our ills, and that the proper method of dealing with social problems is to transfer power from the private to the public sector, and within the public sector from state and local governments to the ultimate power center in Washington." The necessary change "is nothing less than a systematic transfer of authority and resources to the states." Reagan argued that such a transfer of authority "would reduce the outlay of the federal government by more than ninety-billion dollars." With these savings, the federal government could balance the budget, pay against the national debt, and reduce income taxes by about 23 percent. Those won over by Reagan's ambitious speech favored reducing the federal bureaucracy. Whether a social–welfare program was worthwhile would now be the decision of "the people of our states" rather than the federal government.[20]

There was much that was appealing in the speech presented in Chicago early in the campaign, but Ford's chief political strategist Stuart Spencer smelled blood. Explaining that Reagan's proposal was problematic in a climate of public mistrust for government taxation, Spencer looked to the New Hampshire primary in late February to hit Reagan hard. He acquired the text of the Chicago speech and the Ford team planned to ambush Reagan on the problem of how state and local governments could possibly finance and run additional programs. A few days after Reagan formally entered the race, the press also probed the candidate about how state governments would be able to take up the slack without state and local governments raising taxes. This was of special concern in New Hampshire where there was no sales tax or state income tax.

As correspondent Bob Clark asked: "In candor, wouldn't you have to tell the people of New Hampshire that you are going to have to increase your tax burden and that probably means either a sales tax or a state income tax?" Having to be on the defensive was not a good way to start any political campaign. For Reagan's political managers, the speech threatened "to be an albatross around his neck." Lyn Nofziger later admitted: "There's no question we'd have been better off if Reagan had never given it."[21]

Still, Reagan surged in the national polls and the New Year beckoned. When he arrived in New Hampshire on January 5, it was cold, and Ford's campaign was ready to pounce. Peter Kaye, Ford's campaign press secretary, recruited two prominent New Hampshire Republicans to hold a press conference in Concord on Reagan's alleged plan to tax the people of New Hampshire. The press conference was successful as was the handing out of press statements to journalists disembarking from Reagan's plane in Manchester.

Immediately, Reagan did his best to reassure New Hampshirites that he did not "have some devious plot to impose the sales or income tax on them." He stayed on message, but the Ford team effectively altered the narrative, and the media pursued the issue until primary day and after. During his three days in New Hampshire, Reagan held 17 open question-and-answer sessions with the public rather than with the press.

At his first stop at a Conway, NH, school gymnasium, he clarified his earlier speech, arguing that the transfer of control "from the federal government to those closer to the people" was an idea like that of earlier presidents. For example, President Kennedy had "protested against centralizing all authority in Washington." In subsequent speeches, Reagan offered a list of ways to finance his ideas without raising state and local taxes. One idea was to transfer to the states the $8 billion collected from federal liquor and cigarette taxes, and another was for the states to receive a portion of federal personal income taxes. Again, his message was that state and local governments would be more efficient and effective in running those programs.[22]

Nevertheless, the Ford team used emotional imagery to blunt Reagan's attempt to regain momentum with what people called his "transfer plan." To a group of reporters in Washington, Ford's campaign manager Bo

Callaway warned that "the American people will not tolerate going back to a system where you don't take care of people in need. The American people don't want elderly people thrown out in the snow." The optics pointed to a heartless Reagan who was uncaring of people in need. Reagan fired back by pointing out the contradictions of the Ford administration. Word got out that Ford himself had considered a plan to pass on parts of federal Medicaid and education programs to the states. But the damage was done. Stuart Spencer appraised the success of the Ford team: "We had to get Reagan off-balance on that first trip in, and I think we succeeded. His trip was a flop; he did not take New Hampshire by storm. He was up there three days or so and he staggered around on that ninety-billion-dollar flap, and then immediately he went to Florida and we nailed him on Social Security." Ford regained lost ground and after New Hampshire "it was a horse race."[23] Ford prevailed in New Hampshire winning by a tiny margin—54,824 to 53,507 for the challenger who demonstrated he could run "dead even" with an incumbent president.[24] Reagan regretted leaving New Hampshire days before the vote to campaign for the Illinois primary: "I'd sent a message to the voters of New Hampshire that I was taking them for granted, that New Hampshire wasn't important to me."[25]

Although polling numbers for Reagan were still good, the media began to write off the Californian after losses in the Massachusetts, Vermont, Florida, and Illinois primaries. On March 23, 1976, he gathered with his closest advisors at the Hotel Stoddard in LaCrosse, Wisconsin, on an unseasonably warm day. But the mood was grim in the old hotel room. There were "the blank sad looks, the quick, darting eyes, the overpoliteness" as the Reagan team wondered when he would quit.[26] The campaign was $2 million in debt and the senior staff had not been paid for weeks. Reagan remained steadfast.

John Sears, the head of the campaign, was not a "dyed-in-the-wool conservative," but his skills as a political tactician were remarkable.[27] He suggested the acceptance of a $100,000 loan from Jimmy Lyon, a flamboyant Texas tycoon fond of wearing open silk shirts exposing a heavy gold chain and hairy chest. A legend in conservative circles, Lyon wanted the campaign to run a Reagan speech on national television blasting Ford and Henry Kissinger for their weak position on national defense. Despite predictions of another loss in North Carolina voting that same day, a determined Reagan liked the idea and announced his intention to fight all the way to the Republican convention in August. Hours later something special happened; Reagan won North Carolina. According to Martin Anderson, "[i]t was the most satisfying political victory I have ever experienced. Not because it was the first (it wasn't), not because it was the most important (it wasn't), but because it was the best. It was the distance we all went that night from the depths of certain defeat to the high hill where all things were once again possible."[28]

The campaign was alive, but there was one notable anomaly when Barry Goldwater accused Reagan of "gross factual errors" for his hardline stand on the United States keeping control of the Panama Canal. Nancy Reagan could not believe it: "I feel as if I have been stabbed…. Of course, everyone knows what my husband did in 1964 for him." The relationship between the Arizona senator and the Reagans was never the same again.[29] Reagan fared well without Goldwater.

With wins in Texas, Alabama, Georgia, California, and several other states, he took the fight to the convention in Kansas City. Some momentum was lost, however, when Reagan gave in to John Sears's bold strategy to announce before the convention that moderate Senator Richard Schweiker would be his running mate. This ploy confused and angered conservatives. Nonetheless, actor John Wayne gave Reagan the benefit of the doubt, telling reporters: "Schweiker was a commie, but if he's good enough for Ronnie, that's enough for me."[30]

At the convention anything could happen, and, in the end, the final decision was close with Ford winning 1187 delegates to Reagan's 1070. When Claire Schweiker, the senator's wife, offered her apologies, Reagan replied: "Claire, you really shouldn't be upset about the outcome because it wasn't part of God's plan."[31] He returned to California, declining an offer from Ford: "I just wasn't interested in being vice-president."[32] The day after the convention, Ford selected Robert Dole as his candidate for vice president.

II

Looking ahead to the first statewide contest for the 1976 Democratic presidential nomination, Jimmy Carter's determination did not waver. When O'Neill, as the Speaker of the House, met Carter for the first time in January 1975, he discovered how confident Carter was in reaching his goal even though at the time he barely registered in the polls. As O'Neill learned, the political outsider Carter had it all figured out: "I know you're boosting Ted Kennedy, but Kennedy won't be running because of Chappaquiddick. Neither will Humphrey. He's got his own problems, and he's still in debt from 1968.... As I look at it, there's only one man who can beat me, and that's Walter Mondale. But he's not running."[33] Carter was certain he would be president. Plus, on the issue of economy, he was confident in his ability to tackle the recession and unemployment (the issue of inflation received less attention). He was a representative of southern liberalism, ready to serve the American people.[34]

Jimmy Carter was born on October 1, 1924, in Plains, Georgia. He grew up in a well-to-do home; his businessman father had significant land holdings and his mother was a nurse. Carter graduated from high school at age 16 and two years later entered the U.S. Naval Academy where he earned excellent marks, ranking in the top 10 percent of his class. He was a naval officer for seven years before returning to Plains to run the family peanut business, a regulated and subsidized industry. Interested in public service, the 38-year-old Carter campaigned for the Georgia Senate in 1962, but lost the election by 139 votes. He took legal action and demanded a recount when he received information about his competition stuffing ballot boxes with the votes of dead people. The revised results gave him victory. Four years later he was a close runner-up in the Georgia Democratic gubernatorial primary. His second run for governor in 1970 was a success.

Carter's strong support for racial justice earned him a place on the cover of *Time* and a story proclaiming him a progressive leader of the "New South."[35] His other successful initiatives were environmental protection, welfare reform, and consumer protection contrasted to the mixed success of his improving the "operation and cost-effectiveness" of the government.[36]

In his 1975 book, *Why Not the Best?*, Carter clarified his passion for reading and understanding the work of experts in various fields; he was a "planner," even taking time to study "the techniques of long-range planning."[37] Wanting government to "express the highest common ideals of human beings," he sought to combine "competent and efficient management of taxpayers' money with the sensitive and effective service needed to alleviate affliction." One of his goals was a comprehensive national health program.[38] Carter said that by way of rational management and planning, and the "personal involvement of the president himself," restoration of the people's confidence in government would be possible.[39]

Having strong ambitions for the presidency, he pored over the detailed plans of chief strategist Hamilton Jordan in August 1974.[40] Jordan was a hard-drinking, tough-talking South Georgian who wore unbuttoned shirts and cowboy boots. His thick black hair "stuck to his head like a plastic football helmet."[41] On December 12, 1974, Carter announced his candidacy, understanding that an early start was crucial. In the months that followed, he invested much time and organized for a serious run, assisted by Jody Powell who had been his press secretary when he was governor.

Born poor and raised near Plains, Georgia, Powell was a scrappy young man with an intense look, constantly on "low-boil simmer." Caught cheating and expelled from the Air Force Academy, his next stop was Georgia State University, followed by graduate studies at Emory University.[42] The issue of integrity rose on several occasions concerning both Powell and Jordan. In 1976, the *Atlantic Monthly* noted the "manipulative" character of 31-year-old campaign manager Jordan and 32-year-old press secretary Powell.[43] One Carter insider wrote that Jordan and Powell looked like "thugs" with "a hint of violence in them."[44]

In his memoirs, Carter recounted his time on the road with Powell: "Jody and I traveled together—for many months there was just the two of us. We drove rented cars, flew in borrowed single-engine airplanes, and slept on couches or in spare rooms of supporters." When they thought they were ready for a full-scale press conference, they rented an expensive room in a downtown Philadelphia hotel and invited scores of reporters. To their embarrassment only one reporter came to the event.[45]

Nevertheless, the hard work paid off in Iowa. Proclaimed the winner, Carter caught the attention of the national media wanting to know more about this moderate who outscored the crowded field of liberal candidates. His victory five weeks later in New Hampshire proved he had a legitimate chance of winning the nomination. Still, there were incidents on the campaign trail that foreshadowed weak support from the progressive wing of the Democratic Party.

One curious incident was Robert Shrum's brief stint as a Carter speech writer. Shrum grew up in a Pennsylvania coal-mining town where his father worked as a tool and die maker. When Robert was eight years old, his father sought a better job and the family packed up the car and moved to Culver City, California. Politics fascinated the young Shrum. In an interview years later, he spoke of his strong political opinions while a teenager: "I knew I would be involved in politics, if not as a politician, then as a historian or political scientist." In high school, Shrum experienced political heaven when he worked for John F. Kennedy's campaign in Los Angeles. After high school, he earned degrees at Georgetown University and Harvard Law School. He taught briefly at Boston College and later took various speechwriting jobs, most notably working for George McGovern when he ran for president in 1972.[46]

In 1976, Carter pollster Pat Caddell recommended that Carter employ Shrum as a speechwriter. The 32-year-old jumped at the opportunity to work for the Carter team, coming one step closer to his goal of being a presidential speechwriter. Less than two weeks later, he made his way to the front desk of the Philadelphia Sheraton with two copies of his letter of resignation for the mailboxes of Caddell and Jody Powell. The first sentence was direct: "Governor Carter, I have decided that in light of my own convictions and in fairness to you, I should leave the campaign without delay." What had happened?

Basically, Shrum, a speechwriter with "bleeding heart" credentials, was unsure of Carter's policies and character. His last work for Carter was writing a victory statement celebrating Carter's Pennsylvania primary win. He decided that his statement about Carter was good, but he himself "didn't believe it." It took little time for him to see that Carter presented contradictory positions on military spending and welfare and economic policies. Shrum was hardly religious, but Carter's private, crass banter about other politicians was inconsistent with his out-front religiosity. In his resignation letter, Shrum wrote: "I am not sure what you truly believe in, other than yourself."[47]

Shrum's exit from Philadelphia was a quiet trip to Washington, an escape from the inevitable tongue-wagging about his abrupt departure. Soul-searching days included time with Democrat writers and Kennedy insiders Doris Kearns and Richard Goodwin. His resignation letter was meant to be private, but political writer Jules Witcover tracked him down after four days of searching. He interviewed Shrum at a Washington office where the "emotionally unstrung" speechwriter had difficulty holding himself together. Nonetheless, he was "deliberate in his speech," offering a critical narrative about Carter that was disputed by Carter in a *Playboy* magazine interview months later.[48] Although only a blip on the campaign, Shrum gave key Democrats reason to be wary of Carter.

Of the well-known progressive Democrats who never warmed up to Carter, Arthur M. Schlesinger Jr. stood out. He was a major voice within the party, rallying behind one progressive idea or person after another as issues arose in Washington's corridors of power. Whether it was politics, media, or entertainment, he was a historian and Kennedy devotee close to many progressive movers and shakers. Having little economic proficiency did not hinder him from stating the necessary and proper policies for America to advance economically. He was confident that progressive economists, such as John Kenneth Galbraith, were correct. Besides, they both shared a Harvard connection and were friends. Neither one was enthusiastic about Carter even if some viewed him as a Southern progressive.

In his private journals, Schlesinger had much to say about candidate Carter and his apparent "authoritarian" instincts. He was after all from the "suspect" South and he had spent years in the navy. For some, he was a moderate lacking the mettle to consistently uphold liberal principles. Schlesinger found Carter an unattractive option—turned off by his "fixed grin, righteousness and ambiguity on issues"—but he knew that Senator Hubert Humphrey's day had passed. Besides there was bad blood between Humphrey and Schlesinger, evidenced by the "acid references" to Schlesinger in Humphrey's memoirs. On February 16, Schlesinger wrote: "I tend to regard Carter as an intelligent, ambitious opportunist, who will move to any position that he thinks would help him in his upward course." Nevertheless, it was prudent not to "denounce him too drastically in the primaries lest we have to support him in the election."[49]

Schlesinger's introduction to Carter on June 24 was at the Waldorf, where other $1000 contributors, including "the darkly handsome but perhaps a little fat" Elizabeth Taylor, gathered to hear Carter. When Dick Dougherty and Schlesinger talked to Carter in a side room, Schlesinger later wrote of Carter as being pleasant. That night he decided not to mention his concern that Carter was occasionally too critical of the government bureaucracy.[50]

In early June, *The New York Times* reported Carter's characterization of the federal bureaucracy as "totally unmanageable."[51] Such talk was a red flag for progressives. At dinner parties, politicians, Hollywood stars, and others wondered about Carter's progressive credentials.[52] Bill Moyers shared with Schlesinger that he neither liked nor disliked Carter: "He's the sort who would burn people at the stake.... I respect him, and I'm afraid of him."[53] Edward (Ted) Kennedy was one important Democrat unsure of where Carter stood, telling Schlesinger in July that he could not reassure other liberals that Carter was trustworthy. Schlesinger wrote: "Ted will serve as the ideological conscience of the Carter administration—and no doubt make Carter a better President than he would be without pressure from the left."[54] If history had passed Kennedy by because of his actions at Chappaquiddick, he still had an important role as senator to support big government.[55]

Jackie Onassis had favored George McGovern rather than Carter whom she described as "that stiff, prissy little man on the [television] screen!" There were plenty of hurt feelings among northeastern progressives who wondered why Carter did not reach out to them for campaign assistance. On this issue, Schlesinger concluded: "He seems a mean little man." Schlesinger appeared to be unaware of his own political baggage and assumed Carter's reason for keeping his distance from Washington insiders was that he did not want Ted Kennedy to overshadow him.[56] With progressive George McGovern as their candidate, the dismal results of the 1972 election was instructive for moderate Democrats willing to give Carter a chance.

One hopeful liberal seeking the nomination was Senator Henry Jackson of Washington who spoke of his three priorities: "Jobs, Jobs. And Jobs!" Catholic intellectual Michael Novak, one of Jackson's supporters, wrote of the difficult economic conditions in his hometown of Johnstown, Pennsylvania, where shuttered steel mills stood silently, and high unemployment was the norm. When the Hollywood production team for the Paul Newman film *Slap Shot* came to town, a dozen Johnstowners were willing to make a little money by having their bare butts filmed, sticking out of the windows of a passing bus.[57] When Jackson lost the Pennsylvania primary in April, despite the endorsement of the state's powerful labor leaders, he withdrew from the race.[58]

Progressives wanted Senator Hubert Humphrey to enter the race and a Gallup Poll gave evidence of his competitiveness. Voicing a common criticism from a conservative, William Simon viewed Humphrey as a big government liberal "who, like most liberals is virtually illiterate in economics."[59] After his consultation with close friends and a *Washington Post* editorial advising him not to discredit his career by entering the race, Humphrey gave a statement that he would not enter the primaries.[60] The path was then clearer for Carter.

As Carter campaigned, he remained virtually unknown in Washington, a fact the candidate wanted to change. One notable Washington gathering gave important Democrats their first introduction to this southern outsider. Dinner guests of columnist Clayton Fritchey and his wife Polly, Clifford Clark and other key people met Carter and went away with a good impression. Clark left the Fritchey's house convinced that he had met the next president of the United States.[61] This was significant coming from someone who had been Harry S Truman's White House Counsel, John F. Kennedy's personal lawyer, and Lyndon B. Johnson's Secretary of Defense.

Carter continued to accumulate delegates in all the primaries and by June the other candidates dropped out, realizing he was unstoppable.[62] His strategy of participating in every primary and his thorough homework about party rules paid off. At the Democratic National Convention on July 14, he gained the necessary votes on the first ballot. His choice of a running mate was a Washington liberal insider—Senator Walter Mondale.[63] Mondale was on the ticket to reassure liberals that Carter—still a mystery to some—would stay true to liberalism. Yet, it was not enough for Arthur Schlesinger; he could not find it in his heart to publicly support Carter. Fortunately for Carter, the lack of support from well-known progressive Democrats was not a serious problem, but there were other glitches.

III

One gift for the Republicans was a serious misstep by Carter strategists. The Carter interview with *Playboy* gave Republicans hope. Urged by Jody Powell and other advisors, Carter did a series of *Playboy* interviews with freelance writer Robert Scheer. The reason for doing the interviews was to go after *Playboy* readers who might be uneasy about Carter. Powell expected that the interviews would be thoughtful but unmemorable; the last page of the 10-page interview was not unmemorable.[64]

The media focused on a few sentences: "I've looked on a lot of women with lust. I've committed adultery in my heart many times…. Christ says, Don't consider yourself better than someone else because one guy screws a whole bunch of women while the other guy is loyal to his wife." These statements read without the context of the whole interview were devastating. Besides, only a small segment of Americans read *Playboy* to know this. Soon after the issue reached the newsstands and the media covered the story, Carter lost 10 points in the polls. Working for Carter, the 25-year-old Harvard-trained pollster Pat Caddell declared: "*Playboy* killed us." Carter admitted that the interview was a mistake: "It demonstrated a confirmation of Ford's proposal to the American people that I was not quite to be trusted—that I was not what I was supposed to be, and that in some ways I was misleading the American voters."[65]

Unable to explain his interview blunder, Carter decided that the best strategy was "to live with it" and try to move forward.[66] Unfortunately for Carter, his next press conference made things worse when he attempted to clarify a derogatory statement he made about Lyndon B. Johnson in the last paragraph of the interview. Reporters believed his explanation was an attempt to mislead them.[67]

Carter relied heavily on Pat Caddell. Having experienced a vagabond childhood, following his Coast Guard father employed on the Atlantic coast, Caddell took an early interest in polling. His first experience consisted of going from house to house asking his neighbors questions. After completing his Harvard degree, he formed the company Cambridge Survey Research. In his run for the presidency in 1972, George McGovern employed the services of Caddell. Nicknamed "the chinless wonder," Caddell stood out with his weak chin, pear-shaped body, and moody demeanor that ranged from exuberance to moroseness. Nonetheless, as an avid reader of history and politics with impressive interviewing techniques, he was smart as a whip.[68]

Still, Carter could be stubborn about taking campaign advice from others. Hamilton Jordan told Carter to stop using the phrase "Nixon-Ford administration" because it was risky to equate Nixon and Ford and, thus, attack the integrity of a man the American people viewed as honest.[69] There was hope in the Ford camp. A good bounce after the Republican convention and the *Playboy* episode gave Ford confidence, but his strategists omitted a key person in the campaign team—Ronald Reagan.[70] When Ford finally reached out to Reagan, time and momentum had been lost.

As Ford and Carter sparred with each other in the press, it was difficult to categorize where Carter stood on economic policy. In college, he did not take an economics course, but as governor he learned from his economic advisor Henry Thomassen, a Georgia State University economist. Given his engineering background, he found details fascinating. With economics, he favored microeconomic problems, such as the economics of energy, over broader macroeconomic ones—that is, employment, inflation, and the gross national product (GNP). Yet there were limits to his interest in economics. According to Stuart Eizenstat, "It was sort of a 'dark science' to him."[71]

The experience of one urban journalist reveals much about Carter the technocrat. Aboard Carter's campaign plane, Ken Auletta received an invitation to join Carter at the front of the 727 for an interview. Sliding into a first-class seat beside Carter, Auletta waited five minutes before

Carter, busy studying a two-page memorandum, acknowledged his presence. After completing his study, Carter gave the journalist a warm greeting and 50 minutes to share his views, including the importance of allocating federal funds to areas worst hit by unemployment. Carter believed the government could plan and allocate funds intelligently.[72]

Carter referred to himself as a nuclear physicist and peanut farmer, but he was neither as some journalists pointed out. More accurately, he was an engineer and an agribusinessman.[73] As a Democrat desiring to shape "our nation's economy," his instincts were for government intervention in economics. Some saw him as a moderate Keynesian with some awareness of the importance of fiscal responsibility and balanced budgets. In some circles, he preferred the label "fiscal conservative."[74] Certainly, on a few issues his words seemed out of place to those Democrats who expected more enthusiasm for government intervention in the economy. For example, he was critical of transportation regulation, arguing that the "present patch-work scheme of rail, truck, and airline regulation at the federal level needlessly costs consumers billions of dollars every year." Yes, "the original purpose of promoting fledgling industry and protecting the public from the tyranny of monopoly or the chaos of predatory competition" was commendable, but the system often discouraged competition.[75]

On welfare policy Carter appeared to side with those who believed the best approach to solving poverty was economic growth and jobs. "Entitlement liberals," on the other hand, were enthusiastic with progressive social programs that gave a guaranteed income for the nonworking poor.[76] With his eye on jobs, Carter proposed to bring unemployment down to 4–4.5 percent, the range viewed as constituting full employment. A lower number was improbable given the time involved for worker transition from job to job, geographically or occupationally.

Having faith in the government's ability to plan economic prosperity, Carter's proposal was like the Humphrey-Hawkins bill under consideration by Washington lawmakers.[77] Senator Hubert Humphrey and Representative August Hawkins were Democratic progressives who were comfortable with taking bold action to lower the unemployment rate. Their bill placed the onus on the federal government to supply jobs if the private sector fell short; however, because the bill lacked any recognition of the dangers of inflation, Carter wanted some modifications before giving his full endorsement.[78] Embracing Keynesian logic, Carter found the bill's goal of three percent unemployment too risky.

Questioned by *Fortune* magazine in 1976 on his commitment to a full employment program, he declared: "I would proceed aggressively, with the first emphasis on jobs. My economic advisers and I agree that until you get the unemployment rate down below 5 percent, there's no real danger of escalating inflationary pressures."[79] Others agreed. Progressive economist Robert L. Heilbroner saw no reason to panic about inflation. Because income and property growth matched inflation over the past 25 years, "the middle class has not been killed—in fact, it has done extremely well."[80]

Milton Friedman called the Humphrey-Hawkins bill "as close to a fraud as has ever served as a campaign document." This "centerpiece" of the fall campaign became "the litmus test of the true-blue Democratic faith of every candidate from Jimmy Carter to the aspirant for dogcatcher." According to Friedman, the best critique of the Democrat's promises of full employment was Adam Smith's *The Wealth of the Nations* (1776). One long sentence stood out: "The statesman, who should attempt to direct private people in what manner they ought to employ their capitals, would not only load himself with a most unnecessary attention, but assume an authority which could safely be trusted, not only to no single person, but to no council or senate whatever, and which would nowhere be so dangerous as in the hands of a man who had folly and presumption enough to fancy himself fit to exercise it." This was a sharp rebuke of Humphrey and Hawkins for a plan absent of any measures to fulfill its promises. Instead of lowering unemployment, the bill would "add to government employment and reduce private employment, in the process making us all poorer and very likely igniting a new inflationary binge."[81]

Friedman charged that it was easy for politicians "to say that the government will be the employer of last resort. But where does her government get the money? Ultimately, from you and me, by hook or crook. If it spends, we don't. If it employs people, we don't." In other words, more government spending would mean higher taxes and less money for taxpayers to spend and hire. If the government also financed its full employment scheme by borrowing, the outcome was no better because lenders would have less to spend. One other avenue was the government printing money, but this taxed Americans indirectly through inflation. Friedman asked: "Is anyone so naïve as to suppose that the government jobs created will be more productive than the private jobs destroyed?"

Nevertheless, the government had an advantage; it usually dodged the blame for its harmful policies because of the visible and invisible effects of government measures: "People hired by government know who is their benefactor. People who lose their jobs or fail to get them because of the government program do not know that that is the source of their problem. The good effects are visible. The bad effects are invisible." People hired by the government return the favor with votes whereas the people who lose their jobs likely direct their discontent to private business.[82] Progressivists viewed Friedman as extreme, but the longevity of his *Newsweek* articles did suggest some degree of support for a dissenting view on the wisdom of government economic policies.

Conservative opponents of Carter saw more evidence of Keynesianism than free-market thinking. If Carter did not share the same degree of intellectual commitment to Keynesianism as progressives, such as John Kenneth Galbraith, conservatives found no major distinction between ardent Keynesians and Carter.[83] They expected no slowing in the growth of government and regulatory agencies. Carter's assessment of the Club of Rome, an organization of scientists promoting government action and a "no-growth" economy (it recommended reducing industrial investment by 40 percent), offered additional clues of his economic thinking. He found the Club of Rome's book *Limits to Growth*—despite its errors—important: "[I]t was a first effort to analyze what's going to happen fifteen or twenty years in the future if we don't correct the problems of population explosion and the decimation of the forests, and so forth. I was impressed by it."[84]

Ronald Reagan had no patience for a pessimistic message of economic decline nor was he happy with the idea of government taking from job creators and giving to others. In his eyes, Carter was a liberal who charted a typical Democratic economic direction of "fairer distribution of wealth, income, and power." These were "code words that to me meant a confiscation of the earnings of people in our country who worked and produced, and their redistribution to people who didn't." Reagan acknowledged that liberals meant well, but the American economy "didn't need master planners."[85]

IV

When Ford met Reagan at the Alameda Plaza Hotel in Kansas City the night Ford won the nomination, the president admitted he was "way behind" in the polls. To win, he needed Reagan's assistance and "a maximum effort by all Republicans" in the fall campaign.[86] For the campaign battle, Republican strategists organized a strategy book with a blunt message: "If past is indeed prologue ... you will lose on November 2—because to win you must do what has never been done: close a gap of about 20 points in seventy-three days from the base of a minority party while spending approximately the same amount of money as your opponent."[87] Having said this, the strategists also expressed confidence that Carter was beatable. With President Ford far behind Carter in the polls, the Republicans had to campaign smart and hope for a Carter stumble. Later to be labeled "the Rose Garden strategy," Ford was to campaign mostly from the safe confines of the White House lawn until the later stage of the campaign.[88] Nerves were on edge. Evidence of friction in the Ford camp was a disagreement between Ford and his staff on whether to make a campaign stop at Bob Dole's hometown of Russel, Kansas. Ford argued it was right to visit the small town and he was glad he did so. The small-town reception for the two was "fantastic" and got the campaign "off to a solid start."[89]

Ford's official fall campaign began at The University of Michigan on September 15. It was a wet day, but approximately 15,000 gathered in Crisler Arena to hear him explain his understanding of good government and economics. There was even a hint of Reaganism in Ford's words: "There are some in this political year who claim that more government, more spending, more taxes and more control [over] our lives will solve our problems. More government is not the solution. Better government is."[90] Although the Ford team failed to invite Reagan to help out in September, Reagan scored points against Democratic policies with his policy essays heard on the radio.

On September 21, he addressed the Humphrey-Hawkins bill and the unfortunate consequence of Americans choosing not to work because government assistance was a better choice. Reagan cited one case of a New Jersey man rejecting a good job offer that fell short of the $15,000 he and his wife received in unemployment insurance, food stamps, and money from moonlighting.[91] Ford himself viewed the Humphrey-Hawkins full employment bill as "an election-year boondoggle."[92]

Following a Democratic Party tradition, Carter launched his campaign for the general election on Labor Day and his choice of location was symbolic, a retreat in Warm Springs, Georgia, where President Franklin D. Roosevelt had gone for renewal and therapy. The hallowed grounds were also where the beloved president died 31 years earlier. In his speech, Carter referenced the low unemployment of Truman and Johnson, declaring that unemployment under President Ford was the highest since

Herbert Hoover.[93] Carter had a good team of Keynesian economists to assist him, but he did not seek out the best-known Keynesian of the day, John Kenneth Galbraith, who was a favorite of the Kennedy family. Although Galbraith offered his assistance, Carter simply responded with a mimeographed note of thanks.[94]

Carter's choice of other Keynesians from "the pool of traditional Democratic economists" began with Lawrence Klein, professor of economics at the University of Pennsylvania. Since his graduate studies at MIT in the 1940s, Klein had embraced Keynesianism. To carry the torch for Carter, he formed a task force on economics that included Carolyn Shaw Bell of Wesley College, Richard Cooper of Yale University, Lester Thurow of MIT, and Albert Sommers, chief economist of the Conference Board. With the Keynesians favoring expansionary policies that targeted the issue of employment, there was less attention to the issue of inflation.[95] The weak economy boosted Carter's argument for more spending, an alternative to Ford's cautious approach of less spending on social programs.[96]

Republicans looked for weaknesses in Carter's economic ideas. One was his tax policy statement reported by the Associated Press in September, revealing that he wanted "a truly progressive tax rate" in which there were higher taxes on those earning above "the mean or median level of income." If implemented, Americans earning above $14,958 to $16,870 were in store for increased taxes.[97] He wanted wealthy Americans to pay more, and one important step was to eliminate tax expenditures (i.e., exclusions, deductions, and credits) that favored the rich.[98]

In front of Washington reporters, Robert Dole took Carter to task for a tax plan hitting the middle class. Anyone doing the math could see that an individual earning $15,000, as one Associated Press reporter told Carter earlier, "is not what people commonly think of as rich."[99] Carter appeared to be disadvantaging the middle class whereas Ford focused on the economic goals of job creation, lower inflation, affordable healthcare, and more home ownership.

Of the three scheduled television debates with Carter, the first took place September 23 at Philadelphia's Walnut Street Theater and covered domestic issues and economic policy. Negotiating the debate details became ludicrous. One Carter aide was serious when he suggested Ford stand in a hole on stage to equal Carter's height and accept the title "Mr. Ford" rather than "Mr. President."[100]

Political journalist James Witcover wrote that Carter approached the debate "like a student accustomed to receiving A's who brushes up on his subjects before a final examination," while Ford used a mock-up of the television set to practice answering questions from Alan Greenspan, Brent Scowcroft, Dick Cheney, and others in a format someone described as "extraordinarily rigorous training."[101] One sore spot for Ford, as it was for other Republicans, was any questions hinting that he lacked compassion.[102] As Democrats often argued, it was greed and indifference to the poor that motivated Republican support for smaller government.

Carter took the first question on how to improve employment from Frank Reynolds of ABC News. Sounding "programed," Witcover wrote, Carter's long and "adequate" response included the importance of having the rich pay more taxes. Pointing out that Carter failed to mention the costly Humphrey-Hawkins full employment bill, Ford countered with the typical Republican solution of tax incentives for the private sector and reduction of federal taxes. Both scored points with Carter accusing Ford of insensitivity toward the unemployed and Ford charging that Carter was set to "raise taxes on about half the working people in this country."[103]

With only a few minutes left in the scheduled 90 minutes, the sound system malfunctioned because of a short circuit. While technicians attempted to solve the problem, Carter and Ford stood in silence for almost half an hour. The theater audience witnessed this embarrassing episode in disbelief. After sound returned, each candidate gave his closing statement. Before the debate, a Gallup Poll had Carter ahead by 18 percent, but after the debate Ford gained ground and was only eight percent behind.[104]

The second debate was on October 7 at San Francisco's Palace of Fine Arts where Ford hurt his campaign with his misunderstanding of Soviet authoritarianism. When Ford stated his belief that there was no Soviet domination of Eastern Europe, advisor Brent Scowcroft "went white." The Carter team welcomed this gift. Stuart Eizenstat declared: "That is the dumbest thing I ever heard!"[105] Another setback was a bad economic report from the Commerce Department and other indicators of a weak GNP growth rate and higher inflation that countered Ford's prediction of economic recovery. Ford admitted that economic uncertainty "was really hurting us politically."[106] Most Americans expected their government to have solutions and resources to keep the economy in good shape, but many of them began to grumble about rising taxes. As the election approached, Milton Friedman declared on NBC's *Meet the Press*: "There are very few taxpayers I believe who think they are getting their money's worth for the forty percent of their income which is being spent for them by government bureaucrats."[107]

Reagan's enthusiasm for Ford was tame. He made campaign appearances with Dole rather than Ford, and annoying to the Ford camp was Reagan's campaigning for Republican candidates who had stood with Reagan when he sought the nomination.[108] In Ford's favor, he made no major errors at the third debate held at the College of William and Mary in Williamsburg, Virginia. In addition, Carter had problems with unenthusiastic progressives. Days before the election, Arthur Schlesinger was upset with Carter for believing in biblical miracles; he wrote: "Two worse candidates I have never seen." Struggling to decide who was more "repulsive," he could not force himself "to vote for a man who believes that Adam and Eve once existed."[109]

A Harris Survey of October 30 had Carter at 45 percent and Ford at 44 percent. Could Ford find the necessary momentum in the final hours of the campaign? Fortunately for Carter, organized labor did not let him down. For example, the Committee on Political Education, which focused on electing labor delegates for the Democratic Party, manned the phones, sent out mass mailings, and stirred up the troops—something it did not do in 1972. November 2 was a day of clear skies and warm temperatures for much of the country when 54.4 percent of voting-age citizens chose Carter by a small margin of 50.0 percent to Ford's 47.9 percent. In the Electoral College, Carter won 297 votes to Ford's 241, the narrowest victory since 1916.[110]

Ford lost the election because of the Nixon pardon and the poor economy, but he concluded that second-guessing the pardon and decisions on economic policy was a "pointless exercise."[111] It was time to move on. Although the American people gave Carter no rousing endorsement, the Keynesian Democratic Party had another shot to fix the economy.

Notes

1. Tip O'Neill with William Novak, *Man of the House: The Life and Political Memoirs of Speaker Tip O'Neill* (New York: Random House, 1987), 299–300.
2. Jimmy Carter, *A Full Life: Reflections at Ninety* (New York: Simon & Schuster, 2015), 110. Bob Woodward, *Shadow: Five Presidents and the Legacy of Watergate* (New York: Simon & Schuster, 1999), 41.
3. Steven F. Hayward, *The Age of Reagan: The Fall of the Old Liberal Order, 1964–1980* (New York: Three Rivers Press, 2001), 398.

4. Robert M. Collins, *Transforming America: Politics and Culture in the Reagan Years* (New York: Columbia University Press, 2007), 30–31. Paul Kengor, *God and Ronald Reagan: A Spiritual Life* (New York: HarperPerennial, 2004), 42.
5. Rowland Evans and Robert Novak, *The Reagan Revolution* (New York: E. P. Dutton, 1981), 86.
6. Dinesh D'Souza, *Ronald Reagan: How an Ordinary Man Became an Extraordinary Leader* (New York: Touchstone, 1999), 52.
7. Lou Cannon, *Governor Reagan: His Rise to Power* (New York: PublicAffairs, 2003), 4.
8. D'Souza, *Ronald Reagan*, 67.
9. Collins, *Transforming America*, 42–43.
10. Rick Perlstein, *The Invisible Bridge, The Fall of Nixon and the Rise of Reagan* (New York: Simon & Schuster, 2015), 311.
11. Ronald Reagan, *Ronald Reagan: An American Life* (New York: Pocket Books, 1990), 200.
12. Ibid., 20–21.
13. Bob Colacello, *Ronnie & Nancy: Their Path to the White House, 1911 to 1980* (New York: Warner Books, 2004), 431.
14. Kiron Skinner et al., eds. *Reagan in His Own Hand: The Writings of Ronald Reagan that Reveal His Revolutionary Vision for America* (New York: Touchstone, 2002).
15. Ibid., 255–256.
16. Perlstein, *The Invisible Bridge*, 538.
17. Reagan, *Ronald Reagan*, 200–201.
18. Milton Friedman, "A Tale of Two Governors," *Newsweek*, March 1, 1976, 71.
19. Reagan, *Ronald Reagan*, 201.
20. Jules Witcover, *Marathon: The Pursuit of the Presidency, 1972–1976* (New York: Viking Press, 1977), 376–377.
21. Ibid., 378–379. Also, see Perlstein, *The Invisible Bridge*, 595–596, and Martin Schram, *Running for President 1976: The Carter Campaign* (New York: Stein and Day, 1977), 227.
22. Witcover, *Marathon*, 380, 382, 384.
23. Ibid., 383, 385, 387.
24. Schram, *Running for President 1976*, 228.
25. Reagan, *Ronald Reagan*, 201.
26. Martin Anderson, *Revolution* (New York: Harcourt Brace Jovanovich, 1988), 41.
27. Colacello, *Ronnie & Nancy*, 437–438.
28. Anderson, *Revolution*, 42–45.
29. Colacello, *Ronnie & Nancy*, 451–452.
30. Quoted in Colacello, *Ronnie & Nancy*, 454.

31. Quoted in Perlstein, *The Invisible Bridge*, 794.
32. Reagan, *Ronald Reagan*, 202.
33. O'Neill, *Man of the House*, 300.
34. On southern liberalism, see Donald Cunnigen, "Jimmy Carter as Spokesman of Southern Liberalism," in *The Presidency and Domestic Policies of Jimmy Carter*, eds. Herbert D. Rosenbaum and Alexej Ugrinsky (Westport, CT: Greenwood Press, 1994): 45–56.
35. Fred I. Greenstein, *Presidential Difference: Leadership Style from FDR to George W. Bush*, Second Edition (Princeton, NJ: Princeton University Press, 2004), 129–132.
36. Burton I. Kaufmann and Scott Kaufman, *The Presidency of James Earl Carter Jr.*, Second Edition, Revised (Lawrence: University Press of Kansas, 2006), 10.
37. Jimmy Carter, *Why Not the Best?* (Nashville, TN: Broadman Press, 1975), 9, 99, 111.
38. Ibid., 11, 131, 152.
39. Ibid., 146–147, 151.
40. Leo P. Ribuffo, "Jimmy Carter and the Selling of the President, 1976–1980," in *The Presidency and Domestic Policies of Jimmy Carter*, 145.
41. Kenneth W. Thompson, ed. *The Carter Presidency: Fourteen Intimate Perspectives of Jimmy Carter* (Lanham, MD: University Press of America, Inc., 1990), 22–23. Patrick Anderson, *Electing Jimmy Carter: The Campaign of 1976* (Baton Rouge: Louisiana State University Press, 1994), 2, 67. Former Carter speech writer, Anderson presents a candid insider's perspective on key people of the Carter campaign of 1976.
42. Thompson, ed., *The Carter Presidency*, 53.
43. Sanford J. Ungar, "How Jimmy Carter Does It," *Atlantic Monthly*, July 1976, 31.
44. Anderson, *Electing Jimmy Carter*, 68.
45. Jimmy Carter, *Keeping Faith: Memoirs of a President* (Fayetteville: University of Arkansas Press, 1995), 43.
46. Chris Hedges, "It's Back to School for a Beaten Political Warrior," *New York Times*, January 27, 2005: http://www.nytimes.com/2005/01/27/nyregion/its-back-to-school-for-a-beaten-political-warrior.html?mcubz=0 (accessed September 12, 2017).
47. Witcover, *Marathon*, 319–325.
48. Ibid., 320–324. A special assistant to President Carter writes of the irreverence, drinking, and profanities of the Carter staff during the campaign, behavior at odds with Carter's religious image. See Peter G. Bourne, *Jimmy Carter: A Comprehensive Biography from Plains to Postpresidency* (New York: A Lisa Drew Book/Scribner, 1997), 315–316.
49. Arthur M. Schlesinger Jr., *Journals 1952–2000*, eds. Andrew Schlesinger and Stephen Schlesinger (New York: Penguin Press, 2007), 406–407, 415.

50. Ibid., 412–413.
51. Charles Mohr, "Carter and His Audiences," *New York Times*, June 2, 1976, A20.
52. Schlesinger, Jr. *Journals 1952–2000*, 415. For example, on July 13, 1976, Schlesinger had dinner with Ted Kennedy, Candice Bergen, and other luminaries.
53. Ibid., 408–409.
54. Ibid., 415.
55. Ibid., 416, 419.
56. Ibid., 420–422.
57. Michael Novak, *Writing from Left to Right: My Journey from Liberal to Conservative* (New York: Image, 2013), 171.
58. Kaufman, *The Presidency of James Earle Carter Jr.*, 15.
59. William E. Simon, *A Time for Truth* (New York: Reader's Digest Press, 1978), 166.
60. Bourne, *Jimmy Carter*, 317.
61. Clark Clifford with Richard Holbrooke, *Counsel to the President: A Memoir* (New York: Random House, 1991), 619.
62. Greenstein, *Presidential Difference*, 133.
63. Kaufman, *The Presidency of James Earle Carter Jr.*, 15–16.
64. Schram, *Running for President 1976*, 300–301.
65. Quoted in Schram, *Running for President 1976*, 303–305.
66. Carter, *A Full Life*, 117.
67. Schram, *Running for President 1976*, 306.
68. Thompson, ed., *The Carter Presidency*, 21–22.
69. Witcover, *Marathon*, 524–525, 529.
70. Ibid., 539.
71. W. Carl Biven, *Jimmy Carter's Economy: Policy in an Age of Limits* (Chapel Hill: The University of North Carolina Press, 2002), 53–56.
72. Ken Auletta, *The Streets Were Paved with Gold* (New York: Random House, 1979), 130–131.
73. Leo P. Ribuffo, "Jimmy Carter and the Selling of the President, 1976–1980," 146.
74. Carter, *Keeping Faith*, 21, 74, 89.
75. Biven, *Jimmy Carter's Economy*, 218.
76. Jeff Bloodworth, "'The Program for Better Jobs and Income': Welfare Reform, Liberalism, and the Failed Presidency of Jimmy Carter," *International Social Science Review*, 82, nos. 3–4 (2006): 136–137.
77. Biven, *Jimmy Carter's Economy*, 31–32.
78. Ibid., 33. Carter explained: "I didn't approve of it the way it was originally written." Advice from various academic economists was that the bill could bring double-digit inflation.

79. Quoted in Biven, *Jimmy Carter's Economy*, 36.
80. Robert L. Heilbroner, "Middle-Class Myths, Middle-Class Realities," *Atlantic Monthly*, October 1976, 40.
81. Milton Friedman, "Humphrey-Hawkins," *Newsweek*, August 2, 1976, 55.
82. Ibid.
83. In his book, *Jimmy Carter's Economy*, Biven argues that Carter lacked the Keynesian rigor of others in the White House, 27; thus, he was a "reluctant Keynesian" (60).
84. Quoted in Biven, *Jimmy Carter's Economy*, 258. His words were from a postpresidency interview.
85. Reagan, *Ronald Reagan*, 205.
86. Gerald R. Ford, *A Time to Heal* (New York: Berkley Books, 1980), 387,
87. Quoted in Witcover, *Marathon*, 532. Ford first saw the strategy book a couple of weeks before the Republican convention.
88. Ibid., 532–533.
89. Ford, *A Time to Heal*, 396.
90. Quoted in Ford, *A Time to Heal*, 400.
91. Skinner et al., eds., *Reagan in His Own Hand*, 266.
92. Richard K. Caputo, *Welfare and Freedom American Style II: The Role of the Federal Government, 1941–1980* (Lanham, MD: University Press of America, 1994), 520.
93. Biven, *Jimmy Carter's Economy*, 29–30. Witcover, *Marathon*, 545–546.
94. Richard Parker, *John Kenneth Galbraith: His Life, His Politics, His Economics* (Chicago: University of Chicago Press, 2006), 551.
95. Biven, *Jimmy Carter's Economy*, 25–27.
96. Stephen Woolcock, "The Economic Policies of the Carter Administration," in *The Carter Years: The President and Policy Making*, eds. M. Glenn Abernathy et al. (New York: St. Martin's Press, 1984), 35–36.
97. Bruce R. Bartlett, *Reaganomics: Supply Side Economics in Action* (Westport, CT: Arlington House Publishers, 1981), 167.
98. W. Elliot Brownlee, *Federal Taxation in America: A Short History* (Cambridge: University of Cambridge Press, 1996), 129, 134.
99. Witcover, *Marathon*, 557–558.
100. Ford, *A Time to Heal*, 397, 400.
101. Witcover, *Marathon*, 573. Ford wrote that the "grueling interrogation boosted my confidence." Ford, *A Time to Heal*, 401.
102. Witcover, *Marathon*, 574.
103. Ibid., 577–578; Ford, *A Time to Heal*, 402.
104. Ford, *A Time to Heal*, 579.
105. Witcover, *Marathon*, 598.
106. Ford, *A Time to Heal*, 415.

107. Quoted in Meg Jacobs, *Panic at the Pump: The Energy Crisis and the Transformation of American Politics in the 1970s* (New York: Hill and Wang, 2017), 155.
108. Colacello, *Ronnie & Nancy*, 462.
109. Schlesinger, Jr. *Journals 1952–2000*, 422–423.
110. Witcover, *Marathon*, 620, 643–644.
111. James A. Baker III, *"Work Hard, Study … and Keep Out of Politics!"* (Evanston, IL: Northwestern University Press, 2006), 72. Ford, *A Time to Heal*, 423.

CHAPTER 6

Carter's Keynesian Start

In March 1977, Jimmy Carter's supposed technocratic skills got full treatment on the comedy show *Saturday Night Live*. Comedian Dan Ackroyd played Carter in a parody of the president taking questions from Americans earlier in the day on live, national radio. In the *SNL* version, the president explains to a troubled Kansas postal worker the proper procedure of operating the "new MarvEx3000 mail sorter"—it was vital to change the "three-digit setting of the caliper post on the first-grid sliding armature."[1] The skit was hilarious, but perhaps Americans did indeed have a president able to solve the problems of the economy. Certainly, celebrated Keynesian economist Paul Samuelson saw 1977 as "a year of opportunity."[2]

So, what economic lessons did Carter learn as he prepared for office? Most biographies on Jimmy Carter give short treatment on his economic education.[3] There is greater attention given to his foreign policy, an unsurprising fact given he spent more time on foreign issues than domestic problems. Carter's training at Georgia Tech and the U.S. Naval Academy was mostly technical with little exposure to liberal arts courses; his strength was naval engineering.[4] Carter recognized the split in the Democratic Party between liberals and conservatives and how neither group saw him as "a member of its faction."[5]

Yet, he understood that "Democrats were the party of government" and he sought to use government "to do 'good'" for the American people. In his first year, there were attempts to win the support of skeptical progressives in the party with his pledge for a national and mandatory

E. R. Crouse, *America's Failing Economy and the Rise of Ronald Reagan*,
https://doi.org/10.1007/978-3-319-70545-3_6

healthcare program, his support for saving New York City from bankruptcy, and his expansion of food stamps.[6] Even if he was a centrist as some believed, Democratic policies drew him to the left.[7] To the relief of progressives, he abandoned his promise to Oklahoma and Texas leaders to decontrol national gas prices. He also tackled an economic stimulus package, tax reform, energy, and the minimum wage.

Writing in his diary on March 11, 1977, Carter speechwriter Hendrik Hertzberg concluded: "If Carter approached society at large the way he approaches reorganizing the government, he would be a real radical."[8] Months later there was a clearer picture on whether Carter was an effective problem solver and whether his own assessment of his performance was realistic. After a year in office, he wrote in his diary: "We're tackling energy, Social Security, minimum wage, and welfare controversies and had solved a couple of them, and had good prospects for energy. In all, 1977 was a good year."[9]

I

Weeks after Carter's victory, one Democrat voiced caution on the limitations of government. Gerson Green of the Office of Economic Opportunity during the Johnson years stated: "The change I discern is that none of us know what to do. In those days, we thought we did. The country has taught the social engineers a lesson."[10] Nevertheless, most Democrats continued to have faith in Keynesianism. Democrat Charles Rangel had an answer to those concerned about the high cost of welfare programs, including the abuse of the system: "The object is to give welfare mothers enough to live on and feed their kids. The poor will never be smart enough to rip off as much as the rich."[11] Seeing Keynesianism in a positive light, Arthur Schlesinger worried more about Carter; at the beginning of 1977 he had "great forebodings" about the president.[12]

Pollster Pat Caddell explained to Carter the importance of an "articulated vision" for the nation, but Carter continued to struggle to point a clear direction for the country.[13] Sidney Lens, a Chicago-based labor leader and activist, acknowledged Carter's delivery of almost 1500 speeches over 22 months; however, like many other Americans, he was unsure what to expect from him. Yes, Carter talked about job creation; reorganizing a "bloated, confused" federal bureaucracy; reforming the tax system; improving the welfare system; controlling inflation; balancing the budget; and establishing a "comprehensive, mandatory national health system." Yet missing was "*philosophical focus*" that gave his individual planks some consistency with each other. It was problematic that his goals were "often contradictory."

A Trotskyist activist in his early years, Lens argued that only "vast injections of government money" prevented the economy from collapsing. Business also depended on subsidies and tax benefits that Lens called "private socialism." Two examples were the shipping industry receiving hundreds of millions of dollars in subsidies and Ford Motor Company benefitting from a $300 million rebate. If government subsidies for business and for poorer Americans did not exist, there would be protest in the streets and talk of revolution.[14]

At his inauguration, Carter spoke of limits and boldness: "We have learned that more is not necessarily better, that even our great Nation has its recognized limits, and that we can neither answer all questions nor solve all problems. We cannot afford to do everything, nor can we afford to lack boldness as we meet the future."[15] Interpreting Carter's message of boldness and limits was not easy. Economic conservatives believed that less regulation could unleash creativity, productivity, and thus create more wealth. This meant a higher standard of living; this was good. When economic conservatives talked limits, their subject was the government. If it was the government that was to be bold, they became uneasy about misguided activism.

Less than a month into his presidency, Carter acknowledged the warnings from others not to spread himself thin trying to tackle too many problems early in his administration. But the rhetoric of limits and the cautious advice of others got lost as he plunged ahead with action. In his diary, he wrote that "it's impossible for me to delay something that I see needs to be done."[16]

Carter's choice of economic advisors also suggested more emphasis on boldness than limits. There was confidence that his team had the necessary qualifications to tackle "the complexities of the modern economy."[17] Even before setting foot in the White House, he demonstrated an ambitious policy style. His transition team, led by Chief Domestic Policy Advisor Stuart E. Eizenstat, prepared a 100-page policy draft that focused on economic stimulus, energy, and welfare reform.[18] Born in Chicago, the Jewish Eizenstat studied political science at the University of North Carolina followed by a Harvard University law degree. His first stint working in the White House was for the Johnson administration. During his second run for governor in 1970, Carter discovered Eizenstat's talents and used him for writing issue papers.

In the White House, the nerdy advisor, with his horn-rimmed glasses and formal suits, was a stoic, hardworking policy "wonk" with deep loyalty to Carter.[19] One journalist suggested that the "skinny and bookish" Eizenstat came "straight out of the mold of the Cistercian monks."[20] At least one other member on the Carter transition team generated criticism. A Texas businessman referred to David Freeman, who favored additional natural gas price controls, as one "philosophically dedicated to socialism and against free enterprise."[21]

Carter's economic team gathered in Georgia with him in late 1976 to discuss stimulating the economy. The centerpiece of policy was unemployment.[22] After arriving in Atlanta, the Carter team traveled by bus for three hours to Plains and stayed at Miss Lillian's Pond House, the home of Carter's mother. Among the key players were Charles Schultze, Michael Blumenthal, Bert Lance, Lawrence Klein, Walter Heller, Arthur Okun, Juanita Kreps, and Ray Marshall.

Schultze, Carter's chief economic strategist and a Keynesian activist on macroeconomic issues, had been the head of the budget bureau in the Johnson government and directed economic policy at the Brookings Institution. Michael Blumenthal had a Ph.D. in economics from Princeton University and served in both the Kennedy and Johnson administrations at the Department of State. Bert Lance was Carter's close friend who was an Atlanta banker without any formal training in economics. Lawrence Klein was a Keynesian economist, Walter Heller was John F. Kennedy's chief economic advisor, Arthur Okun was at the Brookings Institution, and Juanita Kreps was the vice president of Duke University.

A staunch Keynesian, Ray Marshall was an aggressive fighter for expanding employment policies and a strong labor movement. Born in Oak Grove, Louisiana, he served in World War II, and used the GI Bill to earn his economics degree at Millsaps College in Jackson, Mississippi, followed by a master's degree from Louisiana State University. After receiving his Ph.D. in economics from the University of California at Berkeley, he taught at a couple of universities before becoming a Fulbright scholar in Finland. His return to the United States led to more teaching at Louisiana State University and a final stop at the University of Texas where he was a labor economist. With Marshall at the helm, the Department of Labor had almost 30,000 employees, including 750 lawyers, and an annual budget of nearly $30 billion.[23] Marshall pushed for the government to spend more resources on jobs, and one of his strategies to increase his influence was sending memoranda directly to Carter.[24]

The Carter team embraced Keynesianism and belief in government's ability to manage the economy. Nonetheless, Carter's economic plan lacked a catchy slogan or missionary zeal for economic ideas.[25] The focus was on employment, with only some attention paid to inflation, which they believed was manageable. During the months on the campaign trail, Carter heard little about the problem of inflation: "When I met with individual groups or college professors or anybody else, nobody ever brought up the question of inflation. It was not a burning issue. The only thing was, what are we going to do about jobs." It was the same after the election; when he met with the congressional leaders at the Pond House, the only economic discussion was jobs.[26] But then again, should it be surprising that college professors and Democrats, heavily influenced by Keynesianism, talked jobs rather than inflation? Believing that the risk of triggering inflation was minimal, Carter focused on stimulating the economy.

The final drafting of the "stimulus package" took place under an ambitious deadline. Soon to be head of the Council of Economic Advisors (CEA), Schultze crafted the policy in longhand on legal pads (he could not type) late into the evening. College student David Lance, Bert's son, typed the written draft early in the morning. Next step was photocopying courtesy of the state police barracks, which had the closest available copier.

Behind much of the urgency was the dating procedure in the U.S. government for fiscal year budgets. The year assigned is the year they end. For example, Ford's 1977 fiscal year budget began in October 1976. When Carter entered the White House the 1977 fiscal year budget was already in play for three months, to continue for almost nine months unless Carter presented revisions. A revision must take place or else the new president loses any input into budgetary decisions.[27]

Within a few days of Carter's inauguration, the key economic advisors of the White House went before committees of Congress to explain the president's stimulus package of a combination of tax cuts and a jobs program. The tax cuts were for citizens and businesses. Americans would receive a $50 rebate and businesses could choose a refundable four percent employer income tax credit or a two percent increase in the investment tax credit. The jobs stimulus component extended youth and training programs that began with the enactment of the Comprehensive Employment Training Act (CETA) in 1973. By way of grants to states and local governments, there was a call for an almost twofold increase of public service jobs (310,000–600,000) for fiscal year 1977 and another increase of 125,000 jobs for the following year. These wishful numbers had the full support of Ray Marshall, who pushed for "direct job creation and as little tax reduction as possible."[28]

While Carter worked on the stimulus package, his cabinet was slow to take shape, hampered as the president adopted a detailed and lengthy review process for scrutinizing facts and references of his list of potential staff members. When he selected his economic team, notable was the choice of Bert Lance for director of the Office of Management and Budget (OMB), a "once proud presidential staff agency" that received much criticism during the 1970s.[29] Two other key appointments were Michael Blumenthal for Secretary of the Treasury and Charles Schultze for chairman of the CEA. Schultze, Blumenthal, and Lance were the key members of the Economic Policy Group (EPG), the official economic advisory team after Carter entered the White House.

A problem with the CEA was expanding membership to include the Secretary of Commerce, Secretary of Labor, and Secretary of Housing and Urban Development (HUD). With two or three assistants assigned to key members, EPG committee meetings were large, consisting of 30 or more people. Schultze lamented the lack of adequate synthesis: "[There was never enough discipline in the process so that on many issues, the president would get a 25-page memo broken into eight subsections, each with three options, so by the time you finished, you [had] … 18 things to check off."[30]

One economist playing an important advisory role was William Nordhaus, a member of the CEA who worked with chairman Schultze. Nordhaus was coauthor of latter editions of Paul Samuelson's well-known introductory economics textbook. Samuelson stubbornly championed Keynesianism and the belief that the Soviet economy would eventually outperform the American economy.

In his study of Carter's economy, economist W. Carl Biven noted the confidence of the Carter administration: "The Keynesian beliefs that most of Carter's advisers brought with them reinforced the natural optimism of a new team of policy makers and gave them the assurance that they could steer the economy in the right direction."[31] They worked under and were faithful to the idea of the Phillips curve: when the economy expands, unemployment decreases and inflation increases; when the economy detracts, unemployment increases and inflation decreases.

Keynesians such as Samuelson, whose research indicated tolerable tradeoffs between employment and price stability, believed that the unemployment rate could drop as low as four percent without causing any significant rise in inflation.[32] The picture was less rosy when officials at the Bureau of Labor Statistics noted the odd occurrence of numerous job losses despite a decline in unemployment numbers. There was an easy explanation: people became so discouraged looking for a job that they ceased looking.[33]

As instructed by Carter in February, Michael Blumenthal worked on tax reform and his proposals submitted in May included tax deductions for business expenses and a lowering of tax rates that received a cold reaction from others in the White House. For example, Charles Schultze, Stuart Eizenstat, and James Fallows—Carter's chief speechwriter—stalwartly opposed the Blumenthal recommendations that in their eyes favored the rich.[34] Eizenstat was not a trained economist whereas Blumenthal was, but it was the former who had sway over Carter on welfare reform and energy issues.[35]

The Carter administration pegged the cost of the stimulus at $15.5 billion in 1977 and the same amount in 1978, too modest in the eyes of Walter Heller who had advised President Kennedy in the role of chairman of the CEA.[36] Others on the left were wary of Carter and his proposal to stimulate the economy with a $50 rebate for citizens and a $900 million reduction of corporate taxes. Moreover, his increase in public works and job-creating programs was inadequate in their eyes. The U.S. Conference of Mayors expected more assistance for cities and the American Federation of Labor-Congress for Industrial Organization (AFL-CIO) wanted $30 billion for public works in 1977.

Several weeks later, after the negative response of progressive politicians and labor leaders, Carter rescinded the proposed tax rebate for citizens.[37] For decades, the labor unions represented a significant component of the Democrat's voting base. Carter lacked the advantage that Kennedy and Johnson enjoyed; there was no impressive economic growth during the 1970s.

Carter included Vice President Walter Mondale, an enthusiastic supporter of big government, in much of the White House business, in contrast to previous administrations when vice presidents were less well-informed about policy discussions.[38] One of Mondale's jobs was point man with labor leaders.[39] Carter's choice of Joseph Califano for Secretary of Health, Education, and Welfare (HEW) clarified his faith in the power of government to meet people's needs. A major player in Lyndon Johnson's administration, Califano viewed government as "the key factor" in the lives of the poor. HEW gave millions of Americans "the *only* chance of surviving at a minimum level of human dignity."[40] A high-powered Washington, DC, lawyer, he gave up his yearly income of $505,000 to take over HEW—the "poor people's" department. He worked hard to see the bureaucracy operate with "effective compassion" even if it took stepping on some toes: "My years in Washington had given me a confidence that sometimes spilled over into arrogance. Toughness is needed to tackle the issues at HEW and I felt I had acquired it. I'd learned plenty about political street fighting from LBJ.... Second only to the President, the HEW secretary had the most power to affect the lives of Americans. I intended to use that power." To exercise this power effectively, Califano recruited "seasoned experts" and "whiz kids" who he believed were "the brightest the department had ever seen."[41]

When Congress formed HEW in 1953, at the recommendation of President Eisenhower, there were 35,000 employees. With Califano at the helm, the department employed 150,000 full-time people and paid the salaries of more than one million employees at state and local levels. There were also 4500 part-time experts on advisory committees.[42] Impressed with Carter's ability to speak as "an efficient planner," Califano began his duties on a hopeful note.[43] There was, however, one initial glitch. The hiring of a cook to serve HEW insiders caused Califano some media grief, but Tip O'Neill reassured him: "It'll pass. You'll do beautiful things. Just get with it."[44]

O'Neill was a New Deal Democrat who stood 6 feet 2, weighed 265 lbs., and wore Saks Fifth Avenue suits. *Newsweek* described him as an old political operator with lots of character: "He stoically endures a glowing red nose; he plays poker, drinks whisky, sings in public saloons, smokes cigars and tells yarns with eloquent Irish wit."[45] His support for big-government liberalism was solid.

One of Califano's first moves was to fire about 100 Ford/Nixon appointees. His choice of Hale Champion for Under Secretary of HEW was key. Champion's experience included working as a top government official in California during the Governor Pat Brown years and holding a major administrative position at Harvard University. The first Republican appointee that he fired was the head of the Rehabilitation Services Administration, a man crippled for life. When he rolled into Champion's office in a wheelchair, the man shared that he had been the chairman of Democrats for Pat Brown in San Luis Obispo County. This fact did not save his job. Telling him he made "one helluva mistake" for accepting the appointment during a Republican administration, Champion fired him.

It was more difficult to get rid of some of the other Republican appointments. John Ottina held an important administrative post and career job that he was unwilling to relinquish. The message from a Califano lawyer was blunt: "The new Secretary may not be able to fire you… [but] he could send you to Alaska for months in the winter to look at HEW programs, and in the summer to Alabama for the same purpose." Califano got his wish; Ottina resigned.[46]

Califano wanted tough and loyal assistants for the HEW cause. An important member of the team was Eileen Shanahan, an economic reporter and committed feminist selected as Califano's press officer. Other chosen Democrats came with proven backgrounds in law, academia, and labor unions. As for federal appointments, the only instruction Carter gave Califano was for "more blacks, Hispanics, and women, and fewer white males."[47] At one cabinet meeting, Zbigniew Brzezinski noted Califano's tendency to flatter Carter "in a way calculated to please him," whereas Commerce Secretary Juanita Kreps showed a standoffish attitude.[48] Just because Carter team members all shared faith in government action by experts did not mean they got along with each other.

Carter's campaign promise of frugality with the public purse was annoying to some. Tip O'Neill complained about the stinginess of food served to congressional leaders at Tuesday morning White House breakfast meetings. The "breakfast" was coffee, orange juice, and a roll. After he explained to Carter that even "Nixon served us better than this," the meetings scheduled before 9:00 a.m. came with a full breakfast.[49] Carter's "frugality" did not apply to his inner circle. As the White House's personnel director, James Gammil received a pay hike from $7500 to $45,496. Hamilton Jordan and Jody Powell, Carter's closest aides, had their salaries doubled to $56,000.[50] In Carter's eyes, Jordan was a "brilliant political analyst" who was his campaign manager for a successful race for governor in 1970; it was the press that misunderstood and underestimated Jordan more than any other person working for Carter.[51] Yet, others noted Jordan's tendency to act bored at policy meetings.[52]

Carter's reliance on his "southern" advisors and his background as an engineer prompted him to work on problems without consulting and horse-trading with members of Congress.[53] While marveling at Carter's intelligence, media icon Walter Cronkite concluded that the president was naïve on how to get things done in Washington.[54] Also problematic was his "excessive micromanagerial" approach; he was a "control freak who wanted to know exactly what was happening around him at all times."[55] Stuart Eizenstat experienced Carter's passion for accuracy when the president sent back enormous briefing books with corrections of punctuation and spelling errors.

The most frequently used word in Carter's first year in office was "comprehensive," as in comprehensive answers to problems.[56] There were those reluctant to work with Carter. After hearing that Bob S. Bergland had no interest in being the Secretary of Agriculture if asked by Carter, Hubert Humphrey urged him to reconsider: "Well, let me tell you, Carter is not going to be a very good president. He's going to need all the help he can get."[57] Bergland took the job.

Carter stated in his memoirs that good governance depended on his "mastery" of the important issues.[58] But Carter ran into trouble early when he failed to consult with Democrats. From the start, Tip O'Neill was unsuccessful in educating Carter on the importance of working with other national politicians and widening his circle of advisors with Washington, DC—people to get things accomplished. Carter had a blind spot, believing that he could bypass Congress and appeal directly to the American people. In O'Neill's New England eyes, southern politicians were sweet talkers who used charm to "skin you alive." The approach of northern politicians was blunter and more rambunctious. They enjoyed conflict, whereas the southerner avoided skirmishes.

As for Carter, he had another shortcoming; he was blind to "Irish or Jewish politicians, or the nuances of city politics." New England Democrats who campaigned hard for Carter expected rewards when it came to appointments at federal agencies. Yet much to the frustration of O'Neill and others, "nobody they knew was appointed to anything."[59] Even some southerners were angry with the president. After playing tennis with Carter, Texas Democratic Senator Lloyd Bentsen could not believe that Carter left after the game without any conversation or lobbying. Did he not understand how important it was for Bentsen to go back home and tell his constituents that he met with the president?[60]

The actions of the southern Democrats who arrived in Washington with Carter made matters worse. They too were amateurs on the issue of working with Congress, including northern Democrats. Hamilton Jordan had a chip on his shoulder and, like too many of Carter's people, was unwilling to allow other Democrats to be full partners. For example, every time John Brademas, the Democratic whip, phoned the White House he had to spell his name. The relationship between Jordan and Tip O'Neill was poisonous from the start.

Following tradition, members of Congress could buy seats for guests for the inaugural gala held the night before the president was sworn into office. O'Neill purchased 12 tickets for his guests, assuring them they had good seats. When he discovered that someone put them in the last row of the balcony, he exploded with anger at Jordan, knowing this development did not happen by accident. Expecting that a Speaker of the House and the president's top aid would work closely together to accomplish the legislative goals of the administration, O'Neill later wrote that he only saw Jordan three times during Carter's four years. After the first incident, O'Neill's name for Jordan was Hannibal Jerken.[61] O'Neill generated his fair share of criticism too. Offering a biting appraisal, William A. Henry, III, wrote that O'Neill's career in government "has been a boon to his family, his friends, his constituents and liberal causes—in roughly that order."[62]

The lack of basic courtesies was likely an excessive and poorly managed reaction to the favoritism and sense of entitlement common in Washington. In the immediate post-Watergate environment, Carter entered the White House as a political outsider desiring to maintain a higher moral standard than in previous years. Had not anti-Washington rhetoric gained him the White House? Others noted, however, that Hamilton Jordan and Jody Powell did not have the same moralism Carter spoke about. Catholic intellectual and Democrat Michael Novak spent enough time with Governor Carter to "glimpse a contrast between the candidate's supermoralism and two-facedness at the center of the Carter team."[63]

Nevertheless, Powell was a hit with White House reporters who appreciated his joining them for drinks and stories late into the night.[64] According to one insider, he was also "disingenuously deferential" to Carter's cabinet members.[65] Powell, Jordan, Stuart Eizenstat, and Gerald Rafshoon received the label the "Georgia mafia" for their service to Carter both in the governor's mansion and the White House.[66]

There were Democrats who saw Carter as a problematic leader for his ideas that in their eyes were too conservative. The rift between Carter and various important Democrats was because of a different approach to the economy. Progressive ideologues did not warm up to Carter, believing him to lack appreciation for big government; Arthur Schlesinger was one who was watchful of Carter's "economic conservatism." He looked ahead four years and the possibility of having his friend Ted Kennedy challenge

Carter's nomination. Of potential challengers, Kennedy "would plainly make by far the best President of the lot."[67]

Carter did attempt to have more women take important jobs. His pledge to give a woman a high-profile position came true with the appointment of Midge Costanza as head of the White House Office of Public Liaison. Attempting to contact Costanza at her parents' home on Christmas Day, Carter was unaware that she was in mourning over the recent death of John Petrossi, the married man she had had a secret affair with for years. Even her parents did not know she was experiencing "roller-coaster emotions" as she began a secret romantic relationship with Jean O'Leary, codirector of the National Gay Task Force.

Carter wanted Costanza to focus on communication with "groups and interest[s] which traditionally have not had access to the White House." She did consider rejecting his offer, but decided to take the job. With Costanza, the White House had a feminist who was unafraid of peppering her speeches with profanity and sexual banter.[68] The drama that Costanza brought to the White House added to the interesting dynamics of Carter's first year as team members sought to advance government action in a direction more progressive and constructive than during the Nixon and Ford years.

II

On April 5, 1977, on Manhattan's upper West Side, teenagers stood in line for many hours hoping to receive a federally financed job available through community agencies. The part-time jobs paid $2.30 an hour and would be for the summer. Late into the night and early morning, 17-year-old Charles Butcher and others waited in the chilly temperature. In a spirit of compassion, at 3:00 a.m. someone allowed the teenagers to find warmth and get some sleep in the nearby school. At other locations throughout New York City, 20,000 teenagers stood in lines to register for much sought-after jobs.[69] Writing in the *New Republic* later of the perils of "timidity," Melville J. Ulmer called for government "national planning" to solve the riddle of inflation and, most important, put people back to work.[70]

In April, the Carter administration pitched its economic program that included the promise of a balanced budget by fiscal year 1981. What about the threat of inflation? Carter's response to inflation was passive, a view shared by his economic team composed of the "'old gang' of Keynesians" from the Kennedy and Johnson years.[71] Even some important business people underestimated the damaging effects of inflation. For example, in his testimony before the House Ways and Means Committee, Reginald Jones, head of General Electric, explained that "there is so much slack in the economy right now that we believe a fairly sizable program of permanent tax cuts and job oriented action programs would not cause unmanageable inflation or deficits."[72]

Complicating matters was the media reporting imprecise inflation numbers from the Department of Labor and Statistics, based on the Consumer Price Index (CPI). The inflation rate was susceptible to sharp distortions from random short-term events such as exceptionally good or poor weather. The "underlying rate" of inflation not given by the news media was more accurate because it eliminated the price effects of random events. Impressive growing conditions for farmers in 1976 lowered the price of food. This in turn lowered the inflation rate to about five percent; however, the "underlying rate" of six percent told another story.[73]

In seeking to solve economic problems, government departments often worked against each other. For example, both HEW and the Labor departments looked out for their own interests, each unwilling to reconcile their differences. Carter's commitment to broadcast a reformed welfare program within a few months of taking office made the situation worse. The deadline was unrealistic as was his commitment to a "zero-cost" plan that kept spending at existing levels.[74]

Joseph Califano and his key aides Ben Heineman and Henry Aaron pushed to revive the War on Poverty and expected increased spending. Heineman had a background in finance and Aaron was an economist with welfare reform expertise. As the primary author of the Program for Better Jobs and Income (PBJI), Aaron instructed his staff to disregard any social science research that identified Great Society policy failures; saying that such "conservative" research failed to promote "a moral commitment to social equality." Stressing good points and minimizing drawbacks, welfare professionals were clever in advancing their favorite approach. In his book on the Great Society, Aaron disputed the position that the federal budget was "slipping out of control."[75]

As early as April 11, Califano informed Carter that welfare reform required additional spending. In frustration Carter responded: "Are you telling me that there is no way to improve the present welfare system except by spending billions of more dollars? In that case, to hell with it. We're wasting time."[76] Weeks earlier, Richard Nathan, senior fellow of the Brookings Institution, advised the government to "abandon the search for a utopian solution to welfare problems and instead build on the programs we have."[77]

Another problem with Califano's welfare reform process was his failure to work close with the congressional leaders who could be instrumental in seeing a welfare reform bill passed. His sponsorship of public hearings and town meetings over a 10-week period to generate support for the government's plans was not enough. When the May 1 deadline arrived to introduce a bill, the administration was not ready. Announcing that "the complexity of the [welfare] system is almost incomprehensible," Carter could only present a 12-point outline. As the administration fumbled about for a policy, the *Washington Post* stated that "nobody should be under the impression that the President has indicated how he intends to fulfill these ambitious goals."[78]

It took until late July for Califano to present a detailed proposal that included a 1.4 million public service jobs program and a commitment to full employment. Whereas the administration estimated the PBJI to cost an additional $2 billion annually, bringing the total to $31.1 billion, the Congressional Budget Office (CBO) estimated the additional cost to be seven times the administration's estimate. Troubling for the administration was the assessment of Tom Joe, a Carter consultant on welfare, who predicted that the "misguided" PBJI would increase welfare by 67 percent. Having an additional 14.2 million Americans receiving welfare payments would be a fiscal nightmare. Unfazed by the complexity and cost of welfare reform, Carter proceeded and presented the jobs plan on August 6 to a national audience. He was less than accurate when he claimed that the PBJI discouraged welfare dependence and offered "strong incentives to keep families together."[79]

There were encouraging signs of support for the bill in media circles, with particularly compelling editorials in newspapers. In its coverage of the PBJI, *The New York Times* overlooked Carter's campaign promise to be frugal. Additional good news for the Carter administration was a Lou Harris Poll indicating that 70 percent of Americans approved the plan. Nonetheless, Carter's avoidance of congressional input came back to haunt him when key Democrats articulated their increasing unhappiness with the proposal. Without the support of House Ways and Means Chairman Al Ullman, Senate Finance Committee Chairman Russell Long, and Senate Subcommittee on Public Assistance Chairman Daniel Moynihan the task of selling PBJI became much more difficult, especially in the Senate.

Moynihan was a freshman senator, but he demanded respect for having served four successive presidents in various positions, including Nixon's ambassador to India. For months, Moynihan was impatient for a guaranteed income provision. He had told the press in April that someone "with a first-rate mind and three months' experience could draft legislation in a morning."[80] After White House officials leaked that Moynihan was a heavy drinker, he put together a scathing case against the PBJI. As more Democrats realized that the welfare reform proposal was too complex and did not offer enough jobs, public opinion also soured on liberal welfare policy because of reports of welfare cheating.[81] Closer examination of the costs was necessary. In front of a congressional committee in early October, a leading expert on welfare reform pointed out that the proposal was "bigger by a magnitude of two or more in cost than they have said."[82]

Others viewed Carter's PBJI as too radical—a plan that added many people to the welfare rolls and sought "to guarantee incomes for all, even at the risk of making some of the truly needy worse off."[83] The significant increase of people put on welfare was alarming to Democratic Senator Russell Long and conservatives.[84] What initially had appeared promising, Carter's convoluted welfare proposal died in congressional committee during his first year. Democrats outnumbered Republicans 292 to 143 in the House and 61 to 38 in the Senate; however, these large majorities were not enough to see Carter's welfare reform come to fruition. The episode foreshadowed difficult relationships between Carter and other Democrats.

Economic difficulties continued concerning trade with other nations, minimum wage laws, Social Security, and urban blight in the largest cities. Economists, such as Milton Friedman, showed no concern for America's trade deficit, but others did. Walter Mondale visited Japan and the major capitals of Europe the same week of Carter's inauguration to propose joint economic expansion that would cause beneficial spillover effects for everyone. The Carter government wanted Japan and West Germany to adopt policies to stimulate their economies. Although the Japanese appeared to reluctantly bow to American pressure, in the end they "resisted adopting specific growth targets."

The Germans responded coolly, sending the message that Germany did not need any economic lessons from the United States. German leader Helmut Schmidt was much more attentive to the danger of inflation than the Americans.[85] There was also a significant number of German economists who rejected the demand management approach for stimulating the economy. Their favored strategy was to minimize government intervention and distortions in the market: "Development through competition may be compared with a millipede. Locomotion is ensured by a large number of small cogs functioning on [the] all-wheel-drive principle. The concept beloved by international Keynesians of a 'locomotive' as the draught horse of dynamic development is erroneous."[86] As it turned out, some found the American numbers discouraging. The $31 billion merchandise trade deficit in 1977 was three times larger than the deficit during Ford's last year. One significant issue was the rise of American dependence on foreign oil, increasing 60 percent in the period from 1975 to 1977 ($28 billion to $47 billion). Price controls on oil explained the decline in American domestic production.[87]

Despite the threat of higher inflation, Democrats turned their attention to raising the minimum wage. A favorite Democratic initiative since its introduction in 1938, the minimum wage saw an increase in 1974 and was due for another adjustment with a Democrat in the White House. Pennsylvania Representative John Dent submitted a bill to raise the minimum wage from $2.30 to $3.30 by January 1, 1978. Democrats rejected the notion that a higher minimum wage would cause unemployment but were split on how much to raise it. The Labor department favored the increase, whereas the Department of Commerce opposed a major jump in the minimum wage.[88]

In November, Carter signed a bill that would raise the minimum wage to $2.65 in January 1978 and $3.35 by January 1981. Not everyone thought this was good policy. Conservatives argued that it hurt the unskilled, especially young African Americans. Thomas Sowell pointed to minimum wage laws as a major reason for a more than fivefold rise of unemployment of teenage blacks in the first 30 years of the post-World War period. Flawed welfare programs "made it less necessary" for young blacks to work and gain important skills.[89]

Another pressing problem was the financial health of Social Security, a retirement system created in 1935 and financed by taxes on employers and workers. The system saw young and lower-paid wage earners facing a disproportionately high tax burden and retired workers were receiving far more benefits than they put into it. In 1940, Social Security Check No. 1 for $22.54 went to Ida Fuller of Brattleboro, Vermont. She drew her last monthly check 34 years later for $112.60, giving her a total of $20,944.42 over the years. This sum compared favorably to the total $24.75 she paid in Social Security taxes.

Carter discovered that Social Security benefits paid out to recipients far outpaced money going into the system. On May 9, he presented a plan to Congress that called for an increase in Social Security taxes, contradicting his campaign promise not to raise payroll taxes.[90] Inflation reared its ugly head and the cost of Social Security and healthcare rose at the same time the percentage of Americans aged 65 and above grew.[91]

There was also the issue of urban economic stagnation in 1977. In October, after viewing the urban blight in New York City, Carter demanded an economic plan of action for the South Bronx to serve as a model for politicians from other ravaged cities. In his first year in the White House, he supported legislation that increased public service jobs and shifted $12.5 billion for urban aid for the most distressed urban centers. HUD secretary Patricia Harris became the head of the Urban Regional Policy Group (URPG), an agency established by Carter. The Harris task force was confident in its ability to revitalize the cities with federal planning. Yet, the additional billions that the URPG requested was unrealistic in weak economic times.

Carter told the task force: "Give me something worth funding if you want more money."[92] City officials across the nation were on edge. On a cold December day with a chilly fog swirling around the Bay, angry mayors gathered in San Francisco to discuss urban problems and the appropriate response by the Carter government. They demanded more federal money for cities struggling with high urban unemployment.[93]

III

Free-market economists had much to say about Carter's first year. Former Secretary of the Treasury William E. Simon lamented that a "political-social-intellectual elite" promoted the government's ability to control the "complex marketplace by fiat better than the people can by individual choice."[94] Simon's analysis represented standard classical economics, but liberals were effective in portraying him as an extremist. More influential was Milton Friedman, who gave a good account of the shortcomings of Keynesianism. In his *Newsweek* column, Friedman cautioned the forthcoming Carter government to be wary of Keynesian exuberance.

The recent history of Great Britain, Italy, and other nations showed the "folly" of attempting to "spend your way out of a recession." Any short-term gains from Keynesian actions came at the expense of future disastrous inflation. It was far better for the government to limit its spending;

tighten the money supply; and, thus, allow the recovery to proceed at a moderate pace.[95] In early January 1977, Friedman again advocated a "steady as you go" policy that avoided "fine-tuning policies to every wiggle in the economic indicators." The economy was too complex for anyone—especially Keynesians—to manipulate to get the desired results.[96]

In contrast to the progressive wing of the Democratic Party, Friedman saw no evidence of economic conservatism in Carter's proposals. In April, he revealed the real numbers behind the president's proposal to lower taxes for business. The offer for businesses was an investment credit or an employment credit; both would complicate the tax system. The former was an example of "advanced tax gimmickry" and the latter reduced the taxes for some employers from 5.85 percent to 5.62 percent. Behind the smoke and mirrors, the only new jobs Carter's proposals would guarantee were the bureaucrats needed to administer the misguided tax system. With Democrats controlling both the House and the Senate, Friedman was not hopeful.

Even though the House rejected Carter's scheme, the tax credit bill it passed was no less gimmicky. The Senate Committee on Finance took the House bill and made it worse. As Friedman concluded, a better approach to stimulate the economy was simpler: "We do not need more tax gimmickry and more bureaucrats. We need lower government spending, lower taxes and fewer bureaucrats."[97] Friedman's analysis came when Carter stood on solid political ground; in late April, a Gallup survey and Harris Poll had public approval for the president above 70 percent.

Another point of attack by Friedman concerned free trade. In July, he discussed why the Carter government was wrong to negotiate "voluntary" quota agreements with foreign producers. Free trade was a better approach for America than the political tactic of setting import quotas on Japanese television sets or South Korean shoes. Protecting specific domestic industries by "arm-twisting" agreements with other countries ultimately would mean higher prices for U.S. consumers. Besides, the argument that restrictive policies protected American jobs was misleading. For example, while there likely would be fewer jobs in the U.S. television-manufacturing industry if the Japanese sold less expensive televisions, there would be "*more jobs in those industries that [could] … now export more to Japan.*" Friedman had an answer for those worried that all American goods would become more expensive than Japanese goods.

When America imported more from Japan, the Japanese spent their earnings in the United States or elsewhere. An important point was that the American people benefited whether the Japanese hid their earnings under the mattress or burned them: "We are then getting their fine products for the trivial cost of paper and ink." Thus, the Japanese eventually would spend a roughly equal amount of money for American goods and services as the dollar–yen exchange rate adjusted to the transactions between the two countries.[98]

Two months later, Friedman poked fun at media headlines about changes in foreign exchange rates—changes that the Carter administration need not worry about. When the *Wall Street Journal* declared "POUND EASES," in reality there hardly had been any change because the adjustment was from $1.7381 to $1.7380. Media reports on exchange rates often were silly hysteria. When President Nixon "set the dollar free," after 27 years tied to gold, flurries in the exchange markets became a non-issue. With no official exchange rate for the dollar, "there literally is no such thing as a 'balance-of-payments problem.'"

When Americans spend more on Japanese goods and services than the Japanese spend on U.S. goods and services, they must acquire extra Japanese yen (JPY) either through income from investments in Japan, borrowing JPY, selling bonds to the Japanese, or using up JPY balances. Failing to acquire the extra Japanese yen forced Americans to bid up the price of yens, "in the process reducing the amount of foreign currencies they or others seek to acquire and increasing the amount available—just as the price of wheat is bid up if the quantity demanded is greater than the amount available." Intervention by government is unnecessary. A trade "deficit" does not necessarily mean the United States is "borrowing from the future to consume today." Some foreign purchases represent goods and service investments (i.e., factories built in the U.S.) rather than consumption. The important point is that greater "purchases over sales abroad is entirely consistent with an accumulation of capital assets at home and abroad."[99]

Friedman also had much to say about the Carter administration's choice of rhetoric. The theme of "fairness" became more common in government announcements. The energy program was about "fairness," the Federal Communications Commission (FCC) sought a "fairness doctrine," it was important to have "fair trade" laws, and businesses should compete providing it was "fair." But then again, Friedman explained that the word "fair" was not in the Declaration of Independence or the Constitution and the Bill of Rights. The First Amendment was about protecting the "free" exercise of religion and the "freedom" of speech.

Opposite to what the Founding Fathers intended, government became "Big Brother" functioning as "an active participant, entering into every nook and cranny of social and economic activity."[100] Friedman found this thinking troubling and a threat to liberty.

Was there an objective standard to fairness? If something was fair, could it be free? In an economy, sellers see a "fair" price as a high price, whereas buyers see a "fair" price as a low price. How is this conflict solved? Should adjudication be by a competitive free market or by government operating in a "fair" market? Friedman warned of the modern tendency of substituting "fair" for "free," something done even in business circles. There were businessmen who spoke of their allegiance to free enterprise while demanding "fair" competition. Of course, the search for fairness was commendable.

Fairness had an important role "in constructing general rules and adjudication disputes about the rules"; however, this was entirely different from "determining the outcome of our separate activities." Friedman turned the Keynesian notion of fairness on its head. For him, consumers benefited when the competition was more "unfair." When government stepped back and let market forces unfold, there were better chances for lower prices and higher quality for the American consumer.[101]

Commenting on economic theory or philosophical arguments was not likely to attract the attention of working Americans, busy with caring for their families. An easier target for conservatives in Carter's first year was the Bert Lance financial scandal. Of all the Georgians whom Carter brought to Washington, Clifford Clark judged Bert Lance "as the smartest and most politically astute." Still, the Director of the OMB was in trouble. By September, the "Lance affair" had the White House in a virtual state of siege. Since 1966, the burly, amiable Lance had been Carter's close friend.

The Georgian banker often played tennis with Carter and when he became governor, he appointed Lance director of the Georgia Department of Transportation. President-elect Carter chose Lance to be the director of the OMB. At his confirmation hearing, Lance promised to divest his stocks in two Georgian banks. His later request that the Senate give him additional time to sell the stocks brought him under greater scrutiny. The Comptroller of the Currency discovered Lance violated banking regulations while he was a bank president in Georgia. For example, he permitted family members to overdraw checking accounts by hundreds of thousands of dollars. There was no clear evidence of illegality, but the episode looked bad for Carter who had promised a higher moral standard in Washington.

Clifford Clark decided to represent Lance as his lawyer, counseling him to confront the charges coming from the Senate Governmental Affairs Committee. With Clark in his corner, Lance put up a good fight, but the optics were not good for the president. Carter suggested that he step down, a move that infuriated Lance's wife, LaBelle, who felt Carter was not giving him the support he deserved.[102] On September 21, 1977, Lance resigned, and Carter's approval rating continued to fall. A Harris Poll in late September showed public approval at 50 percent, a decline of 25 percent from March.

The episode tainted others in the White House, including Jody Powell. When Senator Charles Percy of Illinois proclaimed his outrage, in front of television cameras, that Lance flew to University of Georgia football games using his bank's plane, Powell alerted several reporters that Senator Percy was a hypocrite who regularly used a Bell and Howell corporate plane for his Washington flights. What followed was a story by the *Chicago Sun-Times* criticizing Powell's attempt to discredit a U.S. senator using information that was false.

In his memoirs, Powell's defense is weak: "I was sick and outraged. In my view, I had been passing on an off-the-record tip—a common practice in Washington—never claiming that I could verify its accuracy. That was up to the reporters." The claim that Carter's government would take the high moral road fell short. Rhetoric and the hint of "Watergate-style 'dirty tricks'" occasionally clashed.[103] In addition to the Lance and other questionable episodes concerning moral character, it was common knowledge among many reporters that there were high-ranking Carter staffers who smoked marijuana.[104] Nor was it helpful when Powell responded to media stories with profanity, including using the f-bomb.[105]

William Safire, a *New York Times* columnist who had been a Nixon speechwriter, thought it fair justice for the Democrats to receive the same scrutiny as had been the case for the Nixon administration. In his columns on "Lancegate," Safire held the Carter administration to the same standard of the Watergate years.[106] To conservatives, this was wishful thinking. When it came to missteps of governance, the record showed Democrats receiving more leeway by the media. As Tom Bethell wrote in *Harper's* magazine, the idea of an adversary press was a myth. Ultimately,

The New York Times or other media chose the "only important side—that of big government and all its works."[107]

Carter could use the favors. After a year in the White House, he still faced an economy with few bright spots. There was the role of the CBO, the organization created in 1974 that allowed economic forecasting by Congress and, thus, ending the monopoly of the White House. Stuart Eizenstat, Carter's assistant for domestic policy, found it shocking that the CBO number for the cost of the 1977 welfare program was $17 billion compared to the $7 billion estimated by the White House. Eizenstat described what followed with the welfare reform proposal: "The program was dead as of that moment—and could never be resurrected after the CBO estimate."[108] In September, Pat Caddell warned Carter that the American people saw "the past, present, and future as quite similar." Many expected difficult economic times to continue.[109] When the third quarter growth rate was lower than expected, in October Charles Schultze told Carter that without additional stimulus "the rate of expansion will fall well short of our 5 percent target for next year."[110]

Before getting the Democratic nomination in 1976, Carter had promised his support for a comprehensive and mandatory system of national health insurance (NHI). Politics overrode economics with Carter's proposed NHI plan which was contrary to the advice of Treasury secretary Blumenthal, CEA chairman Charles Schultze, and Budget director James McIntyre.[111] The sluggish economy forced Carter to delay any action much to the frustration of Senator Ted Kennedy who demanded a NHI plan. Although Schultze and McIntyre outlined a phased-in plan, where the government and private sector would share the cost, Carter declined to pursue the issue.[112]

In November, Arthur Schlesinger watched Carter's decline with satisfaction. He saw no coherent, liberal vision that progressive ideologues yearned to champion. Roosevelt had the New Deal, Truman the Fair Deal, Kennedy the New Frontier, and Johnson the Great Society. Carter had no label for his program.[113] Whereas economic conservatives saw typical Keynesian solutions to the economy, liberal Democrats worried that Carter would stray from progressive economic thinking. Carter told Clark Clifford that Truman was one of his heroes, though Clifford thought it odd that Carter never asked him a single question about Truman.[114] Democrats controlled both the House and the Senate, yet the year was a challenging one for Carter. Progressives wanted bolder action. Would 1978 be a better year for the economy?

Notes

1. Robert M. Collins, *Transforming America: Politics and Culture in the Reagan Years* (New York: Columbia University Press, 2007), 20.
2. Paul A. Samuelson, "A Year of Opportunity," *Newsweek*, January 31, 1977, 63.
3. One example is Randall Balmer, *Redeemer: The Life of Jimmy Carter* (New York: Basic Books, 2014).
4. Betty Glad, *An Outsider in the White House: Jimmy Carter, His Advisors, and the Making of American Foreign Policy* (Ithaca, NY: Cornell University Press, 2009), 19.
5. Jimmy Carter, *Keeping Faith: Memoirs of a President* (New York: Bantam Books, 1982), 68.
6. Stuart E. Eizenstat, "President Carter, the Democratic Party, and the Making of Domestic Policy," in *The Presidency and Domestic Policies of Jimmy Carter*, eds. Herbert D. Rosenbaum and Alexej Ugrinsky (Westport, CT: Greenwood Press, 1994): 4–5, 7.
7. Meg Jacobs, *Panic at the Pump: The Energy Crisis and the Transformation of American Politics in the 1970s* (New York: Hill and Wang, 2017), 171.
8. Quoted in Douglas Brinkley, *The Unfinished Presidency: Jimmy Carter's Journey Beyond the White House* (New York: Viking 1998), 31.
9. Jimmy Carter, *White House Diary* (New York: Farrar, Straus and Giroux, 2010), 163. Paul Samuelson agreed that it was "a pretty good year." See Paul A. Samuelson, "The Year That Was," *Newsweek*, January 2, 1978, 52.
10. Quoted in William E. Simon, *A Time for Truth* (New York: Reader's Digest Press, 1978), 122.
11. Quoted in Joseph A. Califano Jr., *Governing America: An Insider's Report from the White House and the Cabinet* (New York: Simon & Schuster, 1981), 322–323.
12. Arthur M. Schlesinger Jr., *Journals 1952–2000*, eds. Andrew Schlesinger and Stephen Schlesinger (New York: Penguin Press, 2007), 429.
13. Burton I. Kaufmann and Scott Kaufman, *The Presidency of James Earl Carter Jr.*, Second Edition, Revised (Lawrence: University Press of Kansas, 2006), 27–28.
14. Sidney Lens, "Jimmy Carter and the New Reality," *Christian Century*, 10–12. However, without being clear on what was the answer, Lens wanted something better than "the cold concepts of Keynesianism."
15. Jimmy Carter: "Inaugural Address," January 20, 1977. Online by Gerhard Peters and John T. Woolley, The American Presidency Project: http://www.presidency.ucsb.edu/ws/?pid=6575 (accessed August 22, 2017).
16. Fred I. Greenstein, *Presidential Difference: Leadership Style from FDR to George W. Bush*, Second Edition (Princeton, NJ: Princeton University Press, 2004), 127.

17. Stephen Woolcock, "The Economic Policies of the Carter Administration," in *The Carter Years: The President and Policy Making*, eds. M. Glenn Abernathy et al. (New York: St. Martin's Press, 1984): 39–40.
18. Dilys M. Hill, "Domestic Policy," in *The Carter Years: The President and Policy Making*, 13.
19. Kevin Mattson, *"What the Heck Are You Up to Mr. President?": Jimmy Carter, America's "Malaise," and the Speech That Should Have Changed the Country* (New York: Bloomsbury, 2009), 71–72.
20. "In the White House," *Newsweek*, January 24, 1977, 23.
21. Jacobs, *Panic at the Pump*, 164.
22. Herbert Stein, *Presidential Economics: The Making of Economic Policy from Roosevelt to Clinton*, Third Revised Edition (Washington, DC: American Enterprise Institute for Public Policy Research, 1994), 217.
23. Kenneth W. Thompson, ed. *The Carter Presidency: Fourteen Intimate Perspectives of Jimmy Carter* (Lanham, MD: University Press of America, Inc., 1990), 39–40, 48.
24. W. Carl Biven, *Jimmy Carter's Economy: Policy in an Age of Limits* (Chapel Hill: The University of North Carolina Press, 2002), 49.
25. Thompson, ed., *The Carter Presidency*, 122.
26. Quoted in Biven, *Jimmy Carter's Economy*, 85.
27. Biven, *Jimmy Carter's Economy*, 40, 79–80, 271n1.
28. Ibid., 61–62, 72–73.
29. Larry Berman, *The Office of Management and Budget and the Presidency, 1921–1979* (Princeton, NJ: Princeton University Press, 1979), ix, 128–129.
30. Quoted in Biven, *Jimmy Carter's Economy*, 45.
31. Ibid., 123.
32. Ibid., 123–125.
33. Quoted in Ken Auletta, *The Streets Were Paved with Gold* (New York: Vintage Books, 1980), 18.
34. Kaufman, *The Presidency of James Earl Carter Jr.*, 71–72.
35. Ibid., 90.
36. Biven, *Jimmy Carter's Economy*, 72, 82. The final signed by Carter had $6 billion for 1977 and $17 billion for 1978.
37. Kaufman, *The Presidency of James Earl Carter Jr.*, 33–35; Biven, *Jimmy Carter's Economy*, 77–78.
38. Biven, *Jimmy Carter's Economy*, 49–50.
39. Ibid., 131–132.
40. Califano, *Governing America*, 18, 42. Italics are mine.
41. Joseph A. Califano Jr., *Inside: A Public and Private Life* (New York: PublicAffairs, 2004), 324–325, 328–329, 331.
42. Califano, *Governing America*, 21, 24.

43. Ibid., 26.
44. Quoted in Califano, *Inside*, 332.
45. "The Man of the House," *Newsweek*, January 17, 1977, 18.
46. Califano, *Governing America*, 28–29, 36–37.
47. Ibid., 41.
48. Zbigniew Brzezinski, *Power and Principle: Memoirs of the National Security Adviser 1977–1981* (New York: Farrar, Straus and Giroux, 1983), 13–14.
49. Tip O'Neill with William Novak, *Man of the House: The Life and Political Memoirs of Speaker Tip O'Neill* (New York: Random House, 1987), 315.
50. Auletta, *The Streets Were Paved with Gold*, 316.
51. Carter, *Keeping Faith*, 41.
52. This was the view Califano painted in *Governing America*, 25.
53. Greenstein, *Presidential Difference*, 128.
54. Walter Cronkite, *A Reporter's Life* (New York: Ballantine Books, 1996), 225–226.
55. Brinkley, *The Unfinished Presidency*, 15–16.
56. Eizenstat, "President Carter, the Democratic Party, and the Making of Domestic Policy," 4.
57. Quoted in Thompson, ed., *The Carter Presidency*, 119.
58. Carter, *Keeping Faith*, 57.
59. O'Neill, *Man of the House*, 302, 305, 309.
60. Bob Woodward, *Shadow: Five Presidents and the Legacy of Watergate* (New York: Simon & Schuster, 1999), 55. The following day Bentsen phoned the White House, declaring "What the f---" is with Carter's behavior.
61. O'Neill, *Man of the House*, 308, 310–311.
62. William A. Henry, III, "The Unlikely Cult Figure," *New Republic*, February 11, 1978, 20.
63. Michael Novak, *Writing from Left to Right: My Journey from Liberal to Conservative* (New York: Image, 2013), 170.
64. Q. Whitfield Ayres, "The Carter White House Staff," in *The Carter Years: The President and Policy Making*, 144, 153.
65. Califano, *Governing America*, 25.
66. Mattson, *"What the Heck Are You Up to Mr. President?,"* 3.
67. Schlesinger, Jr. *Journals 1952–2000*, 434.
68. Peter G. Bourne, *Jimmy Carter: A Comprehensive Biography from Plains to Postpresidency* (New York: A Lisa Drew Book/Scribner, 1997), 363. Kaufman, *The Presidency of James Earl Carter Jr.*, 64.

Doreen J. Mattingly, *A Feminist in the White House: Midge Costanza, the Carter Years, and America's Culture Wars* (New York: Oxford University Press, 2016), 83–87.

69. "Waiting for Jobs," *Nation*, April 23, 1977, 484.
70. Melville J. Ulmer, "Stagflation," *New Republic*, October 29, 1977, 12–13.
71. Robert M. Collins, *More: The Politics of Economic Growth in Postwar America* (New York: Oxford University Press, 2000), 157.
72. Quoted in Biven, *Jimmy Carter's Economy*, 87.
73. Ibid.
74. Kaufman, *The Presidency of James Earl Carter Jr.*, 65–66.
75. Jeff Bloodworth, "'The Program for Better Jobs and Income': Welfare Reform, Liberalism, and the Failed Presidency of Jimmy Carter," *International Social Science Review*, 82, nos. 3–4 (2006): 139. Anderson, *Welfare*, 178. Henry J. Aaron, *Politics and the Professors: The Great Society in Perspective* (Washington, DC: The Brookings Institution, 1978), 6.
76. Bloodworth, "'The Program for Better Jobs and Income,'" 140.
77. Martin Anderson, *Welfare: The Political Economy of Welfare Reform in the United* States (Stanford, CA: Hoover Institution, 1978), 147.
78. Ibid., 12. Bloodworth, "'The Program for Better Jobs and Income,'" 140.
79. Bloodworth, "'The Program for Better Jobs and Income,'" 141–142.
80. Quoted in Anderson, *Welfare*, 171.
81. Bloodworth, "'The Program for Better Jobs and Income,'" 142–144.
82. Richard Nathan had served as the Assistant Director of the Office of Management and Budget in the Nixon years; see Anderson, *Welfare*, 185–186.
83. Ibid., 193.
84. Kaufman, *The Presidency of James Earl Carter Jr.*, 65–67.
85. Biven, *Jimmy Carter's Economy*, 95–99, 102–103, 112.
86. Ibid., 149.
87. Ibid., 113.
88. Ibid., 211–212.
89. Thomas Sowell was one of the early American scholars who studied the injurious consequences of minimum wage laws. For example, see Thomas Sowell, *Ethnic America: A History* (New York: Basic Books, Inc., 1981), 223.
90. Kaufman, *The Presidency of James Earl Carter Jr.*, 91.
91. Ibid., 25.
92. Ibid., 93–94.
93. *Time*, December 12, 1977, 12–16.
94. Simon, *A Time for Truth*, 41.
95. Milton Friedman, "To Jimmy from James," *Newsweek*, December 6, 1976, 87.
96. Milton Friedman, "Steady as You Go," *Newsweek*, January 10, 1977, 58–59.

97. Milton Friedman, "Tax Gimmickry at Its Finest," *Newsweek*, April 11, 1977, 90.
98. Milton Friedman, "The Missing Advocates," *Newsweek*, July 25, 1977, 67.
99. Milton Friedman, "Exchange-Rate Jitters," *Newsweek*, September 5, 1977, 74.
100. Milton Friedman, "Fair versus Free," *Newsweek*, July 4, 1977, 70.
101. Ibid.
102. Clark Clifford with Richard Holbrooke, *Counsel to the President: A Memoir* (New York: Random House, 1991), 628–632. Also, see Woodward, *Shadow*, 59–61. Also, Kaufman, *The Presidency of James Earl Carter, Jr.*, 73–77.
103. Jody Powell, *The Other Side of the Story* (New York: William Morrow, 1984), 50–51.
104. Ibid., 177. One blow to the Carter administration was the allegation of Hamilton Jordan using cocaine in the New York disco Studio 54. For Powell's interpretation, see Powell, *The Other Side of the Story*, 135–156.
105. Ibid., 229.
106. Woodward, *Shadow*, 57–58.
107. Tom Bethell, "The Myth of an Adversary Press," *Harper's*, January 1977, 33–34.
108. Biven, *Jimmy Carter's Economy*, 53.
109. Kaufman, *The Presidency of James Earl Carter Jr.*, 78.
110. Quoted in Kaufman, *The Presidency of James Earl Carter Jr.*, 73.
111. Friedman, "The Politics of Economics," *Newsweek*, October 16, 1978, 92.
112. Kaufman, *The Presidency of James Earl Carter Jr.*, 125.
113. Schlesinger, Jr. *Journals 1952–2000*, 436–437.
114. Clifford, *Counsel to the President*, 620.

CHAPTER 7

Inflation and Taxes in 1978

Howard Jarvis was not everyone's idea of a hero. At a television studio in California's San Joaquin where the agenda was to discuss the upcoming vote on the tax-reducing Proposition 13, onlookers looked on in shock when the 75-year-old Jarvis, making his way to a table loaded with sandwiches lost his balance and fell face first on the studio's orange carpet. Dusting himself off, he declared: "That shows how stupid I am." Changing the subject to the Proposition 13 debate, the moderator "gingerly asked" Jarvis about going "over the format." The wisecracking Jarvis responded in a "loud, bull frog bass" manner: "You're going over the *floormat*? I just did."[1] If Jarvis was as silly as he appeared on occasion, he certainly outfoxed many impressive politicians on tax policy.

Carter's political honeymoon was not a long one for a modern Democratic president. His public approval rating went from the low 70s in the early weeks of his presidency to the low 50s by the end of 1977. After his first year, spending and job opportunities for the American people continued to be the narrative for Democratic politicians, but it became difficult to avoid the significance of inflation. Unfortunately, well-known Keynesians gave questionable advice, as was the case when Walter Heller said in January 1977 that the $70 billion deficit was "minor" and no threat to raising "'even a specter' of inflation."

In the same month, Alice Rivlin, director of the Congressional Budget Office (CBO), dismissed the possibility of the deficit crowding out business investment and raising interest rates.[2] In May 1978, the Council on

E. R. Crouse, *America's Failing Economy and the Rise of Ronald Reagan*,
https://doi.org/10.1007/978-3-319-70545-3_7

Wage and Price Stability (COWPS) reported the slowing of labor productivity and the escalation of unit labor costs over the past year.[3] It did not help matters that the momentum for spending was especially robust during the year of the midterm elections. The anxiety and anger over inflation merged with the protest about high taxes. In fact, taxes offered a more straightforward target than the problem of inflation for Americans who wanted to be heard. The dramatic tax protests that unfolded disrupted Keynesian thinking at both state and federal levels.

I

In early 1978, the Department of Commerce organized the White House Conference on Balanced National Growth and Economic Development, what the media branded "the nation's first town meeting on growth." Governor John D. Rockefeller IV of West Virginia was the chairman and Michael S. Koleda, vice president of the National Planning Association, served as conference director for the five-day event that attracted 500 official delegates to Washington, DC. Comprised of many mayors and governors, the conference tackled the difficult task of integrating growth, environmental protection, and resource conservation. Some at the conference suggested slower growth was a wiser course. In the eyes of Henry Ford II, this so-called "balanced growth" represented the misguided approach of sacrificing industrial growth "on the altar of environmental purity." Overall, any achievements of the conference were at best modest. One of Carter's objectives was for the conference to deflect attention from the White House by promoting decentralization. As one White House aid explained: "We have to pull away from this notion that everything has to fall squarely into the lap of the federal government."[4]

Political leaders across the nation looked to the Carter administration for assistance to deal with financial difficulties in their respective jurisdictions and a few did not find a warm welcome. For example, Jody Powell was no fan of New York Governor Hugh Carey and New York City Mayor Ed Koch: "No more slippery pair of political ingrates had ever sidled into the Oval Office, hat in one hand, shiv in the other."[5] Bad feelings went both ways. To discuss New York City's economic mess, Senator Daniel Moynihan met with journalist Ken Auletta for lunch at the Edwardian Room of the Plaza Hotel. An engaging man who enjoyed hearing his voice, Moynihan told Auletta that Washington shortchanged the state of New York by more than $7 billion (i.e., the state sent $36 but received

$29 back). Working on his fourth Guinness stout before the arrival of his pea soup, Moynihan presented deficit calculations that did not make sense to him. He believed the federal government was "systematically deflating the economy of ... New York State."[6]

On the primary campaign trial in 1976, Moynihan had supported Henry Jackson rather than Carter. Still weakened by his failure to produce tax and welfare reform in his first year, Carter did not need a fight with Moynihan and other unhappy Democrats. The problem for Carter went beyond his relationship with politicians seeking financial support; a major obstacle for the Carter administration was a weak economy burdened by rising inflation. The Democratic administrations of Kennedy and Johnson delivered on a significant number of promises because the economic years before they entered office were good ones.[7] The rising inflation of the 1970s made governance for Carter more challenging.

Conservative critics, such as Richard Viguerie, viewed inflation as a hidden tax that hit "the poor harder than other forms of taxation." In fact, because blacks were disproportionately poorer, they were "among the chief victims of liberal fiscal irresponsibility."[8] Born in Texas in 1933 and graduating from the University of Houston with a B.Sc in political science and a minor in economics, Viguerie was a Catholic with a burning desire to make a difference in politics. He became the executive secretary of Young Americans for Freedom, and one of his responsibilities was fundraising. He wrote many letters to wealthy contributors, a process that led to starting his own direct mail company in 1964. By the late 1960s he was a success story, attracting the attention of politicians who understood how mailing lists could grow votes. Using new technology in the 1970s, Viguerie operated a direct mail system that bypassed liberals' "near-monopoly of the national news media."[9] Direct mail was costly with postage accounting for 40 percent of total costs; however, done correctly it was an effective advertising medium.[10]

Viguerie was a health-food nut who stashed jars of wheat germ and dried fruit in his office and served guests coffee but chose V-8 juice for himself. Although a formidable opponent of the Democratic Party, he spoke softly and his manner, according to the *Atlantic Monthly*, was "polite, professional, deferential, controlled, and consciously affable."[11] With his economics background, he found it curious how liberals pressed for more jobs for Americans while showing "contempt" for job creators in the private sector: "How can you be for eggs but against chickens? Or for milk but against cows? Where do they think jobs come from?"[12]

Although Carter's opponents cited full-employment schemes backed by federal money as clear examples of idealism instigating fiscal irresponsibility, the White House thought otherwise. At a Congressional Black Caucus dinner in September, Carter declared: "I continue to regard the passage of the Humphrey-Hawkins bill as one of the highest legislative priorities of my Administration."[13] The Black Caucus believed it was the answer for job creation, but the members wondered whether Carter's actions would match his words.

At one meeting, Parren J. Mitchell of Maryland (chairman of the caucus) got in a loud argument with Carter and Walter Mondale. An angry John Conyers of Michigan walked out of the meeting.[14] Caucus leaders demanded action, but were the bill's ambitious goals of four percent unemployment and three percent inflation possible?[15] For Milton Friedman, it was best to see employment as "a means to the production of goods and services that we can enjoy." Having full employment was unsatisfactory if it meant "employment at unproductive jobs, digging holes for others to fill."[16]

As for inflation, it was costly to creditors who lent money in fixed amounts, allowing debtors to pay off their loans with cheaper money. Inflation was a serious issue for businesses because uncertainty weakened incentives for industry to invest and expand, and less business activity meant fewer jobs. Unless workers had automatic cost-of-living adjustments, they suffered when the price for goods and services outpaced any rise in wages and salary. Although there were homeowners who benefited from rising house prices, those seeking to buy their first home faced out-of-reach prices made worse with high interest rates.[17]

With job programs and spending projects, inflationary pressure caused major problems for the Carter government still faithful to Keynesian thinking. Seeking to win the favor of the feminist movement, Carter appointed Bella Abzug to serve as a cochair of the President's Advisory Committee for Women. This appointment became questionable when Abzug openly criticized his anti-inflationary policies.[18] Whether Carter's policies were against inflation depended on one's interpretation. In *Harper's* magazine, Tom Bethel wrote that Carter's "record is turning out to be indistinguishable from that of an old-fashioned FDR-inspired liberal, complete with [a] seal of approval from Americans for Democratic Action."[19]

A major concern for Carter was his declining popularity as the inflation rate rose. By April, a Harris poll indicated that on the issue of the economy only 24 percent of Americans gave Carter a favorable rating, down from the

47 percent it was 10 months before. Delivering a speech to the American Society of Newspaper Editors shortly after the release of poor poll numbers, Carter promised "to take the lead in breaking the wage and price spiral by holding Federal pay increases down." One important step was to limit Federal white-collar salaries to 5.5 percent compared to the more than 7 percent the previous year, thus "setting the example for labor and industry to moderate price and wage increases." Carter also used government purchasing as a weapon against businesses unwilling to hold prices in check, declaring: "All executive branch agencies will avoid or reduce the purchase of goods or services whose prices are rapidly rising, unless by so doing we would seriously jeopardize our national security or create serious unemployment."[20]

To help persuade business and labor leaders to comply, Carter appointed Robert Strauss, a special trade representative known for his persuasion skills, to be his "official jaw-boner." Some major businesses in various industries signaled their support for Carter's program, but Strauss had far less success with labor leaders who established multiyear contracts for their members. Once locked into a contract, workers without a cost-of-living adjustment had less purchasing power when inflation drove prices higher. One meeting with George Meany and Lane Kirkland of the AFL-CIO was unpleasant without much progress. Before labor unions would commit to Carter's program, price inflation had to slow down.[21]

On September 1, 1978, Carter's communication advisor Jerry Rafshoon sent him a candid message: "It is impossible to overestimate the importance of the inflation issue to your presidency." Alarmed by the level of anxiety and insecurity among Americans, Rafshoon wanted Carter to adopt a tough anti-inflation program even though this would upset George Meany and other labor leaders. Carter's economic advisors wanted formal and tougher wage and price guidelines; they outlined an anti-inflation policy that would limit annual wage increases to seven percent.

In addition, they received Carter's support for a procurement sanction that required the compliance to the policy of those firms doing business with the government. The OMB thought that such coercion was a bad idea because the cost of administering the plan would be high and the results trifling.[22] Carter addressed the nation on October 24 to outline new initiatives including the reduction of the federal budget deficit to $33 billion for fiscal year 1980.[23] For free-market economists, it was still too much spending. The administration continued to avoid what many economists understood: It was impossible to defeat substantial inflation without experiencing an interim period of slow economic growth.[24]

The Keynesianism of Carter's administration was also on display three months earlier with world leaders at the Bonn, West Germany, NATO summit when Carter argued for stimulative fiscal policy. One scholar described it as "the high-water mark of a Keynesian type of demand management" and an example of "the futility of attempting international macroeconomic coordination."[25] Adding to this failure was a disappointing domestic anti-inflation plan that fell flat in slowing the inflation rate; the results of the government's call for businesses and labor unions to control increases in prices and wages remained dismal.[26]

II

For Milton Friedman, any discussion of solving high inflation had to include the work of the Federal Reserve System (Fed), an agency created in 1913 that he often criticized. As far as he knew, the Fed had "never admitted error in any official statement" since its creation. A private business cannot hide mistakes; it must correct them or there is bankruptcy: "That is why the *loss* component of the *profit* and *loss* system is far more important than the profit component."[27] Mistakes by the Fed had significant consequences for the economy.

As a creation of Congress, the Fed is an independent government agency that controls monetary policy. One of its major objectives is to maintain a healthy money supply that allows job growth without overheating the economy and causing inflation. Composed of a Board of Governors that oversees 12 District Reserve Banks, it reports to Congress. The president appoints the governors, but occasionally there is tension between the president and the chairman. Whereas Friedman was wary of the Fed pumping too much money into the economy, the Carter administration worried about monetary restraint.

The Fed chairman was Arthur Burns, appointed by Richard Nixon in 1972. Before Carter met with Burns, he received a warning from Charles Schultze: "Arthur Burns has waged a life-long fight against big government, deficit spending and inflation. He regards budget deficits as the principal source of inflation, and his views on budget deficits are as much a matter of moral conviction as they are of analytic reasoning." Burns was "an intellectually stubborn man" who opposed the need for a stimulus package.[28]

A former professor at Columbia University and senior researcher at the National Bureau of Economic Research, Burns earned the respect of many as an eminent statesman. At Columbia, the avuncular, pipe-smoking professor found it rewarding "to provoke disagreements" in his graduate classes. Contrary to the economic mainstream, he favored empirical evidence and deductive logic. In the early 1950s while Allan Greenspan was a Columbia graduate student, he got this lesson from Burns: excessive "government spending causes inflation!"[29]

The White House did not need to worry too much about Burns. When it came to important economic decisions, there was a divergence of rhetoric and reality at the Fed. The rise in inflation in 1978 indicated that the Fed had failed to restrict money.[30] As it was, Burns's term ended in January 1978, and there was no chance of Carter reappointing him for another four-year term. Carter did not like him, and Burns fell short in giving attention to both unemployment and inflation.

In a memorandum to the president, Michael Blumenthal and Charles Schultze wrote: "Arthur Burns has stirred up opposition to many of your policies, and will continue to do so. He is not committed to the same fundamental goals as the Administration, and positively relishes in leading the opposition when he thinks it important."[31] Carter's advisors wanted someone more in line with their policies, so the president announced the appointment of William Miller as the Fed chairman; he assumed office in March 1978. Miller enjoyed the Metropolitan Opera, bourbon, and polkas.[32] A graduate of Coast Guard Academy, his college education was like Carter's, although later he earned a law degree. He was no economist. Carter's advisors told him that Miller had the right views and would "be cooperative and easy to work with."[33]

This decision left Friedman unenthusiastic. While he was chairman, Burns had repeatedly warned of the perils of inflation and the necessity of reducing spending and government's interference with private businesses. He also reported to Congress and the media on how the Fed reduced its target rates of money growth, but in truth the monetary supply increased rather than decreased. Was Burns deceitful? Friedman did not blame him for the divergence of rhetoric and reality; it was one more "example of how an individual may be unable to bend an institution, subject to many pressures and forces, to his will."[34]

Much of the pressure on the Fed to print money came from Americans who wanted more goodies from the government without paying for them with higher taxes. Friedman was blunt: It was John Q. Public "demanding inflation and aborting every attempt to stop inflation." Politicians also benefited because inflation acted as a hidden tax, a clever way for them to pay for government spending. The rise of prices and incomes pushed people into higher tax brackets.[35] Friedman expected even higher inflation when the Fed leadership was someone the Democrats praised.

Friedman explained to *Newsweek* readers that over the years the federal government demonstrated a reluctance to cure inflation with the necessary medicine. The basic cause of inflation was straightforward: "too high a rate of growth in the quantity of money—too much money chasing the available supply of goods and services." Inflation was not the result of militant trade unions, greedy capitalists, uncontrolled consumerism, poor crops, harsh weather, or OPEC cartels. They might be "consequences of inflation" or "sources of temporary blips of inflation" but nothing else. The cause of too much money was the Federal Reserve System.

When Washington politicians wanted money for federal spending, the "independent" Fed typically conceded. According to Friedman, "the Fed refrains from using its independence because it is afraid of losing it."[36] Even the words of Burns did nothing to undermine the plausibility of Friedman's claim. Testifying before the House of Representatives in 1977, Burns declared: "The trend of growth in monetary aggregates, I regret to say, is still too rapid. Even though the Federal Reserve has steadily sought during the past two years to achieve lower ranges for monetary expansion, the evolution of its projections has been extremely gradual; indeed, at the pace we have been moving *[note: with respect to projections, not behavior]* it would require perhaps a decade to reach rates of growth consistent with price stability."[37]

It seemed to Friedman that there was a link between the economic irresponsibility of spendthrift politicians and the Federal Reserve's inflationary behavior. There were ample words from the Fed, but no serious action of restraint. If Congress wanted to do something useful, it could demand Fed accountability: "Instead of simply requiring the Federal Reserve to *report* its 'projections' or 'targets' for monetary growth, let the Congress require the Fed to *achieve* specified rates of monetary growth (or specified levels of the quantity of money) within specified ranges of tolerance." This would identify to the American people who was responsible for inflation.[38] Friedman predicted inflation would be worse in the future unless the Carter administration and the Fed supported the strategy of gradually reducing the monetary growth rates and staying the course regardless of public pressure.[39]

The government's problem with inflation stemmed from misguided commitment to a significant Keynesian construct. Freidman argued that the faith of Carter's economic advisors in the Phillips curve and the idea of tolerable tradeoffs between unemployment and inflation was a delusion. When there was inflation, wages rose, and workers responded by supplying more labor. This caused the unemployment rate to drop. In time, however, workers learned that their higher wages were inadequate to compensate for the higher price of food and other goods and services. Because there was no improvement to their "real" wage, they decreased their labor. In the whole process, the unemployment rate rose to its earlier rate, "but at a now higher level of prices."

The analysis of other economists complemented Friedman's research. University of Chicago economist Robert Lucas examined the "rational expectations" of workers, revising Friedman's argument that a tradeoff existed for a short time as workers learned the truth about their real wages. The "rational expectations" school claimed that workers learned to anticipate inflation, thus not even a short-term tradeoff existed. The practical implication of these academic assaults cast doubt on the government's confident Keynesianism and its ability to manage the level of unemployment.[40]

In September 1978, Friedman wrote that Carter and his advisors wanted to put more money into welfare programs and national health insurance, displaying "supreme confidence in their ability to fine-tune the economy—to promote growth now and to do something about inflation later." Pointing to the administration's "overconfidence in its ability to manipulate the economy," Friedman predicted a bleak situation of double-digit inflation by 1980, plus a recession and high unemployment.[41]

III

Throughout the 1970s, Friedman wrote often about taxes and government waste. Months before Carter took office, the economist's comparison of New Hampshire and Vermont tested C. Northcote Parkinson's formulation that "[e]xpenditures rise to meet income." New Hampshire had no state income tax or state sales tax, but Vermont had both. So how did they compare on spending? In the third most taxed state in the nation, Vermont residents gave 50 percent more of their personal income for expenditures than was the case in New Hampshire. It was clear that Vermont's expenditures rose to meet its income. Nevertheless, Vermont's extra spending did not translate into improved education and welfare services. For example, teachers' salaries and mean Scholastic Aptitude Test scores were roughly the same in New Hampshire and Vermont. Vermont, however had a state and local debt "more than twice as large a percentage of personal income as New Hampshire."

Friedman's conclusion: "Apparently, extra income and sales taxes only whet the appetite of the ambitious public servant." What could a taxpayer do? One option with local government was to move from the small community that "is taxing much and returning little in services." This option was more difficult with the state and federal government because competition was less. The American people got less for their money "from the state than from the local government, and even less from the Federal government."[42]

Given that the total budget of a government is the sum of all appropriations, it is important that no single appropriation exceed a certain limit on spending. Yet, what happens is that each separate appropriation has the support of special-interest groups. When politicians fight for a specific "pet" proposal, they argue that the costs—spread thinly over all taxpayers—is minimal for each voter. The politician knows that voters are unlikely to vote against them if the tax increase is barely noticeable, but it becomes more of a problem when many politicians fight for their pet programs.

Another defect in the political system is that each program has the support of "an un-holy coalition of well-meaning reformers and self-interest groups." What often happens is that self-interest groups dominate the reformers. According to Friedman, these two issues caused excessive government spending. Government spending in 1928 was approximately 10 percent and 50 years later it was about 40 percent. Were taxpayers "getting their money's worth?"[43]

Certainly, taxes were a big story in 1978. When a reporter asked Friedman to assess Carter's decision to abandon a proposed $25 billion tax cut, the economist explained that there was "no proposal to cut taxes, only to shift their form, while in fact proposing to raise them."[44] Whether at the federal, state, or local level, people seeking political office seldom found it beneficial to promise voters future spending cuts. Simply put, spending brought jobs, which usually neutralized the problem of deficits that otherwise might have caused the Democrats political trouble. A proven strategy was working with special-interest groups and promising attractive government handouts "while talking in vague generalities or not at all about how the handouts were to be financed."[45] Still, the strategy was not perfect. A politician could dodge talking about taxation only to the point when Americans began to feel the effects on their wallets.

The tax revolt of 1978 elevated the national profile of non-Keynesian activists and economists. One source of headaches for the White House and Keynesians came from Californian Howard Arnold Jarvis. Labeled "a briny old brawler" by *Newsweek*, he led a tax revolt with the tea bag as its symbol, harkening back to the Boston Tea Party.[46] Born in 1902 in the small copper-mining town of Magna, Utah, Jarvis found his way to the University of Utah where he earned a law degree.

Rather than practicing law, he borrowed money to buy a weekly newspaper, the first of several. One anti-government exploit was hiding on a rooftop and photographing officials engaged in the moonshine whisky trade: "I got a hell of a lot of politicians put in the penitentiary." He wanted more than what Utah offered, so after selling his newspapers for $105,000 Jarvis moved to California. His resentment of "Big Government" grew when, days after the Japanese attack on Pearl Harbor, the federal government shut down a factory in which he had invested his capital. Nevertheless, all was not lost. His company, which manufactured products ranging from aircraft parts to garbage disposals, was a financial success during the postwar period.

In the early 1960s, Jarvis retired and turned his attention to fighting high taxes that caused seniors to lose their homes. Although he tried his hand at running for office, he suffered large losses in a Republican primary and a bid for mayor of Los Angeles; his profanity was not an asset on the campaign trail. He labeled himself a "Jack Mormon." Jarvis swore, drank vodka, smoked a pipe, and stayed clear of churches on Sunday. When he led the Proposition 13 fight, he was old and in poor health, taking medication for his narrowing arteries. None of these ailments stopped him from fighting high taxes; for example, his property tax bill for his West Los Angeles home, assessed at $80,000, was almost $3000.[47]

As reported by the *Los Angeles Times*, property assessments in the city rose 120 percent between the years 1974 and 1978. Homeowners clamored for relief not knowing whether their protests would bear fruit with property assessors hamstrung by an earlier scandal in which an assessor received "consulting" fees from businesses in exchange for lower assessments. Responding to the conviction of the assessor in the 1960s, Democratic Governor Pat Brown signed a law preventing any assessor from tampering with the numbers. Unfortunately, local government continued to have the upper hand. More painful to homeowners was when the assessed value of homes became higher than previous assessments of most homes across the state. County assessors depended on voter approval for reelection, but they no longer had the ability to resist pressure from local governments demanding more tax dollars for their favorite projects.[48]

Inflation drove up the paper value of homes and governments dutifully raised the taxes on homeowners. One research report indicated that there were Los Angeles citizens earning between $10,000 and $15,000 a year who paid $2500 in property taxes. Unable to afford taxes that came with excessive assessments, people lost their homes. State environmental regulations slowed the rate of homes being built and, thus, demand outpaced supply, contributing to the rising house assessments in California. "Revenge is in the air," declared San Francisco columnist Herb Caen.[49]

Nonetheless, victory for Proposition 13 was not a sure thing. Since the adoption of the initiative process in California in 1911, most proposals for new legislation went down in defeat at the polls. Recent examples were the 1968 and 1972 tax relief proposals, which failed when the state legislature ushered in tax relief measures to diffuse the anger of homeowners. Although Proposition 13 began with "an awkwardly phrased, eight-paragraph blunderbuss that slashed the tax rate from 3 percent of market value to 1 percent," Jarvis succeeded in gathering over one million signatures, more than enough to get the proposition on the June 6 ballot.

To bolster his campaign, Jarvis joined retired real estate man and tax-cut advocate Paul Gann (described as a "gentler type" by the *Atlantic Monthly*), hired a consulting firm, and gained the support of key people such as economist Milton Friedman. Known as the Jarvis-Gann Initiative, the momentum of Proposition 13 was unstoppable with Jarvis as the front man who captivated people with his flamboyant and funny character and his focus on big government: "The only way to cut government spending is not to give them the money in the first place." Arguing that Proposition 13 benefited the rich with handsome profits, opponents were unable to redirect "public attention on the windfall of business."[50] In a letter to the editor of the *San Francisco Chronicle*, Norman I. Arnold captured the sentiment of many Californians supporting the proposition: "We are not anarchists, we are not radicals and we do not think we are irresponsible. We are simply full sick and tired of having our pockets picked at every level of government."[51]

Slow to respond to this anti-tax climate and what to do with the state's $5 billion surplus, Governor Jerry Brown's government made a last-minute attempt to sidetrack the Jarvis proposal with its own proposal. Some called Brown flaky, but there were few politicians as canny and opportunistic as the fourth-generation Californian who won the race for governor in 1974 by a close margin of 2.9 percentage points. Identifying himself with the religion of Zen Buddhism, he had a knack for diverting attention from troublesome news.[52]

When California's unemployment rate hit above 9.8 percent in late 1975, the Brown government acted with the "important announcement" of getting rid of the nativity scene that had been on display at the capitol for decades during the Christmas season. His diversion tactics were creative. Responding to a newspaper story of a housing project rife with criminal activity, Brown paid a surprise visit to see the plight of residents. He spoke forcefully that people step forward and help the tenants and not ignore the problem. The next day the governor was off to watch the migration of whales near San Luis Obispo County. An aid in his office admitted later that Brown's visit to the housing project "was one of the most cynical things we've ever done."[53]

Joining the Democratic Party's opposition to Proposition 13 were labor leaders, education administrators, and liberals who forecast the loss of numerous jobs. Not what Brown intended, his government's alternative proposal to the Jarvis plan "confirmed the average tax-payer's feeling that an across-the-board tax cut was not all that difficult to bring off."[54] It became obvious to Proposition 13 opponents that additional scare tactics were necessary because there was more at stake than the capping of property tax rates. If passed, the amendment also would limit the power of local governments to raise revenue. State- and local-level government officials warned of the shutdown of schools and libraries, the loss of fire and police protection, and the abandonment of poor people.[55]

These tactics were sweeping. Legislative analyst A. Alan Post expected literal "chaos" and California State Assembly speaker, Leo McCarthy, predicted the destruction of the school system.[56] Education organizations sent notices to teachers warning of their automatic dismissal if the amendment passed. Various cartoons in the *Los Angeles Times* illustrated scenarios of tough times; for example, one of a police station front door displaying the message, "In Case of Burglary Call Howard Jarvis"; and an image of an empty classroom with the message on the blackboard, "Call Howard Jarvis."[57] Dr. Ralph Wilson, school superintendent of the suburban community of Redwood City, said Proposition 13 would result in a 48 percent reduction of total education revenue. A possible outcome would be the closure of "the entire school system at the end of January." Jarvis responded that the "doomsday predictions were 'a crock of manure,'" though he used much more colorful language.[58]

Critics hoped to win the day by focusing on Jarvis's connection with rental owners. As Ed Salzman of the *California Journal* pointed out: "All you need to know about the Jarvis-Gann Initiative is that Howard Jarvis is the paid director of an association of apartment house owners in Los Angeles. The proposition should be called the Apartment House Owners Enactment Act of 1978." State Finance Office analyst Clifford Allenby reported that landlords and businesses would receive the bulk of the tax relief. Arguing that lower property taxes would not guarantee lower housing rents, anti-Proposition 13 forces predicted that the tax initiative would hit renters harder than homeowners because they would get no tax relief. Given that renters constituted almost half of California households, opponents hoped their votes would defeat Proposition 13.[59]

Milton Friedman acknowledged that the campaign against the proposition was massive, but "the public refused to be bamboozled this time, as they had been so often before while watching taxes mount and government services deteriorate." His observation rang true for many; the scare tactics produced a "backlash."[60] There were Californians who expected chaos, and they were fine with it. In a letter to the *San Francisco Chronicle*, one angry person explained: "We know [Jarvis-Gann] will severely disrupt state and city governments. We are also saying we want severe disruption. We do not think we are being irresponsible. We are simply tired of having our pockets picked by a horde of thieves."[61]

Eileen Porras and her husband witnessed the property tax on their three-bedroom home in southwest San Francisco rise from $300 to $2240 over a period of 19 years. She had had enough: "I honestly don't care if they close the library, the schools, some firehouses." Although few likely held this position, there were plenty of people disgusted with government waste. Retired construction worker William Peterson believed that politicians were out of control. Proposition 13 was "a notification to the legislature—they're talking about inflation while they're the ones creating inflation." Even Berkeley government worker Elsie Garwood took issue with too many people getting "a free ride in government—five people standing around to dig a hole when you need only one."[62]

Three weeks before the election, Proposition 13 led the polls by a slim three percent, but there was a shockwave when newspapers reported large increases in new assessments of California properties. The tide turned and voters sent a message that "the cynical purchase of special-interest votes can no longer be readily concealed behind the pretense of serving the public interest."[63] On June 6, the proposition received about 65 percent of

Californians votes; *Newsweek* explained the outcome: "taxpayers are mad as hell and aren't going to take it anymore."[64] Taking an opposing position in his article, "Mutiny in California," Richard L. Strout of the *New Republic* wanted Proposition 13 "discarded."[65]

Although Governor Brown had fought the amendment, he appeared to dance politically closer to being "a charter member of the Proposition 13 fan club," earning the nickname "Jerry Jarvis."[66] David Broder of the *Atlantic Monthly* wrote: "At one level, Brown's political trick is quite simple: he is a product of the Democratic Left who says things with great appeal to the Republican Right."[67] He was up for reelection in the fall, and Brown had his share of angry letters from Californians stating why they voted for Proposition 13. One woman wrote: "I'm tired of paying for politicians' dinners and lunches when my family can't afford to go out to dinner even once a month.... I'm tired of doing without so that you all can have everything."[68]

Brown would, however, have to shave government spending projects "including his pet plan for a space satellite."[69] In addition, he would have to abandon the idea of having any assistance from Washington when Carter clarified that the government would not "single out California for special Federal programs just because they have lowered property taxes."[70] One curious outcome was that Howard Jarvis helped Brown's campaign for reelection in November by doing a political commercial for him.[71]

IV

In June 1978, a Philadelphia audience of 700 cheered Ronald Reagan when he praised tax reform in California, hoping it would unleash a "prairie fire" across the nation and ignite enthusiasm for "limited government and unlimited freedom."[72] Although not happy about it, Robert Lekachman of the *New Republic* predicted that "Jarvis fever" would infect Americans beyond the Golden State: "California of course is special because much of the nation's kookiness starts there and spreads east."[73]

Keynesians nationwide feared a tax revolt was a realistic concern given that there were anti-tax movements elsewhere before the California vote on Proposition 13. Attacking federal taxation was a tall order, but the anti-government movement had greater success targeting state and local taxation.[74] In May, Milton Friedman and about 200 others, representing 38 states, gathered in Illinois for the first national convention of the National Tax Limitation Committee. Over a period of two days there was important discussion on tactics to confront the problem of excessive government spending and high taxes.

Voters scored victories at various levels of government. For example, 70 percent of the electorate went to the polls in Elgin, Illinois, to defeat a school district tax hike. On the other side of the aisle, Democratic politicians fought back with their defense of heavy spending. Nonetheless, as they discovered, wins were not easy. Illinois Governor James Thompson, weeks before that National Tax Limitation Committee met, defeated a tax-limitation amendment by "threatening a veto, twisting arms, and calling in every political chip he could muster."[75] That the Keynesian defense required such energy demonstrated that momentum was with taxpayer protests.

In the larger picture, labor union leaders expressed concern as often as politicians. Like other critics nationwide, they sought to protect their own political turfs. When Californians approved Proposition 13, the Public Employee Department of the AFL-CIO discussed ways to prevent any similar tax revolts elsewhere. Rather than dismissing the idea of tax cuts, their main strategy was to call for more modest tax cuts. Jerry Wurf, president of the American Federation of State, County and Municipal Employees (AFSCME), feared "that demagoguery in the wake of Proposition 13 will destroy the viability of the nation's cities and states."

Representing one million members, the AFSCME made plans to buy space in newspapers to sell its ideas for tax reform. Wurf and other union leaders understood the danger of Proposition 13-type revolts. More than 40 percent of government workers in California voted for Proposition 13, a remarkable number given the possibility of lost government jobs. An Urban Institute study of the 1971 to 1976 period revealed that municipal workers in various major cities lost as much as one-third of their purchasing power.[76]

Progressive journalists, such as Carey McWilliams of the *Nation,* argued that middle-class homeowners did not see the true source of their grievances. Homeowners had good cause to be angry, but at fault was a government that was not progressive enough. "Wrongheaded" government wasted money on defense spending, allowed corporations "to rake in profits," and gave bankers and lenders preferential treatment, while social services for the poor declined. In New York City, for example, did not politicians care more about paying the bankers than the reality of the city poor scavenging food from garbage cans? McWilliams believed that the "economic establishment," for some time, could lessen the burden of inflation on the middle class by denying the assistance entitled to "ghetto blacks, [and the] chronically unemployed and unemployable." Not paying property taxes themselves, the "down-and-outers" took revolt to another stage "with bank robberies, stickups, burglaries, assaults and an increase in arson."[77]

Discord among leftist activists, notable during the 1960s, reared its head over Proposition 13. McWilliams's critique did not go far enough for Peter Connolly, a lawyer working for a senator in Washington. Proposition 13 could never be "a healthy phenomenon," something he believed McWilliams did not recognize. When Howard Jarvis speaks, Connolly said, "one hears the voice of an America one thought was blessedly gone, a country of raw economic greed, unmodulated by the precarious though real moral accomplishments of U.S. during the past thirty years." Had not the social justice policies of the post-World War II period vanquished greed? The immediate need was for a stronger denunciation of Proposition 13—"the harbinger of a reactionary counterrevolution in American politics." Connolly warned "serious radicals" to resist the temptation to bang the "Populist drum" that undermined the legitimacy of government and the hope of "humane collective action" bringing "a more decent society."[78]

Victory in California advanced "the credibility and visibility of the taxpayer movement."[79] Proponents relished the timing. Jim McGuinn, a supporter of the Association for Taxpayers in Massachusetts, declared: "If California can do it, so can we." Political scientist Jeff Bell, a 34-year-old who had never run for public office, scored a surprising victory in the GOP primary in New Jersey against liberal four-term Senator Clifford Case. To explain his victory, Bell pointed to "the tidal wave of tax revolt."[80]

Populism was evident in voting patterns and polling numbers. A Gallup Poll indicated that most Americans (57 percent) supported "a Jarvis-style tax cut in their states." Many working families believed that they had gained little economic progress in a decade. Some working families only inched ahead when wives entered the labor force. There was also the issue of higher tax brackets. One did not need to be an economist to understand that high inflation, caused by increased government spending and taxes, hurt many who struggled to find ways to pay their taxes. *Newsweek* reported that "many political scientists" saw signs of a new consensus replacing the liberal hegemony that had been dominant since the 1930s.[81]

Most media focus was on economic and political personalities, especially conservatives who were in the process of reformulating conservative economic thinking. The media began to pay more attention to Arthur

Laffer and the Laffer curve. As reported in *Newsweek*, before boarding the Washington shuttle at New York's La Guardia, Laffer received praise from a New York policeman burdened with property taxes of more than $3000 for his Nassau County house. Recognizing him, the policeman took Laffer's hand and congratulated him for standing for "the little guy."

Laffer taught business economics at the University of Southern California, but he played no part in the planning of Proposition 13.[82] So why pay any attention to an academic economist? Economists, such as Milton Friedman, were rare; the public perception was that most academic economists were boring scholars immersed in their academic world of economic theory and technicality. Like Friedman, Laffer had a welcome message that made sense and resonated with the broader public. The New York policeman and others at the grass roots became aware of Laffer because of his numerous talks across the nation, some televised, explaining how tax cuts stimulated economic growth. He had sung this song for years, and in 1978 Americans were ready, more so than ever before, for this music.

Journalists found Laffer captivating. He slept in a rare Chippendale bed, swam with his pet terrapin named Bobby, wore alligator-skin cowboy boots, drove an old battered Ford station wagon, was a fan of country singer Waylon Jennings, was serious about antique crystal, and had admitted to a friend his desire to become a biologist after he turned 40 because "after 40 all your ideas as an economist become obsolete." The picture *Newsweek* chose in its story on the economic "guru" was Laffer standing, eyeing the camera with his left hand in his pants pocket and his right hand holding his blue macaw.

Laffer's wife and four children shared the house with the macaw, five parrots, two cockatoos, four turtles, and a ferret named Fern.[83] The *New Republic* described him as an ambitious, likable guy who "talks as though somebody had pulled the trigger of a machine gun." He had quick and intense gestures: "[W]hen he mentions holding down taxes his hands hold them down, like somebody kneading dough."[84]

Laffer represented a new wave of supply-side economics that entered the political picture during the late 1970s, bolstering the free-market challenge to Keynesian ideas. Supply-side economists reasoned, in less-than perfect language, that supply created its own demand. They promoted the Laffer curve that explained how high taxation became counterproductive and caused economic "malaise." Such thinking was not new. In the late eighteenth century, Adam Smith wrote: "High taxes, sometimes by diminishing the consumption of the taxed commodities, and sometimes by encouraging smuggling, frequently afford a smaller revenue to government than what might be drawn from more moderate taxes."[85]

The U.S. government had lost billions in uncollected taxes from people working under the table in the so-called "subterranean economy." In addition, liberal states, especially in the northeast, lost revenue because businesses found the lower taxes of the Sunbelt region more attractive. New York City was the "capital of liberal compassion and concern" but at a high cost; New Yorkers paid twice as much in taxes as the average tax for the next 26 largest cities.[86]

Laffer acknowledged that the data for proving the superiority of tax cuts was incomplete and that there were questions concerning the Laffer curve. At what point did less taxation begin to hurt government revenues? Could one calculate the optimum point on the curve measuring government tax revenues and the tax rate? William Felner of the American Enterprise Institute agreed "that, at some point, less punishing tax rates would produce more revenue as well as more private output. But where the U.S. economy sits along such a curve is completely undocumented, unexplored and unknown."

One thing Laffer knew was that status quo thinking was a failure. It was time to try something new. His unorthodox message of tax cuts won him many converts and the enthusiasm of some fans was remarkable. Charles Walker, a former high-ranking official in the Treasury department, stated: "He has had a more rapid impact on the political scene than any economist since Keynes in the 1930s."[87]

An additional supply-side criticism of Keynesianism was that politicians ignored its original purpose of temporarily boosting the economy during times of distress. Rather, they employed it primarily to rationalize their income-redistribution programs. Jude Wanniski, one of the leading promoters of supply-side thinking, argued that "liberals who at one time viewed the Keynesian magic as an antidote to Marxist impulse are attracted more and more to collectivist notions—central planning, detailed regulation of commerce, wage and price controls."[88] Was he talking about Carter?

One setback for Carter was when the House approved a $16 billion tax cut. The White House argued that it gave preferential treatment to high-income taxpayers by reducing the capital gains tax. The tax reduction from 49 percent to 35 percent on assets (e.g., stocks, bonds, and real estate) was, according to Stuart Eizenstat, "the most regressive tax change ever proposed in Congress."[89] But then again, opposition to tax reduction appeared out of touch with those who sold stock in an age of high inflation. If someone paid $100 for stock and sold it for $110 when inflation was at 10 percent, they made no gain. Yet, the IRS said otherwise. People were unhappy that they owed capital gains taxes in cases where they broke even at best or lost money.[90]

The AEI entered the battle, focusing on lowering capital gains taxes to free more capital for investment in dynamic companies. Carrying the torch was Republican Representative William Steiger of Wisconsin, the "baby-faced" and "slightly portly, non-imposing" man who was not short on courage and skill.[91] Steiger sought to reduce the capital gains tax from 50 percent to 25 percent, a plan Democrats claimed would gut government revenues and fail the "fairness" test. Treasury secretary Michael Blumenthal warned Congress that reducing the capital gains tax rate "would sharply erode the progressivity and horizontal equity of the income tax system." He said it was paramount that every American "pay a fair share of the nation's tax burden, according to ability to pay."[92] Michael Kinsley in the *New Republic* argued that a reduction of the capital gains tax rate was a handout for the rich that promised neither a catalyst for investment nor an increase in tax revenues.[93]

In support of Steiger, Ronald Reagan gave a history lesson in two radio broadcasts. In June, he pointed out that in 1968 (the last year before the capital gains tax doubled) the government collected $7.2 billion, but only $4.7 billion the first year the capital gains tax was at 50 percent. In a broadcast the following month, he praised the statesmanship of earlier AFL leaders who understood, during the early 1940s, that a reduced capital gains tax encouraged "the investment of capital needed to create jobs for their members."

Reagan noted that those leaders demonstrated sounder economic wisdom than recent AFL-CIO leaders who wanted a larger capital gains tax and a more progressive income tax system. He told his listeners that Carter's talk of a reduced capital gains tax producing a "windfall for millionaires" ignored the fact that half of Americans who reported capital gains had "adjusted gross incomes below $15,000," far from millionaire status. Moreover, Reagan said, it was a "false idea that business can be made to pay a larger share of the tax burden thus relieving individuals." Excessive taxes were part of the cost of business, passed on to individuals who paid higher prices for consumer products.[94]

Despite Democrats dominating the House, Steiger secured the necessary 19 votes for a majority in the Ways and Means Committee that totaled

37 members. The White House orchestrated a major attack on Steiger's proposal and, on the stump, Carter referred to the "three-martini lunch" of millionaires who paid no income taxes. Given the force of Democratic opposition, it is notable that arguments against him crumbled and his amendment passed in December 1978.[95] Democrats who supported Steiger realized that many Democratic voters translated the rhetoric of "fairness" into "higher taxes for me."[96] The amendment, Jude Wanniski wrote, was "the cutting edge of an important intellectual and financial breakthrough."[97]

V

It was too early to celebrate that Keynesianism was dead, but the reality of stagflation began to change many people's minds. Ronald Reagan had strong words for Carter: When the president told his platform committee that the "'tax structure is a disgrace—it must be made more progressive,' he was only right about one thing—it is a disgrace." Carter's plan to increase the progressivity of income taxes guaranteed "little or no relief for anyone making $20,000 or more." For example, any family of four that earned $20,000 would receive a $270 income tax cut but lose $261 from an increase in the social security contribution, thus a net gain of $9. A family of four at $25,000 would see no tax reduction. Reagan asked, "can we steepen the tax brackets any more than they are without being totally unfair to those who work & earn & make this country go?"[98]

Reagan had much praise for New York Republican Congressman Jack Kemp and Delaware's Senator William Roth. Economist Paul Craig Roberts wrote that Kemp "was the first supply-side politician," a man among the few who brought about a "revolution" that "captured the imagination of the Congress." The traditional thinking held by the Carter administration and various Republicans was that tax cuts could happen only after other policies revitalized the economy, whereas Kemp saw tax cuts as the means to improve the economy. The key to a stronger economy for Kemp was to have a tax rate that gave incentives for people to work and entrepreneurs to invest. By 1978, more Republicans were aware that their previous emphasis on balancing the budget through raising taxes and cutting spending was politically unattractive.[99]

Kemp was a good candidate to lead the charge for the new Republican economic thinking. Before he entered politics, he had a successful professional football career as a quarterback, winning a championship for the

Buffalo Bills. Since his entrance into Congress in 1971, representing New York's 38th Congressional District, he focused on economic policy—a timely decision given the shifting economic uncertainties of the 1970s. In 1977, Senator Roth's interest in tax cuts prompted him to seek Kemp's collaboration on policy. Although not generating much fanfare when introduced in July, the Kemp-Roth Tax Reduction Act set the foundation for official Republican policy.

Key was the reduction of the highest income tax rate of 70 percent to 50 percent and a drop of the lowest tax rate from 14 percent to 8 percent.[100] The following year, the Kemp-Roth bill generated much debate in the press, in large part because of the passage of Proposition 13. After losing a close vote in the House early in 1978, Kemp brought the bill for a vote again in August with no better success. Roth tried in the Senate, but the Kemp-Roth bill lost 36 to 60 in October.[101] Did the failed bill achieve anything?

The *Nation* suggested that "the tax-cut craze" was both "a fad and a mania" only providing "relief for the greedy."[102] Nevertheless, the tax-cutting climate did have an effect on Carter's policies and, in a speech on October 24, 1978, he declared: "Next year, with tough restraints on Federal spending and moderate economic growth in prospect, I plan to reduce the budget deficit to less than one-half what it was when I ran for office—to $30 billion or less."[103] Carter was unsure about giving any numerical pledge in the speech, but at the last moment he sided with Secretary Blumenthal and gave the $30 billion commitment (there was a last-minute change on the teleprompter), much to the anger of Eizenstat.[104] Hoping to get the cooperation of labor for his inflation speech, Carter announced his intention "to ask congress next January to enact a program that workers who observe the standards would be eligible for a tax rebate if the inflation rate is more than 7 percent."[105] The Tax Incentive Plan, favored by Charles Schultze, went nowhere with union leaders, Congress, or business and financial leaders.[106]

As Americans went to the polls for the midterm elections in November, Democrats tried to cope with the "tax-cut craze." Asked by Bill Moyers in November whether the Democratic Party had coopted the Republican philosophy, Carter responded: "No, I don't think so. The Democrats have always been a party of compassion and concern about the people of our country."[107] As opponents to the anti-tax movement, the Democrats fought hard, but there were limitations to what they could do to change people's thinking. Presenting the outcome of the November elections, the *Wall Street Journal* had a message for the pundits who declared Kemp-

Roth a failure: "Republicans enjoyed their greatest political success in many years—winning 57 percent of the Senate races, capturing 6 governorships and gaining 300 seats in state legislatures—all by running on the wrong issue!"[108]

For those in the thick of economic theory and policy, 1978 was a major turning point. *Wall Street Journal* editor Robert L. Bartley wrote: "Almost unconsciously, it seemed, the body politic rejected the gestalt that had dominated tax policy since" the late 1960s when Democratic leaders began their hunt for any rich Americans who did not pay their "fair" share of taxes. Free-market economists, anti-tax activists, and new guard Republicans sought to reset the narrative. The change in thinking on taxes came back to one issue: Keynesians "had no answer to inflation."[109] This was a major problem for the White House as was the challenge of responding effectively to the energy crisis that hit home for ordinary Americans.

Notes

1. "Mr. Proposition 13," *Newsweek*, June 19, 1978, 25.
2. Paul Craig Roberts, *The Supply-Side Revolution: An Insider's Account of Policymaking in Washington* (Cambridge, MA: Harvard University Press, 1984), 26.
3. W. Carl Biven, *Jimmy Carter's Economy: Policy in an Age of Limits* (Chapel Hill: The University of North Carolina Press, 2002), 136.
4. Robert M. Collins, *More: The Politics of Economic Growth in Postwar America* (New York: Oxford University Press, 2000), 148–151.
5. Jody Powell, *The Other Side of the Story* (New York: William Morrow, 1984), 241–242.
6. Ken Auletta, *The Streets Were Paved with Gold* (New York: Vintage Books, 1980), 123–129.
7. On Kennedy and Johnson promising "more," see Herbert Stein, *Presidential Economics: The Making of Economic Policy from Roosevelt to Clinton*, Third Revised Edition (Washington, DC: American Enterprise Institute for Public Policy Research, 1994), 94.
8. Richard A. Viguerie, *The New Right: We're Ready to Lead* (Falls Church, VA: The Viguerie Company, 1981), 166.
9. Ibid., 6, 27, 29, 32, 34–35.
10. Ibid., 95.
11. Nick Kotz, "King Midas of 'The New Right,'" *Atlantic Monthly*, November 1978, 53.
12. Viguerie, *The New Right*, 21.

13. Quoted in Gary M. Fink, "Fragile Alliance: Jimmy Carter and the American Labor Movement," in *The Presidency and Domestic Policies of Jimmy Carter*, eds. Herbert D. Rosenbaum and Alexej Ugrinsky (Westport, CT: Greenwood Press, 1994): 792.
14. Burton I. Kaufmann and Scott Kaufman, *The Presidency of James Earl Carter Jr.,* Second Edition, Revised (Lawrence: University Press of Kansas, 2006), 134.
15. Milton Friedman, "Implementing Humphrey-Hawkings," *Newsweek*, March 5, 1979, 87.
16. Milton Friedman, "In Defense of Dumping," *Newsweek*, February 20, 1978, 73.
17. Biven, *Jimmy Carter's Economy*, 4–5.
18. Donald T. Critchlow, Phyllis Schafly, and Grassroots Conservatism. *A Woman's Crusade* (Princeton, NJ: Princeton University Press, 2005), 254.
19. Tom Bethell, "The Liberal Character," *Harper's*, August 1978, 18.
20. Quoted in Biven, *Jimmy Carter's Economy*, 137.
21. Ibid., 138.
22. Ibid., 186.
23. Bruce J. Schulman, *The Seventies: The Great Shift in American Culture, Society, and Politics* (Boston: Da Capo Press, 2002), 133.
24. Milton Friedman, "Inflation and Jobs," *Newsweek*, November 12, 1979, 97.
25. Biven, *Jimmy Carter's Economy*, 178.
26. Ibid., 185.
27. Milton Friedman, "Inertia and the Fed," *Newsweek*, July 24, 1978, 70.
28. Biven, *Jimmy Carter's Economy*, 89.
29. Alan Greenspan, *The Age of Turbulence: Adventures in a New World* (New York: Penguin Press, 2007), 35.
30. Biven, *Jimmy Carter's Economy*, 92.
31. Quoted in Biven, *Jimmy Carter's Economy*, 92.
32. "Miller: Images of Jimmy," *Newsweek*, January 9, 1978, 51.
33. Biven, *Jimmy Carter's Economy*, 140. Also, see Paul A. Samuelson, "Reappoint Burns?" *Newsweek*, November 21, 1977, 81. The Keynesian Samuelson wrote: "the President should appoint his own man as chairman."
34. Milton Friedman, "Burns on the Outside," *Newsweek*, January 9, 1978, 52–53.
35. Ibid.
36. Milton Friedman, "Why Inflation Persists," *Newsweek*, October 3, 1977, 84.
37. Quoted in Friedman, "Why Inflation Persists," 84.
38. Ibid.
39. Friedman, "Burns on the Outside," 52–53.

40. Biven, *Jimmy Carter's Economy*, 126.
41. Milton Friedman, "Options for 1980," *Newsweek*, September 18, 1978, 76. Friedman listed two extremes for 1980: 8–12 percent inflation and a recession or 10–15 percent inflation and a severe recession (rising unemployment).
42. Milton Friedman, "Parkinson Revisted," *Newsweek*, July 12, 1976, 58.
43. Friedman, "After the Elections," *Newsweek*, November 15, 1976, 100.
44. Milton Friedman and Paul A. Samuelson, "Answering the Big Questions," *Newsweek*, May 29, 1978, 80.
45. Milton Friedman, "The Message from California," *Newsweek*, June 19, 1978, 26.
46. "Mr. Proposition 13," 25. "The Big Tax Revolt," *Newsweek*, June 19, 1978, 20.
47. "Mr. Proposition 13," 25.
48. Chuck McFadden, *Trailblazer: A Biography of Jerry Brown* (Berkeley: University of California Press, 2013), 85.
49. Michael Castleman, "The Jarvis-Gann Tea Party," *Nation*, June 3, 1978, 656.
50. "California: The Property Tax War," *Atlantic Monthly*, May 1978, 20. "The Big Tax Revolt," *Newsweek*, June 19, 1978, 27.
51. Quoted in Friedman, "A Progress Report," *Newsweek*, April 10, 1978, 80.
52. Rick Perlstein, *The Invisible Bridge, The Fall of Nixon and the Rise of Reagan* (New York: Simon & Schuster, 2015), 685.
53. McFadden, *Trailblazer*, 10. J. D. Lorenz, *Jerry Brown: The Man on the White Horse* (Boston: Houghton Mifflin, 1978), 243–44.
54. "California Earthquake," *Nation*, June 17, 1978, 714.
55. "The Big Tax Revolt," 20.
56. Michael Castleman, "The Jarvis-Gann Tea Party," *Nation*, June 3, 1978, 655.
57. "The Big Tax Revolt," 28.
58. Castleman, "The Jarvis-Gann Tea Party," 655–656.
59. Ibid., 657.
60. Friedman, "The Message from California," 26.
61. Castleman, "The Jarvis-Gann Tea Party," 656.
62. "The Big Tax Revolt," 27–28.
63. Ibid., 27. Friedman, "The Message from California," 26.
64. "Mr. Proposition 13," 25. "The Big Tax Revolt," 20.
65. "Mutiny in California," *New Republic*, June 3, 1978, 6.
66. "The Big Tax Revolt," 23. McFadden, *Trailblazer*, 87.
67. David S. Broder, "The Canniness of the Long-Distance Runner," *Atlantic Monthly*, January 1978, 39.
68. Quoted in Schulman, *The Seventies*, 209.
69. "Taxquake Tremors," *Newsweek*, June 26, 1978, 22.

70. Ibid., 23.
71. McFadden, *Trailblazer*, 87.
72. Craig Shirley, *Reagan Rising: The Decisive Years, 1976–1980* (New York: Broadside Books, 2017), 38, 122.
73. Robert Lekachman, "Distribution Wars," *New Republic*, July 29, 15.
74. W. Elliot Brownlee, *Federal Taxation in America: A Short History* (Cambridge: University of Cambridge Press, 1996), 139.
75. Friedman, "The Message from California," 26.
76. "Union Blues," *Newsweek*, June 26, 1978, 25.
77. "California Earthquake," 714–715.
78. Peter Connolly, "The Voice of Raw Greed," *Nation*, July 22–29, 1978, 77–78.
79. "The Big Tax Revolt," 28.
80. Ibid., 20. Viguerie, *The New Right*, 138.
81. "The Big Tax Revolt," 21, 30.
82. "The Tax Revolt's Guru," *Newsweek*, June 26, 1978, 24.
83. Ibid., 24–25.
84. TRB, "Nitroglycerine," *New Republic*, September 23, 1978, 3.
85. Adam Smith, *Wealth of Nations*, Books IV–V, ed. Andrew Skinner (London: Penguin Books, 1999), 479.
86. Auletta, *The Streets Were Paved with Gold*, 162, 203, 215. On Americans taking extra jobs on the side, see "The Middle Class Poor," *Newsweek*, September 12, 1977, 30.
87. "The Tax Revolt's Guru," 25.
88. Jude Wanniski, *The Way the World Works*, Fourth Edition (Washington, DC: Regnery Publishing, Inc., 1998), 171.
89. Kaufman, *The Presidency of James Earl Carter Jr.*, 122.
90. Robert L. Bartley, *The Seven Fat Years: And How to Do It Again* (New York: The Free Press, 1992), 65.
91. "About-Face on Capital Games," *Time*, June 12, 1978, 42. Michael Novak, *Writing from Left to Right: My Journey from Liberal to Conservative* (New York: Image, 2013), 179.
92. Quoted in Bartley, *The Seven Fat Years*, 69.
93. Michael Kinsley, "Alms for the Rich," *New Republic*, August 19, 1978, 26.
94. Kiron Skinner et al., eds. *Reagan in His Own Hand: The Writings of Ronald Reagan that Reveal His Revolutionary Vision for America* (New York: Touchstone, 2002), 260, 277–278.
95. Novak, *Writing from Left to Right*, 180–181.
96. Ibid., 180.
97. Quoted in Bartley, *The Seven Fat Years*, 64.
98. Skinner et al., *Reagan in His Own Hand*, 277–278.
99. Roberts, *The Supply-Side Revolution*, 1, 4–5, 20.

100. Bruce R. Bartlett, *Reaganomics: Supply Side Economics in Action* (Westport, CT: Arlington House Publishers, 1981), 130.
101. Ibid., 133.
102. "Relief for the Greedy," *Nation*, October 7, 1978, 329.
103. Quoted in Biven, *Jimmy Carter's Economy*, 186–187.
104. Biven, *Jimmy Carter's Economy*, 187–188.
105. Quoted in Biven, *Jimmy Carter's Economy*, 189.
106. Kaufman, *The Presidency of James Earl Carter Jr.*, 137.
107. Don Richardson, ed., *Conversations with Carter* (Boulder, CO: Lynne Rienner Publishers, 1998), 166.
108. Quoted in Bartlett, *Reaganomics*, 133.
109. Bartley, *The Seven Fat Years*, 61–62, 75.

CHAPTER 8

The Energy Crisis

It was Independence Day of 1979. The celebration in Washington, DC, was a bust—rain canceled the nation's biggest fireworks show. The mood was no sunnier the day after when key members of Carter's staff prepared to board a helicopter to join the president at Camp David to discuss the shortage of gas for car owners and other energy problems. There were few gas stations open for business in DC; those not closed had long lineups and wait times of up to three hours. On the ground, Hamilton Jordan boiled in anger and frustration, Jody Powell chain smoked his cigarettes, Jerry Rafshoon paced and pulled on his curly hair, and Stuart Eizenstat blurted out criticisms. In the helicopter, they appeared nervous and even "a little punch-drunk."[1]

The White House was struggling to fine-tune the economy, and *New Republic* writer Robert Lekachman predicted that slow economic growth would likely last for the rest of the century.[2] Farmers protested in early 1979 by crowding Washington streets with tractors, complaining that the family farm was under assault. The government had no better success with its urban-renewal programs, including the public housing projects that became "a hotbed of crime and a breeding ground of poverty." Milton Friedman wrote that costly social programs with noble intentions "repeatedly failed to achieve their intended objectives."[3]

Critics worried about environmental and no-growth movements "in making it ever more difficult to build new houses, apartments, factories or what have you."[4] Inflation worsened. Alfred Kahn, the president's chief

E. R. Crouse, *America's Failing Economy and the Rise of Ronald Reagan*,
https://doi.org/10.1007/978-3-319-70545-3_8

inflation fighter, told Carter in February "that neither your economic nor your political advisors are ever going to present you with *the* solution to the problem of inflation, ready-made."[5] Kahn also had his hands full with the issue of deregulating oil. Union leaders fought deregulation, warning that they would "kiss" wage and price standards "goodbye" if their workers had to pay a dollar for gasoline.[6]

The high price of gasoline became a problem during the 1970s, causing substantial "panic at the pump."[7] In his critique of government intervention in early 1976, Friedman pointed out that apart from World War II, America had never experienced an energy crisis. It did not occur "until [the] government interfered on a large scale." In 1954, setting the ceiling price on natural gas was the first federal government action and resulted in lower production. In 1971, Richard Nixon's ill-advised price and wage control policy was another economic blunder. A smaller group who favored the gold standard also criticized his decision to drop it. Gerald Ford's rhetoric suggested a change in energy policy, but his "opposition" to oil price controls did not stop him from "expanding" them. Friedman said that "further extension of government intervention into a crucial industry" promised higher prices for consumers in the future.[8]

The nervousness of the Carter staff was understandable. What took place in the first half of July was the unprecedented cancellation of a planned July 5 television speech to the nation, followed by days of soul-searching with Carter reflecting on the advice of a string of people invited to Camp David to share their thoughts. Then came the extraordinary speech to the nation on July 15 that became known as the "malaise" address. This affair and the larger issue of the energy crisis during the Carter administration gave non-Keynesians an opening to exploit their ideas on what was needed for America to get back on track.

I

Energy policy had been a major headache for Gerald Ford. He often resisted the strategy of progressive Republicans, but one major exception was his acceptance of the Energy Policy and Conservation Act (EPCA) of 1975 that would continue the controls on domestic crude oil prices until mid-1979.[9] William Simon, who served as Nixon's energy czar, and Treasury secretary for both Nixon and Ford, judged it to be "the worst error of the Ford administration." Simon pointed out three major problems with the EPCA: there was no serious attempt to eliminate the barriers on energy production, its focus on conservation was a short-range strategy, and the act ushered in controls on "all energy-using industries—*which is to say, for virtually all industry in the United States.*" The outcome would be a more "centralized, controlled economy."[10]

During the Ford years, a *Wall Street Journal* reporter asked Simon whether it was a good idea to extend the life of the Federal Energy Administration (FEA). The thought horrified Simon: "Extend its life! That place is a menace. It's strangling the energy industry at the very time when we need production. It should be wiped out of existence." When he heard that Ford chose to support "this bureaucratic abortion," he stomped over to the White House "with blood in [his] … eye." Economic counselors Alan Greenspan, Paul MacAvoy, and Paul O'Neill likewise opposed extending the life of the FEA. But it was to no avail.

Frank Zarb, the FEA director explained: "At least we're keeping all the garbage in one place, so *we* can control it rather than distribute it all over government." This was not reassuring for those looking ahead to when the Democrats would retake the White House. Simon responded: "You've forgotten one thing. One day *you're* not going to be here, and *I'm* not going to be here; but *that horrible thing* is still going to be here."[11]

Another problem for Simon was environmental activism that opposed nuclear energy production. With any energy production there were risks, but some environmentalists appeared incapable of differentiating between the small risk that might affect a minuscule number of people and the certain calamity to society when government regulation paralyzed energy production. Simon's solution to prevent energy chaos was straightforward: "deregulate the tortured productive system; drop price controls, destructive bans, and crippling subsidies; and let exploration and production rip with the profit motive as guide, allowing prices to find their true market value."[12]

In 1975, a persisting economic fallacy was "that decontrolling the price of 'old' oil—produced from domestic wells—would mean a higher price of gasoline and fuel oil to final consumers." As Milton Friedman explained to his *Newsweek* readers, the government pegged the price of "old" at \$5.25 a barrel, about half the price of imported oil. Those who favored this price ceiling only considered the visible effect of the policy without any consideration of the invisible effect.

Yes, elimination of the price ceiling would cause the price to rise, but the higher cost for gas that consumers paid would be short term. It was basic economics. Taking advantage of the promise of more profits, oil producers would act and produce a greater supply of oil. Friedman wanted to know "[h]ow can more oil be produced yet the final price of petroleum products be higher?" Although often shouting in the Keynesian wind that encouraged government regulation, he continued to drive home his major point: "Bad economics makes bad policy."[13]

Others concurred. In a 1976 paper presented at Hillsdale College, economist Alan Reynolds pointed the finger at government regulations for the "made in the USA" energy problems. The policies of the Federal Power Commission and the Environmental Protection Agency (1970) pushed "utilities and industries out of coal and into fuel and natural gas," and the Coal Mine Health and Safety Act (1969) meant fewer coal mines in operation. Even though these regulations increased the demand for oil, they did not cause an actual shortage of oil and gas; there was enough oil and gas in the United States to last for generations.

A shortage is when "consumers want to buy more at some specific price than producers want to sell at that price. If the price were higher, initially, consumers would demand less and producers would supply more, and the shortage would disappear." By increasing demand and restricting supply, government regulations guaranteed that demand outran supply. When domestic oil fell short of the needs of the American people, the government had no choice but to turn to foreign oil producers, then in an "enviable bargaining position."[14]

Faced with the issue of greater dependency on foreign oil, Washington politicians responded with price controls on domestic oil and gas. This policy resulted in a five percent decline in 1974 and a seven percent decline in 1975 of "marketed production of natural gas."[15] Explaining the diminished supply of gas, Reynolds wrote: "We have been eating everything in the cupboard, and not making enough trips to the grocery store." Confusing the issue was the "propaganda" pamphlet distributed by the House Subcommittee on Oversight and Investigations entitled "Questions and Answers About the Nature and Causes of the Natural Gas Shortage." It declared that falling supplies and higher demand for natural gas "had nothing to do with price." At fault were natural gas producers who withheld production, waiting for a better day of higher prices.[16]

Fighting to keep price and control policies in place, the House passed one bill that exempted small producers from price controls, giving those who produced about one-third of the gas supply the incentive to stay small. Not benefiting from this government favoritism, "big firms would become small through bankruptcy." In its "egalitarian approach to shortages," the House bill also extended price controls on "intrastate gas development" that had experienced a recent boom. As Reynolds lamented, the politicians figured there was no point in allowing healthy gas production when "the whole country easily could be made miserable." Absent was any acknowledgment that decontrolling the gas industry would result in "larger supplies of natural gas to replace more expensive substitute fuels."[17]

Price controls on heating oil in 1971 resulted in a serious oil shortage in winter 1972, and Reynolds questioned the policies of the Federal Energy Office (FEO), a regulatory agency created in 1973. Embarrassing decisions by the FEO prompted a name change to the Federal Energy Administration in 1974; however, misguided thinking continued, including the requirement of all new homes to be electrically heated. This, according to Reynolds, would double the heating cost and "put an additional strain on our already inadequate electric generating capacity."

Not to be outdone, the EPCA (also known as the "Cold Homes and Dark Factories Act") had its share of "curious ideas, like forcing Detroit to build tiny cars while simultaneously trying to keep gasoline cheap so those cars won't sell."[18] Equally worrisome was Nelson Rockefeller's proposed Hundred Billion Dollar Plan, a plan "to get taxpayers to underwrite ventures which are too risky to attract sensible investors." Reynolds explained why they were too risky: "[T]hey are based on the curious idea of using our most expensive energy resources first, and saving the oil and gas until later, when it will probably be obsolete."[19]

The oil and gas industry is unique compared to many other industries more suited to self-regulation in which market prices dictate production toward market equilibrium. What sets it apart from many other industries is the high cost of exploration and development and the low incremental cost once the oil flows. With production facilities in place it was possible to have "runaway supply" in the short run that could lead to widely fluctuating prices. This fact opened the door for government regulation to stabilize the flow of oil to market. America's heavy reliance on imported oil from the Middle East complicated the situation for both Washington policymakers and consumers.

Despite the difference between the energy industry and other industries where self-regulation is more straightforward, there were solid arguments for a free-market approach that assumed the existence of large supplies of world oil, much of it yet undiscovered.[20] Supply-sider Jude

Wanniski wrote that "the planet is not energy 'scarce' now, nor will it be at the end of the century—or at the end of the next thousand centuries."[21] Nonetheless, the optics were bad for oil companies, viewed as greed-driven with no concern for Americans' day-to-day struggle to make ends meet. Environmentalists also pointed to disturbing pollution. Ford signing the EPCA clarified that the oil companies would not get much help from the White House.

II

On the campaign trail in 1976, Carter delivered proposals on energy, promising the creation of a Department of Energy and a commitment to deregulate the price of natural gas. Although the deregulation promise gave him much-needed votes in Texas and Oklahoma, he abandoned this commitment once in office and continued controls much to the satisfaction of his economic advisors. Stuart Eizenstat later suggested that this was Carter's "most fateful domestic decision."[22] Another promise was to deliver a national energy policy within 90 days of taking office.

One omen on Inauguration Day was the malfunction of a solar-heated reviewing stand setup to keep people warm.[23] The winter of 1976 to 1977 was extremely cold and stories of hardship were heartbreaking. Pinkey Carson, 66, died of exposure in an unheated room in a New York City hotel. Chicago experienced its "coldest day of the century," and southern Florida was hit with snow. One Good Samaritan paid a steep price for assisting people stranded in a stalled automobile on the side of the highway. When Lewis Cline stopped his pickup, a man stuck a pistol in his ribs and he and two others stole his truck.[24] On storm-hit Interstate 65 in Indiana, a fleet of 23 snowmobiles rescued 400 stranded motorists.

As the cold continued, natural gas shortages caused the closure of schools and factories from coast to coast. In its early February coverage of the gas crisis, *Newsweek* reported that Pennsylvania shut down "every school" and that 400,000 workers lost their jobs in Ohio.[25] Some took the cold in stride with humor. An Alabama waitress said it was so cold that she "saw two beagles with a jumper cable trying to start a rabbit."[26] The effects of the severe winter were uneven between states with free-market prices and those states burdened by federal price controls; the former had concentrations of natural gas and the latter ran short. Although the lesson seemed obvious to William Simon, "many in the liberal world learned nothing at all." The Carter administration chose centralized planning as the best strategy to solve the energy crisis.[27]

Carter took symbolic action at the White House by barring limousine service for staff and by setting the thermostats at 65 degrees. His first televised "fireside chat" took place on February 2, 1977, when he told the American people of his commitment to conservation and the creation of a new energy department so as "to bring order out of chaos." He wanted the oil and natural gas industries to be honest about their reserves and profits and to clarify "the difference between real shortages and artificial ones."

Any solution to the energy problem depended on the sacrifice of both citizens and private companies.[28] In his memoirs, Carter wrote of his concern over the oil industry's "unearned profits from higher prices" and the problem of allowing the free market to decide the price and distribution of energy products. Free-market theories to solve the energy crisis had little influence on him; he said they were useless ideas promoted by the special-interest lobbies of the energy industry.[29]

Sitting in the White House library, Carter delivered his speech wearing a cardigan sweater. Some remarked of the odd sight of the fireplace in the background with only *one* log burning.[30] Tip O'Neill found Carter's words "terrific," but the president was a poor communicator and the American people were unwilling to lower their thermostats.[31] A Harris poll in mid-April indicated less than 10 percent of Americans had lowered the thermostats of their homes to 65 degrees.[32] Carter's energy czar also had concerns.

Carter's pick for planning and leading an energy program was James Schlesinger, a Ph.D. economist who went from the RAND Corporation to various jobs in the Nixon and Ford administrations, including Secretary of Defense. Schlesinger was a man passionate about his hobby of bird-watching and his work in government. During the Ford years, Washington politicians noted his arrogant attitude and the president himself reprimanded Schlesinger for some of his questionable actions.[33] He made few friends with his "haughty and gruff" manner, aggravated people when he smoked a pipe during cabinet meetings, contradicted Carter in public, and failed to work well with Congress.[34] The *New Republic* portrayed him as a tough guy, a man who took his family to Amchitka, Alaska, when head of the Atomic Energy Commission, to prove to environmentalists that a nearby nuclear test explosion would be harmless.[35]

Predicting that Americans might exhaust all the world's proven oil reserves "by the end of the next decade," Carter viewed energy as the most pressing issue in the early stages of his government.[36] The main objectives of a "comprehensive" program were energy conservation, greater domestic fuel production, and "the long-range development of alternate forms of energy which could begin to replace oil and natural gas in future years." In his mind, there was a struggle between the American people and the oil industry.[37] Carter expected Schlesinger to create an energy program within the 90-day target he established.

This did not come easily because Schlesinger also was responsible for the preliminary work of setting up the Department of Energy (DOE), a task that required working in secrecy to prevent leaks that might build opposition. One drawback of this secrecy was the lack of interagency review typical for legislative proposals. When Schlesinger asked for more time, Carter told him: "I made the pledge and I intend to keep it." Keeping to his 90-day promise, Carter introduced his energy program on television on April 18.

The plan included a "crude oil equalization tax" and development of solar power, which corresponded with Schlesinger's warning that America "had to stop depending on crude oil for economic growth."[38] Carter declared to the American people that the energy crisis was America's greatest challenge—"the moral equivalent of war."[39] It was unfortunate for the Carter administration that opponents used the acronym "Meow" when referring to the energy program.[40]

Tip O'Neill groaned when he discovered that the energy plan filled four phonebook-size volumes.[41] There were more than 100 separate provisions, but only a few garnered the attention of most Americans. One item not lost in policy jargon was the imposition of a "gasguzzler" tax on automobiles. For Carter, it was crucial for government to act, given the recent cold winter and suffering in the northeastern states from severe shortages of gas. In his memoirs, he wrote: "[T]here was never a moment when I did not consider the creation of a national energy policy equal in importance to any other goal we had."

The shutting down of many factories and schools was "another stark reminder of the need for quick and vigorous action."[42] Opposed to the free-market approach of the past, Carter wanted an energy policy that made sense to his way of thinking. Others thought differently. Energy challenges throughout his administration marked how divisive the energy issue had become among Americans.

Those supportive of Carter were unable to see any major problem with government controls and regulations. James Nathan Miller, roving editor of *Reader's Digest*, argued that the data validating gas deregulation was "at best doubtful and at worse false."[43] Democrats thought government intervention made good politics, and much of the media were supportive of government action. When the nation experienced extreme cold weather, media reports linked oil shortages to the cold weather rather than to policy. But then again, was the extreme cold the culprit behind the shortage?

In late February 1977, Milton Friedman explained that the extreme winter was not the reason for the energy crisis; the problem was Washington with its federal control of the prices of natural gas and oil that clearly discouraged production. In Friedman's home state of Illinois, Senator Adlai Stevenson's support for low price ceilings on natural gas may have looked good to those who talked about "greedy gas producers," but it ultimately guaranteed shortages. A more constructive and long-term approach to ensure efficient fuel use and the development of future supplies would be to "abolish the Federal Energy Administration and eliminate the authority of the Federal Power Commission to fix the price of natural gas—or any other product."[44]

After several extensions, the FEA saw its staff grow "from zero to 4000 in less than four years." In Friedman's eyes, the establishment of a DOE, starting with 20,000 employees and far-reaching power, was further harmful policymaking. Again, Democrats were confident that government experts with a Keynesian mindset had the answer for solving the energy crisis, whereas Friedman saw the Department of Energy as a bad idea that decreased economic freedom. Given the vital importance of energy, this department would have a major impact on "the life-blood of our economic system." Its tentacles reached into the lives of consumers and the business of industries. Moreover, "it enthrones a bureaucracy that would have a self-interest in expanding in size and power and would have the means to do so—both directly, through exercising price control and other powers, and indirectly, through propagandizing the public and the Congress for still broader powers."[45]

There was considerable pressure on factories and utilities to shift to coal or else face heavy taxation. Friedman explained that taxing an industry was a misnomer. An industry cannot pay a tax; only people pay a tax: "The burden of the tax is borne either by the stockholders, or the employees, or the customers—and, in the long run, for a tax on a specific product, primarily by the customers." In addition, a tax often caused a stifling of investment and employment, as was the case with the taxing of big cars. If the market was free and all Americans paid the full cost of energy, each person would decide how best to meet the cost; one person might drive a large car less miles, another might buy a smaller car, and someone else might conserve on other consumer items.[46]

Conservative journalist George F. Will wrote in *Newsweek* of James Schlesinger's reaction to the American public not buying small energy-efficient cars despite rebates from the automobile companies. Because large cars sold "like hotcakes," Schlesinger tooled "around Washington looking like a funeral director who has heard about a death, sober but not really sad."[47] There were legitimate concerns about gas guzzlers, but it was important to consider tradeoffs, notably the economic viability of automobile industries depending on the sales of bigger, more expensive cars. An ailing automobile industry was a serious issue given the thousands of jobs at stake.

There were ample technical flaws with the energy program, predictable to those calling for a credible review process. Neither Treasury secretary Michael Blumenthal nor CEA chairman Charles Schultze had an opportunity to study the program.[48] Carter's energy package sent to the House was enormous—five volumes of legislation—picked apart by various committees, each having its own agenda. Pulling off an impressive feat, Tip O'Neill streamlined the process by creating an ad hoc Committee on Energy, filled with members supportive of Carter's energy plan, and on August 5, the House passed the energy package 244 to 177. The following year, the Senate gutted the bill and added to the problems Carter continued to face with his energy policy.[49]

Milton Friedman was relentless in his criticism of Carter's energy policy. In a May 1977 *Newsweek* article, he called it a "monstrosity," noting that the United States had experienced no energy crisis for nearly two centuries. What was the secret for America "without the heavy hand of Big Brother making sure that energy was produced by the right people, in the right way, and distributed to the chosen recipients?" The "secret" was straightforward. The physical availability of energy did not change significantly, and free markets organized and allocated energy in a responsible manner that met the needs of consumers and industry; because Americans "paid *directly* the full cost of energy" wasteful consumption that would cause shortages was not an issue. What changed was the greater intervention of government—first the Federal Power Commission, then the FEA, followed by a mushrooming of other agencies.

Explaining there was no "free lunch," Friedman asked: "How do we get better results by paying for energy through taxes rather than prices and letting bureaucrats spend our money for us?" It disturbed him that "a highly trained and intelligent economist" like James Schlesinger favored a political solution rather than an economic one. The correct answer was to eliminate government controls and to allow the free market to work, but this action, of course, "would render unnecessary the agency that he is destined to head!"[50] Months later, Friedman's comparison of the before and after Schlesinger was blunt. When Schlesinger was at the RAND Corporation he was "an able professional economist," but in the White House he was head of a "taxation program in disguise."[51]

In early 1978, Friedman took aim at the philosophy behind Carter's energy policies. One statement in a White House document was particularly worrisome: "The producers have no equitable claim to the enhanced value because it is unrelated to their activities or economic contributions." For example, when proposed deregulation resulted in U.S. oil companies experiencing a rise in value, it was undeserving. Citing the Declaration of Independence and the Fifth Amendment to the Constitution, Friedman made the point that Carter's energy plan was "subversive." The administration appeared to say "that private property is not a right but a privilege that is conferred by an all-powerful state for the purpose of providing incentive."[52]

III

The White House also faced pressure from labor activists. In the winter of 1977 to 1978, the United Mine Workers of America (UMWA) carried out an action that became the longest coal-mining strike in American history. In the early stage of Carter's administration, there was a push to double each year's domestic coal production. In addition to energy conservation, its increased production would minimize America's dependency on OPEC oil. There was a clear understanding that the key success was a good relationship with the UMWA, which mined more than half of America's coal supply. One problem was the combative history of the coal union. The UMWA negotiated contracts with coal employers—the Bituminous Coal Operators Association—every three years, using aggressive tactics including sabotage.[53]

Even after the UMWA agreed to a contract in 1974, wildcat strikes (i.e., strikes not sanctioned by union leaders) by the regular members continued. Thus, there were tense relations between miners and employers and strained relations between some miners and the UMWA. Wildcat strikes in the spring of 1977 closed more than 50 coal mines. In December 1977, the UMWA initiated strike action that resulted in 160,000 miners walking off the job.[54] Careful not to jeopardize its relationship with organized labor, the White House avoided any direct intervention in the strikes.

Carter's call for industry to minimize wage and price increases was a tough sell to coal miners whose focus was on their incomes rather than the nation's macroeconomic problems. The union demand for a 44 percent wage increase over three years was not good news for the Carter administration. Another union demand was equally gloomy. Prepared to fight long and hard, the miners intensely opposed the provision in the new contract that permitted coal employers to fire miners who participated in wildcat strikes. For labor negotiations, the threat of a wildcat strike was too valuable for miners to lose. Aggressive acts of violence by miners demonstrated their defiance. For example, in Pennsylvania armed miners gathered in more than 100 vehicles and traveled to various mining sites still in operation, ordering them to shut down immediately. To make their point clear, the roving miners destroyed property at mining operations.[55]

A couple of months into the coal strike, Carter worried about the larger impact of the mining shutdown as General Motors and Chrysler operations warned of layoffs because of electricity shortages. In Ohio, Indiana, Tennessee, and Pennsylvania, coal-powered electrical utilities were near the point of panic because their coal reserves were dangerously low. Carter wanted industries to convert to coal power and be less dependent on OPEC, but labor conflict in the coal-mining industry made that argument more difficult to advance.

With the UMWA remaining defiant, the political options for Carter were unpleasant. In desperation, the government could invoke the anti-union Taft-Hartley Act, forcing the miners back to work. The last president to do this with the UMWA was Harry Truman in 1950.[56] Union leaders warned that such a move would result in "chaos and bloodshed." David Forms, a West Virginian miner, told *Time* magazine: "You've got $250,000 pieces of equipment in each of these mines, and it wouldn't take much to tear them up. I'm not making any threat. That's just the way it is."[57]

Carter lost patience and invoked Taft-Hartley on March 6, 1978, but of the 160,000 miners less than 100 returned to work. One *Christian*

Science Monitor report explored why miners remained steadfast in their opposition. West Virginian miner Robert White wanted to return to work, but there were other miners determined to keep the mines quiet: "I got a call saying if I went back to work, my home would be blown up and everything in it." The logjam finally broke on March 24 when the miners accepted a new offer giving them a 39 percent wage increase over three years and promising no crackdowns on wildcat strikes.[58] The episode left Carter with a poorer standing with Americans; two-thirds of respondents of an NBC-Associated Press Poll gave him a failing grade for his handling of the conflict.[59]

On the issue of energy, however, Carter had one advantage. Oil companies received much worse press, despite the arguments of companies, such as Mobil Oil, that reminded critics that material wealth was "indispensable if a society is to support such essentials as healthcare, education, and other social services." Selling the virtues of democratic capitalism, Mobil's marketing campaign linked profits and productivity.[60] Mobil officials understood the American public's suspicion of oil companies always making handsome profits in good and bad economic times. The company poured millions of dollars into public relations. For Robert Sherrill of the *Nation*, Mobil was responsible for "one of the longest-running propaganda acts in town."

Whether it was in the pages of *The New York Times* or on television screens in the middle of popular soap operas, advertisements promoting oil cast the company in a good light. Top Mobil official Herman J. Shmidt explained: "A reader sees a Mobil message, and associates it with Big Oil. So, he may be wary." Still, readers became "more receptive" when their favorite television soap opera included Mobil advertisements. The print versions, first on *Times* op-ed page in 1970, sought to capture opinion shapers, and television advertisements targeted middle-class Americans. By 1976, Mobil placed advertisements in more than 100 newspapers, but the role of the prestigious *New York Times* was the reason for much of the irritation of critics such as Michael Gerrad who wrote: "With sheer cash, Mobil has become a *Times* columnist."[61]

Regardless of people's frustration with Mobil propaganda, it was an uphill battle for oil companies in an age when Americans spoke of the "obscene profits" of the industry. In the halls of Congress four years earlier, senior executives stumbled, at televised hearings, before the withering fire of politicians demanding an explanation of huge oil profits at a time when Americans struggled to find an open gas station.[62] The closed stations during the Carter years drove people to commit crazy acts, including violence as angry motorists confronted each other with fists, broken beer bottles, knives, and even guns.[63] It mattered little in defense of the oil companies that the $15 billion in profits in 1978 barely kept up with inflation and fell below the average rate of profit for all American industries.[64]

Fred J. Cook of the *Nation* hit back, referring to oil fraud and oil companies "desperately trying to cover up the rip-off of the American consumer."[65] Pointing to the "giganticism" of Mobil, *New Republic* editor Richard Trout argued that the company portrayed democratic capitalism as a market of small competitors, a Mobil interpretation that "few people" believed.[66] The critique by Henry Fairlie was broader and harsher: Capitalism "is greed and meanness and insecurity. It is abominable. It has to be removed, in the next quarter century."[67]

When it came to public relations, Carter had more political capital than oil companies and a good team of media experts to guide him. Determined to help Carter with speechwriting and a better image, Gerald Rafshoon joined the president's team in July 1978. Born in Brooklyn, New York, Rafshoon and his Jewish family moved to Texas. His majors at the University of Texas were journalism and advertising. One day in 1966 he heard one of Carter's radio announcements for his run for governor, prompting him to join Carter to help with advertisements. With curly locks, an impish smile, loads of energy, and a talent for spin, Rafshoon was a welcome member of the "Georgia mafia." Under his eye, the media saw a different Carter in the summer of 1978: darker suits, a tougher look, and a more forceful way of speaking, imaging that gained the term "Rafshoonery."[68]

Hendrik Hertzberg also helped with speechwriting, considered by some to be Carter's best-ever speechwriter. Hertzberg's father was Jewish and his mother was a Quaker; he came to the Carter camp as a democratic socialist who left his journalist career at the *New Yorker*. Assisting Hertzberg was his friend Gordon Stewart whose master's in drama from Yale University was a bonus for getting Carter to deliver his speeches more effectively.[69]

IV

In January 1979, Keynesian Paul Samuelson gave *Newsweek* readers a somewhat positive prediction: the coming year would likely see a brief and "mild" recession.[70] Others shared Samuelson's faith in government intervention. James Schlesinger favored government action and hoped the oil shock of early 1979 would undermine political opposition to a windfall profits tax.[71] On March 19, Carter wrote in his diary: "We spent all day discussing economics and energy. Inflation was higher than we had anticipated, but the economy was stronger and budget response has been outstanding."[72]

Nevertheless, it became clear that 1979 was not going to be any easier for Carter. His January budget message to Congress meant an eight percent increase in total spending, but this was not enough for Senator Ted Kennedy who later challenged Carter for the next election's nomination. Stuart Eizenstat told the president of problems that the economic advisors faced: "The process of developing the basic crude oil pricing options and the macroeconomic analysis of these approaches has proved more difficult than originally expected."[73] Eliot Cutler, his chief White House energy advisor, warned Carter in mid-March of the growing opposition: There were opponents of inflation, critics of regulations, those against oil profiteering, and others who simply "want to make life politically miserable for us."[74] The nuclear accident at Three Mile Island, Pennsylvania, in April further complicated energy matters, after which opposition to nuclear power grew.

In addition, there was the persistent problem of inflation that the Carter government blamed in part on OPEC's increased oil prices. Secretary of Commerce Juanita Kreps, for example, maintained the argument that OPEC action prevented the government from defeating inflation.[75] The Keynesians appeared oblivious to the impact of Nixon ending gold convertibility in 1971 and international monetary economics. Supply-siders Robert Mundell and Jude Wanniski were among the few who pointed to the breakdown of the international monetary system as the cause of the energy crisis and inflation.[76]

On energy policy, Carter heard four options from his cabinet: full decontrol on June 1, 1979, a phaseout of controls by September 30, 1981, elimination of controls by 1984, or extension of controls by Congress to 1985.[77] Secretary of the Treasury Blumenthal wanted immediate decontrol. As he explained to the president, this was an opportunity for him "to take complete charge of a major problem, which has been locked in political stalemate for 8 years, and to resolve it in the national interest with a single bold stroke." A phased-out option "would invite complaints from all sides and could lead to frequent confusing revisions by the bureaucracy or the Congress."[78]

Blumenthal further argued that immediate decontrol would encourage energy conservation, increase oil production, and eventually reduce the trade deficit and strengthen the dollar. His arguments went nowhere. Carter rejected immediate decontrol and agreed to a phased deregulate starting on June 1 and continuing until October 1, 1981.[79] This decision flouted his commitment at an international summit in Bonn, West Germany, to decontrol oil. Richard Cooper, undersecretary of state for economic affairs, worried that the government's failure to honor the Bonn pledge risked American credibility and offered West Germany and others "an excuse to back away from some of their own already-implemented commitments."[80] Domestic politics trumped foreign matters.

The American people heard Carter's energy plan when he addressed the nation on television on April 5, 1979. Only 30 million watched, a large drop compared to the 80 million for his April 1977 energy speech. He announced the phased decontrol of oil and his support for a 50 percent windfall profits tax "on producer revenues attributable to decontrol or to future price increases by OPEC." Carter got his wish and Congress passed a profits tax bill that he signed later the following year.[81] Carter had no sympathy for oil companies, expecting they would "fight to keep the profits they have not earned."[82] His attitude toward price controls of oil was frustrating for supporters of a free market. When asked how he would respond if Congress extended price controls beyond the 1981 deadline, he declared: "[I]f the House and Senate pass this legislation and send it to me, I will certainly not veto it. We will live with it."[83]

On the other hand, there were notable obstacles for Carter who wrote in his diary on April 30 that Congress was irresponsible for resisting the administration's plan "to handle gasoline rationing and impose conservation measures if necessary in an emergency."[84] The following month, a federal district court ruled that the president exceeded his authority with price controls and the threat of withholding federal contracts to those companies failing to follow price control guidelines.[85]

The month of May saw a return to disturbing acts of violence as the West Coast experienced gas shortages. When Carter visited California early in the month, his motorcade traveled an extra 20 miles to find an open gas station. There was panic-buying by distraught motorists unable to find a gas station willing to sell the quantity of gas they sought.[86] Democratic Senator Daniel Patrick Moynihan suggested that such panic was not unusual for Californians. Nonetheless, desperate measures also were evident in the Eastern states as was the case with the pregnant woman who asked if she could cut in a long gas line. Sympathetic motorists granted her request, but when two pillows "fell out from under her dress," they chased her away. In a letter to the *Washington Post*, one citizen wrote: "Stories of gun-toters, line crashers and the like make one wonder about our own civilization." Hot selling items were siphon hand pumps, large gas cans, and, not surprising, locking gas tank caps.[87]

The protest of independent truckers, who experienced a 34 percent hike in diesel fuel cost in the first half of 1979, generated the most attention. Trucker culture—with a good mix of long-haired men with tattoos, wearing flannel shirts, taking amphetamines if necessary, and communicating with each other on CB radios—symbolized independence and, if demanded, rowdiness. Truck protests beginning in May grew in June with better organization and collective action. In a protest strike, 60 percent of independent truckers parked their trucks, allowing fruit and vegetables to rot in farm fields. More fuel arrived when the federal government repealed an obscure rule concocted earlier by the DOE. It was June 22 before most independent truckers, somewhat satisfied, agreed to return to the highways.[88]

One curious expression of protest was when disc jockey Bo Weaver barricaded himself in a Trenton, New Jersey, radio station where he played the song "Cheaper Crude or No More Food" nonstop for three hours. Appreciative fans ordered pizza for Weaver. Levittown, Pennsylvania, witnessed its own version of defiance. In the town's central intersection, many stoned teenagers gathered mattresses, sofas, and tires then lit them on fire. With flames 30 feet high, the teenagers danced and raised a ruckus. One tow truck driver dropped a junk car in the intersection that teenagers torched. It took a state of emergency and 117 arrests before the police restored order. Such incidents prompted the *Wall Street Journal* to editorialize that "the social fabric of this society is stretched tauter than any time in a decade."[89]

The White House response included an invitation to select thinkers to discuss America's problems "rooted in culture, social structure, and economics." Held on May 30, the event included a diverse number of people who were liberal or left-leaning on economics, hinting of Carter's own preferences. Attendees were Harvard sociologist Daniel Bell, journalist Charles Peters who promoted public service, progressive television journalist Bill Moyers, John Gardner who served as the Department of Health, Education, and Welfare (HEW) secretary in the Johnson administration, civil rights activist Jesse Jackson, journalist Haynes Johnson, and historian

Christopher Lasch. Absent was anyone with a graduate degree in economics.[90] The guests had drinks on the Truman Balcony followed by a meal of lamb chops and asparagus, raspberry ice cream, and coffee.

Throughout the discussion, Carter kept returning to the issue of consumer culture and the difference between wants and needs. The meeting ended at 11:00 p.m. with no sense of accomplishment and three of the invited guests joined Jody Powell and Pat Caddell for drinks at a bar. The following month Carter's public approval rating fell to a "staggering" 30 percent.[91] Even Stuart Eizenstat recognized that many low-income Americans opposed Carter's energy program that had ushered in higher energy costs.[92]

Clearly, Carter's ineffective policies were taking a toll. In June, a *New York Times*-CBS survey showed that only one of three respondents viewed him favorably.[93] Other numbers had him at 25 percent approval in July—lower than Richard Nixon's numbers in the days of Watergate. It was time to do something different to reverse the trend of horrible polling numbers. Carter's staff advised giving another energy speech to the American people, this one planned for July 5. The exhausted Carter left for Camp David on July 3, expecting to rest and wait for the drafted speech. His plan changed, however, and he canceled. His staff scrambled to Camp David where they were in a virtual state of panic. Eizenstat screamed at Caddell and other staff members got heated with each other, while Mondale was on the verge of a nervous breakdown. Carter's solution was to hold a domestic summit with a long list of invited speakers, each to offer their analysis on the state of America.[94]

The president received numerous suggestions. His least favorite discussion topic was economics. In his diary, he wrote: "The worst session of the week was the economic meeting. When you get bankers, labor leaders, economists, financiers around the table, they are so eager to posture and repeat the analyses they've already evolved that it's not helpful. But we had to go through the rote process."[95] Agreeable to Carter was the suggestion from economist John Kenneth Galbraith to have oil rationing. During a meeting of religious leaders, democrat socialist Robert Bellah advised Carter not to blame OPEC. Carter's response reassured him: "It would be rather self-righteous to blame it all on OPEC. Americans don't like it when a foreign country can interfere in our life, but we've been interfering in OPEC countries' and most other countries' lives rather heavily for a long time." Thirty-two-year-old Governor Bill Clinton of Arkansas explained the importance of the federal government playing a role in developing, with the American people, "alternate sources of energy."[96]

Wearing blue jeans and a polo shirt, President Carter sat on the floor taking notes on a yellow pad as numerous leaders and experts spoke. The days of discussion represented an intense reassessment. In his diary, Carter wrote: "I spent 90 percent of my time listening. I worked hard all week, some of the more strenuous work of my life. Also, it's not easy for me to accept criticism and to reassess my way of doing things." It was part political theatre, but Carter wanted to hear what he was doing wrong. With public opinion polling data gathered by pollster Pat Caddell; the advice of economic and energy advisors; and feedback from a variety of governors, members of Congress, and business and labor leaders, Carter formulated a speech "to get the attention of the news media and the public." Speaking from the Oval Office on July 15, 1979, Carter acknowledged there were many who lost confidence in the government, but went on to urge Americans to work together with courage to solve the serious problems.[97]

Initially, the speech earned excellent reviews in the press. "Remarkable" and "extraordinary" were assessments voiced by various newspapers. The White House received a deluge of mostly positive calls and letters from Americans everywhere. More meaningful was that Carter's poll numbers jumped by 11 points.[98] Unfortunately for him, the good numbers soon evaporated. Later, Richard Wirthlin, a Ronald Reagan pollster, declared: "I remember the exact moment I knew Ronald Reagan could beat Jimmy Carter. The date was July 15, 1979."[99] Even Tip O'Neill found the speech shocking: "The responsibility of leadership isn't to dwell on the negative, but to offer a positive way out of the morass. That speech was one of the biggest blunders Jimmy Carter ever made."[100] In the "malaise" speech, he blamed the American people rather than his policies, blame that many saw as another example of Carter's self-righteousness.[101]

O'Neill wrote that Carter also stumbled after the economic malaise speech when he purged his cabinet of some of his best men, including James Schlesinger of the DOE, Michael Blumenthal of Treasury, and Joseph A. Califano Jr. of HEW. The advice Carter accepted from other advisors was that Blumenthal was too conservative, Califano was insufferable to work with and likely the source of information leaks, and the arrogant Schlesinger was mostly responsible for the energy mess. These three resignations and two others the next day gave the impression that "the government was falling apart."[102] Carter's method was distasteful. Rather than requesting specific people to step down, he had the entire cabinet resign "and then accepted the resignations of only those people he wanted to get rid of."[103]

Any staff deemed incompetent, unless they were minorities or women, were at risk of losing their jobs.[104] Califano lost his job, Carter told him, for not getting along with Hamilton Jordan, Jody Powell, and Frank Moore. It was a crushing blow for Califano, made worse when Carter told him he did an outstanding job but later denied this to the media. Califano praised his staff who represented the "best people" from universities, law firms, and foundations.[105]

The "'July Massacre' of Cabinet sackings" made the climate in the White House worse.[106] Carter shifted Fed chairman William Miller to Treasury secretary, moved Housing and Urban Development secretary Patricia Harris to HEW, and appointed Charles Duncan as DOE secretary. Carter also agreed to finally appoint someone to run the White House's day-to-day operations. His choice for Chief of Staff was Hamilton Jordan, the insider with few friends on Capitol Hill. The staff was to accept Jordan's orders "as if they were the President's own."

O'Neill had hated Jordan since January 1977, and many of the White House staff likewise found one of Jordan's first acts insulting—that is, senior members of the administration were sent a questionnaire for grading the work habits and loyalty of subordinates. Was this the first step of more firings—in this case middle management?[107] In August, there was speculation that Jordan himself had used cocaine at a fashionable disco; this did not improve his reputation.[108]

As the White House sought its bearings, Milton Friedman persisted with his message that the Carter administration was out of touch with economic reality. He wrote that neither the oil industry, high consumer consumption, the severe winter of 1979, nor Arab leaders were at fault for the gasoline shortage. The oil industry had been around for many decades, there was no radical change in consumer behavior, there had been many hard winters in the past, and the Arab sheiks had sought wealth for years. Any one of these issues might raise oil prices, but they did not cause a shortage. With its "silly explanations" and its inability to understand how a price system worked, the media was doing America a disservice. Blame for the energy crisis fell squarely on the shoulders of government and bad policy.

Friedman was confident his analysis was correct: "Economists may not know much. But we know one thing well: how to produce surpluses and shortages." Regardless of the commodity, a guaranteed surplus resulted when the government approved an artificially high minimum price above market price. A guaranteed shortage of a commodity occurred when the government legislated a maximum price under market price. The solution to end the energy crisis was simple: get rid of all price controls on oil. Yet, Friedman doubted that Carter would take this necessary step: "[R]emoving price controls would reveal that the emperor is naked—it would show how useless, indeed harmful, are the activities of James Schlesinger and his 20,000 employees. It might even occur to someone how much better off we were before we had a Department of Energy."[109] Many in the media blamed OPEC for the energy crisis, but what power the organization exercised was a consequence of misguided economic policies—notably the many mistakes of the DOE.[110]

Conservatives found it unfortunate that missing in Carter's speech was talk about modifying or canceling the counterproductive price control on oil that was the main reason for America's increased dependency on foreign oil. Echoing conservative economic theorists, the *Newsweek* editorial of July 16, 1979, explained: "Free markets allocate scarce resources more efficiently than government bureaucracies do, so decontrol of oil and gasoline prices is essential to any rational energy policy—and must proceed as quickly as possible." Not only did most economists favor decontrolling crude oil and gasoline prices, but this also became the position of outgoing Energy secretary James Schlesinger. With the elimination of price control and regulation obstacles, private enterprise would find the capital; take the risks; develop other fuel resources; and, thus, solve the energy crisis.[111]

In December, Friedman listed five points for how policymakers could reduce America's dependence on Middle East oil. First, the government needed to appreciate that big oil companies, often a convenient scapegoat, were "a great national resource." Removal of the excise tax on domestic oil production was imperative. Second, the government needed to immediately dismantle the entitlement programs and price controls on oil and natural gas. Third, it was important to waive federal restrictions and allow oil and gas exploration in areas of Alaska, the West, and the coasts. Fourth, curb environmental regulations that were out of balance with the need to offer people affordable energy. Fifth, abolish the government's strategic oil reserve and give private enterprises incentives to grow and manage oil reserves.[112]

Months later, Friedman referred to the "windfall profits" tax as another harmful decision by politicians attempting to impose hidden taxes on the American people.[113] No longer on the periphery, Friedman was successful in undermining the long dominance of a Keynesian mindset, particularly the enduring faith in government experts and their macroeconomic management.

The message from economists was not enough and the next step for conservatives was to see political leaders repeat the arguments of Friedman and other like-minded thinkers. Ronald Reagan was key, especially since a January 1979 Gallup Poll revealed that among Americans he had a name identification of 95 percent.[114] It became clear that Reagan, in radio addresses throughout 1979, was ready to challenge Carter's energy policy philosophy that government action was proper to keep greedy oil companies from exploiting the American people. In January, Reagan cautioned calling oil producers "greedy monsters" without any sober analysis of why there was a rise in oil prices. One reason Middle East oil prices rose was the lower value of the American dollar (the result of poor economic policy) compared to the more stable currencies of the West German mark and the Japanese yen. Moreover, restrictive government regulations resulted in "untapped natural gas" that would break the OPEC monopoly.

Declaring "[y]ou can't sell a pencil for a nickel if it costs a dime to make it," Reagan explained there was no incentive for oil producers to drill if such action put them in the financial hole.[115] In May, he told radio listeners he understood their frustration of sitting in a car for three hours to buy gas. It was no funny matter that of California's 65,000 oil wells there were 23,000 not in operation because the price set by the DOE made them lose money. Reagan concluded his address with a question: "Have you figured out yet who we should be mad at?"[116]

In *Newsweek*, Keynesian Arthur M. Schlesinger Jr. claimed that "the age of cheap energy is over."[117] The *New Republic* editorialized that reliance "on private enterprise alone to solve our energy problem would be an act of piety, not of sound policy." The journal argued that a "fair reduction in our standard of living" was preferable to the unfairness sure to unfold if Keynesian thinking fell to more conservative economic approaches.[118] If these messages represented the "practical economics" of the era, they also were pessimistic ones that rubbed Reagan and many Americans the wrong way.[119] Perhaps it was time to consider the arguments of those who had less confidence in the government's assessment of the economy and its ability to get it right.

An increasing number of Americans viewed Carter's proposals as a clear failure; their calls for the abolishment of the Department of Energy spoke volumes. Even Stuart Eizenstat, assistant to the president for domestic policy, wrote of his own aggravation in finding gas to fill his car: "I sat in several gasoline lines near my house from up to an hour so I could get to the White House to plan how to end them!"[120] America's dependency on Middle East oil was one serious consequence of bad economic decisions that discouraged domestic production.

The energy crisis of the Carter years exposed the shortcomings of Keynesian management of the economy and helped shift American politics in a conservative direction.[121] Carter was confident that his comprehensive energy program "reversed the movement toward disaster"; however, Americans seeking gasoline for their cars, heating oil for their furnaces, and general energy stability found the government's solutions wanting.[122] Carter said he consulted a cross-section of Americans, but he had little time for oil producers.[123] The White House had good reason to be nervous as Carter pondered ways to reassure the American people that the nation, despite discouraging economic indicators, was on the correct track for economic renewal.

The brainstorming and the soul-searching of the Camp David episode reflected both Carter's desire to improve America's fortunes and to set the foundation for a successful bid for a second term. After Carter's "malaise" speech, there was greater hope among conservatives that a 69-year-old conservative from California had a legitimate shot of defeating Carter and his talk "about an age of limits." If the energy crisis generated effective criticism of the economic decision making of Keynesian experts, it also resulted in more attention to what Ronald Reagan had to say.

Notes

1. Kevin Mattson, "What the Heck Are You Up to Mr. President?": Jimmy Carter, America's "Malaise," and the Speech That Should Have Changed the Country (New York: Bloomsbury, 2009), 1–2, 4, 6.
2. He made this prediction in 1978; see Robert Lekachman, "Distribution Wars," *New Republic*, July 29, 15.
3. Milton Friedman, "What Carter Should Do," *Newsweek*, June 18, 1979, 66.
4. Milton Friedman, "Three Mini-Columns," *Newsweek*, June 12, 1978, 88.

5. Burton I. Kaufmann and Scott Kaufman, *The Presidency of James Earl Carter Jr.* Second Edition, Revised (Lawrence: University Press of Kansas, 2006), 168.
6. W. Carl Biven, *Jimmy Carter's Economy: Policy in an Age of Limits* (Chapel Hill: The University of North Carolina Press, 2002), 165.
7. See the recent study, Meg Jacobs, *Panic at the Pump: The Energy Crisis and the Transformation of American Politics in the 1970s* (New York: Hill and Wang, 2017).
8. Milton Friedman, "Rising above Principle," *Newsweek*, January 19, 1976, 68.
9. Friedman, "What Carter Should Do," 66. Biven, *Jimmy Carter's Economy*, 163.
10. William E. Simon, *A Time for Truth* (New York: Reader's Digest Press, 1978), 79–81.
11. Ibid., 75–76, 82.
12. Ibid., 74, 81.
13. Milton Friedman, "Two Economic Fallacies," *Newsweek*, May 12, 1975, 83.
14. Alan Reynolds, "The Federal Energy Agencies: The Solution or the Problem?" *Imprimis*, 5, no. 9 (1976): 1.
15. Ibid., 2.
16. Ibid., 3.
17. Ibid.
18. Ibid., 5.
19. Ibid., 6. Also, see Daniel Yergin, *The Prize: The Epic Quest for Oil, Money, and Power* (New York: Free Press, 1992), 660.
20. Marilu Hunt McCarty, "Economic Aspects of the Carter Energy Program," in *The Presidency and Domestic Policies of Jimmy Carter*, 556, 559.
21. Jude Wanniski, *The Way the World Works*, Fourth Edition (Washington, DC: Regnery Publishing, Inc., 1998), 307.
22. Biven, *Jimmy Carter's Economy*, 157.
23. Steven F. Hayward, *The Age of Reagan: The Fall of the Old Liberal Order, 1964–1980* (New York: Three Rivers Press, 2001), 521.
24. "The Deep Freeze!" *Newsweek*, January 31, 1977, 34, 37.
25. "Now, the Gas Crisis," *Newsweek*, February 7, 1977, 14–15.
26. "Guntersville, ALA—Life Below Zero," *Newsweek*, February 14, 1977, 26.
27. Simon, *A Time for Truth*, 81–82.
28. Jimmy Carter, *Keeping Faith: Memoirs of a President* (New York: Bantam Books, 1982), 94.
29. Ibid., 94, 96, 98–99.
30. Tip O'Neill with William Novak, *Man of the House: The Life and Political Memoirs of Speaker Tip O'Neill* (New York: Random House, 1987), 319.

O'Neill wrote that the one log burning was "a preposterous sight" for a New Englander.

31. Ibid., 320.
32. Russell D. Motter, "Seeking Limits: The Passage of the National Energy Act as a Microcosm of the Carter Presidency," in *The Presidency and Domestic Policies of Jimmy Carter*, 575.
33. Gerald R. Ford, *A Time to Heal* (New York: Berkley Books, 1980), 129, 133.
34. Mattson, *"What the Heck Are You Up to Mr. President?,"* 71.
35. Eliot Marshall, "James Schlesinger—Back Again," *New Republic*, January 29, 1977, 15.
36. "Reserves: The New Math," *Newsweek*, June 27, 1977, 71.
37. Carter, *Keeping Faith*, 92.
38. Biven, *Jimmy Carter's Economy*, 157. Yergin, *The Prize*, 661–663. It took until November 1978 before Congress passed an energy bill.
39. O'Neill, *Man of the House*, 320. Yergin, *The Prize*, 662–663.
40. Yergin, *The Prize*, 663.
41. Hayward, *The Age of Reagan*, 522.
42. Carter, *Keeping Faith*, 91–93.
43. James Nathan Miller, "They're Giving Us Gas, All Right," *New Republic*, February 12, 1977, 15.
44. Milton Friedman, "Gas Crisis: Weather or Washington?," *Newsweek*, February 28, 1977, 69.
45. Milton Friedman, "A Department of Energy?," *Newsweek*, May 23, 1977, 62.
46. Milton Friedman, "Energy Rhetoric," *Newsweek*, June 13, 1977, 82.
47. George F. Will, "Cold Comfort," *Newsweek*, February 7, 80.
48. Kaufman, *The Presidency of James Earl Carter Jr.*, 38–39.
49. Ibid., 70–71, 85.
50. Milton Friedman, "A Monstrosity," *Newsweek*, May 2, 1977, 20.
51. Milton Friedman, "To Jimmy from James," *Newsweek*, October 17, 1977, 99.
52. Milton Friedman, "What Belongs to Whom?," *Newsweek*, March 13, 1978, 71.
53. Michael Camp, "Carter's Energy Insecurity: The Political Economy of Coal in the 1970s," *The Journal of Policy History*, 26, no. 4 (2004): 461.
54. Ibid., 462.
55. Ibid., 463, 465.
56. Ibid., 464, 467–468.
57. Ibid., 470.
58. Ibid., 471–472.
59. Kaufman, *The Presidency of James Earl Carter Jr.*, 98.

60. For example, "Business and the Rational Mind, Part II," *Atlantic Monthly*, March 1978, 25.
61. Robert Sherrill, "Mobil News That's Fit to Print," *Nation*, January 27, 1979, 3, 71.
62. The early battles of government hearings took place in 1974, the year Senator Henry Jackson coined the phrase "obscene profits." See Yergin, *The Prize*, 656–657. Most Americans believed Big Oil "created an artificial shortage." See Jacobs, *Panic at the Pump*, 5, 44.
63. Kaufman, *The Presidency of James Earl Carter Jr.*, 170.
64. Yergin, *The Prize*, 658–659.
65. Fred J. Cook, "How Big Oil Turned Off the Gas," *Nation*, July 28–August 4, 1979, 65. Fred J. Cook, "Heating Oil Goes Through the Roof," *Nation*, October 20, 1979, 369–372.
66. TRB, "Why Mobil Isn't Loved," *New Republic*, October 14, 1978, 3.
67. Henry Fairlie, "The Passionate Socialist," *New Republic,* March 26, 1977, 19.
68. Kenneth W. Thompson, ed., *The Carter Presidency: Fourteen Intimate Perspectives of Jimmy Carter* (Lanham, MD: University Press of America, Inc., 1990), 57.
69. Ibid., 63–64.
70. Paul A. Samuelson, "Year-end Questions," *Newsweek*, January 1, 1979, 45.
71. McCarty, "Economic Aspects of the Carter Energy Program," 565.
72. Jimmy Carter, *White House Diary* (New York: Farrar, Straus and Giroux, 2010), 305.
73. Quoted in Biven, *Jimmy Carter's Economy*, 172.
74. Yergin, *The Prize*, 693.
75. Thompson, ed., *The Carter Presidency*, 90.
76. Wanniski, *The Way the World Works*, 222, 307, 315. Also, see Brian Domitrovic, *Econoclasts: The Rebels Who Sparked the Supply-Side Revolution and Restored American Prosperity* (Wilmington, DE: ISI Books, 2009), 33.
77. Biven, *Jimmy Carter's Economy*, 172.
78. Quoted in Biven, *Jimmy Carter's Economy*, 173.
79. Ibid., 174,
80. Quoted in Biven, *Jimmy Carter's Economy*, 176.
81. Ibid, 177.
82. Kaufman, *The Presidency of James Earl Carter, Jr.*, 171.
83. Quoted in Biven, *Jimmy Carter's Economy*, 303–304n54.
84. Carter, *Keeping Faith*, 111.
85. Kaufman, *The Presidency of James Earl Carter Jr.*, 172.
86. Hayward, *The Age of Reagan*, 572.
87. Mattson, *"What the Heck Are You Up to Mr. President?,"* 110–111.

88. Ibid., 113–117.
89. Ibid., 117–119.
90. Daniel Bell, a close friend of Irving Kristol, "had an immense intellectual curiosity" and probably understood economics better than most in his social-democratic circle. See Irving Kristol, *Neoconservatism: The Autobiography of an Idea* (Chicago: Elephant Paperbacks, 1999), 476.
91. Mattson, *"What the Heck Are You Up to Mr. President?,"* 89–94, 98.
92. Kaufman, *The Presidency of James Earl Carter Jr.*, 183.
93. Ibid., 173.
94. Mattson, *"What the Heck Are You Up to Mr. President?,"* 130–134.
95. Carter, *White House Diary*, 342–343.
96. Mattson, *"What the Heck Are You Up to Mr. President?,"* 141, 143, 147.
97. Carter, *Keeping Faith*, 114–115, 118, 120–121. Warned that there would be a media backlash to his speech, Carter responded: "F*%* the press." Randall Balmer, *Redeemer: The Life of Jimmy Carter* (New York: Basic Books, 2014), 114–115. Carter apparently said the same about Ben Bradlee of the *Washington Post*. See Ben Bradlee, *A Good Life: Newspapering and Other Adventures* (New York: Simon & Schuster, 1995), 426.
98. Thompson, ed., *The Carter Presidency*, 7–8.
99. Quoted in Mattson, *"What the Heck Are You Up to Mr. President?,"* 167.
100. O'Neill, *Man of the House*, 318. Joseph Califano wrote: "After the speech, Carter walked through the room briefly. On cue, we all rose and applauded as he entered, more out of hope than conviction." See Joseph A. Califano Jr., *Governing America: An Insider's Report from the White House and the Cabinet* (New York: Simon & Schuster, 1981), 428.
101. Jeffrey Hart, *The Making of the American Conservative Mind:* National Review *and Its Times* (Wilmington, DE: Intercollegiate Studies Institute, 2007), 259.
102. Kaufman, *The Presidency of James Earl Carter Jr.*, 179.
103. O'Neill, *Man of the House*, 318.
104. Califano, *Governing America*, 431.
105. Ibid., 435, 438–439, 444. Bob Woodward, *Shadow: Five Presidents and the Legacy of Watergate* (New York: Simon & Schuster, 1999), 86–87.
106. Dilys M. Hill, "Domestic Policy," in *The Carter Years: The President and Policy Making*, eds. M. Glenn Abernathy et al. (New York: St. Martin's Press, 1984): 18.
107. Kaufman, *The Presidency of James Earl Carter, Jr.*, 180–181.
108. Ibid., 184.
109. Milton Friedman, "Blaming the Obstetrician," *Newsweek*, June 4, 1979, 70.
110. Friedman, "What Carter Should Do," 66.

111. Friedman cites the July 16 editorial in Milton Friedman, "The Energy Boondoggle," *Newsweek*, July 30, 1979, 56.
112. Milton Friedman, "Iran and Energy Policy," *Newsweek*, December 31, 1979, 61.
113. Milton Friedman, "Our New Hidden Taxes," *Newsweek*, April 14, 1980, 90.
114. Craig Shirley, *Reagan Rising: The Decisive Years, 1976–1980* (New York: Broadside Books, 2017), 147.
115. Kiron Skinner et al., eds. *Reagan in His Own Hand: The Writings of Ronald Reagan that Reveal His Revolutionary Vision for America* (New York: Touchstone, 2002), 321.
116. Ibid., 322–323.
117. Arthur M. Schlesinger Jr., "Can We Control Our World?," *Newsweek*, November 19, 1979, 136.
118. "Energy Politics," *New Republic*, July 7 and 14, 1979; TRB, "The Fed Needs Help," *New Republic*, October 20, 1979, 6.
119. Hayward, *The Age of Reagan*, 579.
120. Quoted in Biven, *Jimmy Carter's Economy*, 1
121. Although not focusing on economic theory, Meg Jacobs argues that "the energy crisis ultimately helped shift American politics to the right in the 1970s and bring an end to [John Kenneth] Galbraith's conception of the American system." See Jacobs, *Panic at the Pump*, 6–7.
122. Carter, *Keeping Faith*, 91.
123. Jude Wanniski, "Oil in Abundance," *Harper's*, October 1979, 26.

CHAPTER 9

On the Brink of Economic Revolution

Tom Bethell's economic education began in the late 1950s when his Oxford University tutor assigned him Paul Samuelson's "heavy textbook" as a source for an essay assignment on money. Bethel found the textbook's articulation about money of no use and his attendance at an academic economics lecture soon after was equally disappointing. Twenty-one years later, he visited Oxford to discover his economics tutor was still in residence, ready to offer him a glass of sherry and conversation. When asked, however, the tutor was unable to offer his assessment of the Laffer curve because he was unfamiliar with it. Bethel wrote: "As I looked out of the mullioned windows, I confess, thoughts of ivied towers crossed my mind. I had a suspicion that I might have been keeping up with the dismal [economic] developments a little more enthusiastically than the professor."[1]

The Laffer curve and supply-side economics caught many by surprise. Rather than Arthur Laffer-types, the best-known free-market economist throughout most of the 1970s was Milton Friedman who also gained television stardom in 1980 with his PBS-sponsored *Free to Choose* series. Bethel wrote that those Keynesians who were aware of the rise of supply-side economics were not too happy, including Samuelson who disparaged the "Washington hot air about 'supply-side economics.'" The Keynesian macroeconomics of the past, which depended on computer models and fine-tuning, was clearly under assault by those who favored "a return to micro, or classical, economics."

E. R. Crouse, *America's Failing Economy and the Rise of Ronald Reagan*,
https://doi.org/10.1007/978-3-319-70545-3_9

Macroeconomics favors mathematics, statistics, and computer models, but it is microeconomics that comes closer to economic reality because "it deals with such unmeasurable qualities as motive, desire, aspiration, and expectation." To clarify his criticism of Keynesianism, Bethell cited economist Henry Hazlitt who argued that the mistakes of Keynes's *The General Theory* was because of his focus on "averages and aggregates that conceal the very causal relations he is trying to study. This aggregate, in-block, or lump thinking is the exact opposite of economic analysis."[2]

In his Nobel-prize lecture in 1974, Friedrich Hayek identified the problem of economists believing they had "exact knowledge" to solve inflation and unemployment. He declared that "economists are at this moment called upon to say how to extricate the free world from the serious threat of accelerating inflation which, it must be admitted, has been brought about by policies which the majority of economists recommended and even urged governments to pursue."[3] Keynesian theory sputtered at the end of the Carter years as one after another major economic episode signaled it was time to consider new thinking. The best-known politician supportive of supply-side thinking was Ronald Reagan who became a believer in late 1976. For him, supply-side economics projected a philosophy more hopeful than the dour budget-balancing of old-school Republicanism. He and other supply-siders pushed aside the ineffective policies of the Democratic Party and gave political expression to a modern version of classical economics that warranted serious consideration.

I

In a 1978 conference paper, economist Robert E. Lucas of the University of Chicago discussed the collapse of "Keynesian macroeconomics." He said that Keynesianism was victim to the faulty thinking behind the Phillips curve, which said people spent the money overprinted by the government without considering that their real income did not rise. Lucas argued that currency overprinting caused people to be doubtful about the value of their money. His work offered a credible approach to better understand stagflation.[4] It was another example of Keynesianism losing ground in academic circles. Additional damage to Keynesian theory came from individuals who had both academic credentials and real-life business experience.

Ira G. Corn was born in 1921 at Little Rock, Arkansas. In 1948, he received a master's degree in business administration from the University of Chicago and was a professor at Southern Methodist University in Dallas until 1954. Next came a successful business career in which he founded or cofounded 24 companies. In 1969, Corn outbid others and paid $404,000 for an original copy of the Declaration of Independence.[5] His testimony was representative of many entrepreneurs who went beyond economic theory on paper and achieved business success. Published in *Imprimis* in January 1980, his economics lecture at Hillsdale College linked creative capitalism with "personal and collective freedoms."

An important aspect of those freedoms was the economic freedom that meant less poverty and a higher standard of living. In Corn's interpretation, the terrible economic state of many Irish people during the 1840s was mainly the result of a feudal society not yet unshackled by the entrepreneurial spirit of the industrial revolution. England experienced greater employment opportunities and more food and goods, "a gift from the young entrepreneurs of the budding Industrial Revolution—no doubt seeking their own narrow ends—who had the wit and resources to devise new instruments of production and new methods of administering industry." This change was mostly positive. As capitalism increased in England and elsewhere, it was "possible for children to be excluded from the productive work force."[6] Many families no longer depended on their children's labor, and there were greater opportunities for women to work outside the home as new types of jobs did not necessarily favor the physical strength of men.

For Corn, American history also was illustrative of the positive aspects of entrepreneurialism. By the twentieth century, America's economic standing was the model for the world with the post-World War II period especially impressive. As Keynesian thinking dominated economic policy, Americans witnessed a rate of economic growth and accumulation of wealth never seen before. So why was America struggling during the 1970s? Corn believed that those critical of business were themselves blind to the problem of Keynesian government growth, including how its dominance reduced the personal freedom of many Americans. Going beyond their original mission and prodded by special-interest groups with their favorite pet projects, bureaucracies expanded to justify new hirings and larger budgets.[7]

Even Secretary of Commerce Juanita Kreps acknowledged how bureaucracies thrived on minutia complicated by the need "to delegate an important problem to several departments or agencies, each of which tend to study it endlessly and report at great length."[8] Keynes's idea of priming the economic pump during downturns occurred nonstop rather than when needed. Missing was the necessary political will to reign in bureaucratic excess; politicians benefited handsomely when they colluded with special-interest groups and the growing bureaucracies. Citing one comparison, Corn noted the modest 15 percent turnover rate in the House of Representatives from one Congress to the next, far less than the average 50 percent rate of the previous century.[9]

Another notable *Imprimis* article presented the analysis of an African American scholar who drew from daily experience and academic research. In his sharp criticism of government intervention, Temple University economist Walter Williams blamed government coercion and the lack of free markets for many of the problems that poor people faced. For example, the high unemployment of young black people was a "national scandal" especially because unemployment of young African Americans had been much lower (and about the same as young whites) in the immediate post-World War years. Did the rate of unemployment of black youths more than triple from 1948 to the 1970s because of greater racial discrimination, lower education of blacks, or changing economic cycles? No, Williams argued.

A better explanation was "foolish government intervention" and the introduction of minimum wage laws that "effectively discriminates against the unemployment of low skilled workers." It seemed to him that those who benefited the most from "massive government programs" were politicians and bureaucrats.[10] As someone with modest economic origins, Williams garnered the attention of those who sought a voice with both experience and education.[11] He was a black academic and libertarian economist offering fresh ideas on improving the daily economic experiences of ordinary people.

If the cozy relationship between politicians and bureaucrats hurt the economy, conservatives pointed to overregulation as further evidence of harmful intervention. Momentum for government regulation of business began in the late nineteenth century with the regulation of railroads and then extended to the trucking industry in the 1920s and 1930s. Other industries operated with various degrees of government regulation, all done with the intention of protecting the public interest.[12] Free-market economists argued that the opposite occurred, pointing out that regulation became a tool of both industry and labor in protecting narrow interests.

Economist George Stigler of the University of Chicago presented compelling arguments against regulation in his "The Theory of Economic

Regulation." A future Nobel-Prize winner, Stigler joined a growing number of respected economists who discouraged the overregulation of private monopolies.[13] An AEI project led by Murray Weidenbaum of Washington University of St. Louis calculated the high costs of regulation, both time and money.[14] The media also reported on the "regulation mess." For example, one Illinois dairy company with 27 employers reported to "twelve different regulators."[15]

Carter made some progress on the issue of government regulation with the appointment of Alfred Kahn as chairman of the Civil Aeronautics Board; this signaled his openness to deregulation. Having established a well-deserved academic reputation as an expert on regulation at Cornell University, Kahn gained national recognition for his regulatory work as chairman of the New York Service Commission in 1974.[16] His success in deregulating the nation's airline industry was a notable achievement. There was less triumph elsewhere.

The story of Lido Anthony "Lee" Iacocca and Chrysler said much about regulation and the American automobile industry. Educated as an engineer, Lee Iaccoca switched to sales after he began working for the Ford Motor Company following World War II. By 1970, this son of immigrant parents was president of the company, but the final step to chairman did not happen as he planned. On June 13, 1978, Henry Ford II fired Iaccoca, telling him: "Sometimes you don't like somebody." Five months later, Iaccoca became president of Chrysler Corporation and in less than a year was the new chairman. In late 1979, American television viewers saw Chrysler's new commercials showcasing Iaccoca himself. A man of contradictions—sometimes going on profanity-spiced meltdowns and at other times shy and insecure—his commercials helped Chrysler sell its new line of Omni-Horizon subcompacts.[17]

Despite these sales, Chrysler remained in financial trouble, and Iaccoca turned to the government for loan guarantees. Facing large federal penalties, Chrysler began retooling to make the larger models smaller even though there was greater consumer demand for large cars. In fact, many Americans bought commercial vans, initially exempted from mileage regulations, and turned them into family vehicles. The gas mileage was less than 10 miles a gallon, but they offered prized space to haul families and all their luggage and extras. Caught by surprise, Chrysler and other auto companies struggled to keep up with the demand for vans.[18]

Arguing that government regulations, in large part, were to blame for Chrysler's decline, Iaccoca believed he had a good case.[19] His first meeting with Speaker of the House Tip O'Neill did not go well. Iaccoca descended on O'Neill's office with an entourage of Chrysler board members, lawyers, and lobbyists. After the meeting, Iaccoca referred to O'Neill as "the coldest bastard he ever met." When he heard this, O'Neill replied: "Do you think I'm going to tell him how to get the job done in front of all those lawyers and lobbyists? They'll just take credit for my ideas."[20] The second meeting between O'Neill and Iaccoca went well and the Democrats fought for more money for Chrysler, not because they favored capitalists but because the automobile jobs were in jeopardy and union leaders' pressure. With the United Auto Workers (UAW) and the Michigan governor behind him, Carter supported a $1.5 billion guaranteed loan to prevent a possible takeover by an "aggressive" Japanese automobile company.[21] Iaccoca always favored the Republican Party, but this changed when he arrived at Chrysler: "There's no question in my mind that if there had been a Republican administration in 1979, Chrysler wouldn't be around."[22]

Responding to "the high-powered" Chrysler bailout campaign, Milton Friedman wrote "hogwash." Clearly the misinformation and scaremongering were profuse. Supporters of the bailout pointed to bankruptcy and the potential loss of 500,000 jobs—Chrysler employees plus those employed by automobile parts suppliers—if the government did not intervene. But then again, could bankruptcy be this disastrous? Friedman's argument was that companies declaring bankruptcy generally continued production with court instructions to eventually pay off debts as much as possible. In other words, many companies survived the interim stage of bankruptcy going on to resume operations under new management.

Even if Chrysler was unable to survive intact as a single enterprise, its facilities would not stand idle. Other automobile companies or manufacturers would find value in the Chrysler properties, potentially running a more efficient operation that created new jobs. As for the automobile parts industry, it would continue operations for the revised Chrysler company and other car companies that would inherit any business lost by Chrysler. Friedman reminded readers that businesses seeking profits in the free-market system ran the risk of financial loss. Carter's high-profile bailout was an indication of too much government control and a lack of understanding of how such control had reversed productivity during the 1970s.

The sad reality, according to Friedman, was that short-term political gains mattered more than a lasting and sound economy.[23] Federal deficits got larger and continued to distort the allocation of resources, cause unstable financial markets, and inhibit capital investment in the private sector.[24] The American people did not need to understand the intricacies of economic policy to recognize economic malaise and the failure of government to respond effectively. A Gallup Poll in August 1979 revealed that a record 84 percent of Americans believed that the United States was on the wrong track.[25]

In 1980, journalist Ken Auletta wrote what few others in the media admitted: "To the public, government dispenses protection but also programs, grants and subsidies the way a counterman dispenses mashed potatoes and meat loaf.... Politicians know that few care about the chef's wisdom, judgment or diet recommendations.... They know the press tends to focus on now, on politics not government." Farmers expected their crop subsidies; tenants looked for their rent subsidies; big businesses anticipated federal loan guarantees; and cities, counties, and states counted on federal grants.[26] All this was apparently fine with those who stood solidly with government.

The poor results of government action did not slow enthusiasm for government intervention whether it was social programs or price controls. Throughout the 1970s, the federal government funneled hundreds of millions of dollars to fight poverty, but the results were discouraging with net poverty at 6.2 percent in 1979, down only by 0.1 percent from 1972. An equally troubling statistic concerned the percentage of the population dependent on government transfer payments, referred to as the "latent poor." The percentage was 19 percent in 1972 and 22 percent at the end of the decade.[27] Conservative critics claimed that welfare programs for the well-being of the poor and unemployed, despite the best intentions, strained traditional family life, resulting in a diminishing role of husbands supporting the family.

Nonetheless, another problem for government programs was the reality of an inflating dollar that got worse in the last stage of Carter's presidency. Further evidence of economic malaise was the struggles of New York City where politicians ignored the fiscal crisis and continued to stuff budgets with goodies. Burdened with a huge deficit, city officials returned to Congress with hat in hand.[28] With many groups demanding assistance, federal spending remained rampant, so Carter had no success reaching his objective of a balanced budget; the federal deficit in 1980 was $60 billion compared to $45 billion in 1977.[29]

Economist Alan Blinder, no champion of conservative economics, wrote in 1979 that politicians "did not learn to steer clear of wage-price controls."[30] Alfred Kahn's appointment as chairman of the Council on Wage and Price Stability (COWPS) suggests the pressure for Carter to solve high inflation was greater than the burden for him to stay pure to Keynesian ideas as defined by the more liberal wing of the Democratic Party. Inflation czar Kahn clarified the enormity of fixing inflation: "I knew that I was taking on something that probably any God could do." He explained that inflation was more than an economic problem; it was a disturbing social problem "in which individuals and groups seek their self-interest and demand money compensation and government programs that simply add up to more than the economy is capable of supplying."[31]

Kahn was a curmudgeon whose brashness irked others including the White House staff and Barry Bosworth, the director of COWPS; however, the American public saw him in a favorable light. In typical independent fashion, he declared Carter's wage and price controls "a catastrophe." He was pessimistic about inflation, informing the president "that neither your economic nor your political advisors are ever going to present you with *the* solution to the problem of inflation, readymade."[32] In February 1979 Kahn declared: "I suggest that if my earlier diagnosis of the unhealthy condition of the anti-inflation program is at all close to accurate, your political and economic advisors had better bestir themselves to think of some dramatic actions [that could have an immediate impact on prices]."[33] The best answer he had was to reimburse workers with real wage insurance to offset the detrimental effects of inflation.

An assessment by Charles Schultze in March was grim: "While we expected high inflation to continue in the first part of 1979, before the anti-inflation program had time to bite, price increases in the last several months have actually accelerated."[34] There was a significant increase in home ownership costs, but the reported numbers made it appear worse than was the case. A flawed method of calculating the Consumer Price Index (CPI) by the Bureau of Labor Statistics in turn distorted the numbers for wage increases in union contracts.[35] In late 1979, Kahn warned Carter not to wait until January—after the State of Union address—to introduce additional anti-inflationary measures.[36]

Seeing low industrial productivity as a major cause of inflation, Schultze suggested the implementation of a $6–8 billion "productivity package."[37] Henry Aaron acknowledged the "climate of doubt about the capacity of government" to effectively tackle the economic problems of the 1970s. Yet he remained hopeful: "[S]ober attempts rationally to solve increasingly complex problems may be advanced if we retain a bit of that sense of mutual obligation and community that flowed from" the Great Depression and World War II.[38]

II

One of the most consistent defenders of government action was the *Nation*, the small weekly magazine founded in New York City in 1865. In 1977, the yearly cost of the magazine to service its approximate 25,000 subscribers with 47 issues was $250,000. For the year, the *Nation* lost more than $120,000, consistent with other small opinion journals that almost always ran at a deficit.[39] Progressive thinkers writing in the *Nation* saw that the solution for full employment and price stability was "a smarter crowd in the White House." On economic matters, the magazine found the "mumbling mumbo jumbo" of conservativism and the misuse of popular resentment by the "right-wing extremists" tragic.

To counter these "hyenas of economic life," it was critical to enact immediate and comprehensive progressive action. With the assistance of his undergraduate students, Hunter College Professor Bertram M. Gross prepared a 10-point anti-inflation program to prevent corporate control of society.[40] Price controls were essential and, according to Robert Lekachman, something the American people wanted. On whether to save Chrysler, Lekachman preferred "outright nationalization," but he understood America was not quite ready for "this clean-cut resolution."[41]

Lekachman had many biting words for conservatives, including Jewish ex-leftist Norman Podhoretz who broke ranks with radicalism and became an influential neoconservative writer in *Commentary* magazine. Lekachman wrote of Podhoretz's "crass egocentricity," his "utterly humorless" and "leaden prose," his rejection of reform, and his inflated college grades of A+; he asked: "Did Lionel Trilling and Fred Dupree really award A+s to our Norman?"[42] The prominence of neoconservatives was not because of their "intellectual power and originality." Rather it was the patronage of the business community that explained the status of these "superficial purveyors of the scraps."[43]

It was simple, the intelligence of those who promoted conservative economics was suspect. *Nation* writer E. L. Doctorow questioned the intellect of Ronald Reagan, someone who was "a third-rate student at a fifth-rate college."[44] Missing in progressive literature, however, was serious analysis of the work of former radical Thomas Sowell whose publications on the promise of the free market began to receive national attention.[45] More substantive than personal, Ralph Nader's critique of those who challenged government intervention in the *Nation* was far-ranging. In March 1980, he called for the business class and corporations "to stop stealing, stop deceiving, stop corrupting politicians with money, stop monopolizing, stop poisoning the earth, air and water, stop selling dangerous products, stop exposing workers to cruel hazards, stop tyrannizing people of conscience within the company and start respecting long-range survival needs and [the] rights of present and future generations."[46]

In a similar vein, City University of New York professor Robert Engler told *Nation* readers that popular organization was paramount to realize the "global cooperation and global planning" necessary to deal with oil resources and environmental protection.[47] Also from City University of New York, economist William K. Tabb and author of *Marxism and the Metropolis* discussed the plans for deregulation and lower social spending in the United States and pointed to the conservative governments in Canada, Britain, and much of Europe that attempted "to prosper by reducing living standards." Tabb said that a "left opposition" was vital to point out that "organized greed" was behind the lack of economic growth in America.[48] James Crotty of the University of Massachusetts was another economics professor who saw "national economic planning rather than laissez faire" as the remedy for America's economic crisis. The "reign" of monetarism and supply-side economics, he predicted, would likely be "short-lived."[49]

The *Nation* took opportunities to undermine popular conservative initiatives, such as Proposition 13, that resulted in California experiencing an economic boom. Approximately one year after California ushered in lower taxes, freelance writer Barbara Koeppel reported in the *Nation* that tenants who voted for Proposition 13 were angry to learn that the legislation was good for landlords but not for them when they experienced higher rental costs. Rising inflation and subsequent increased labor and operating costs pushed landlords to increase rents. A comparison of rents before and after Proposition 13 is instructive.

In 1974, one California couple paid $125 a month for their two-bedroom, but with new owners the rent went to $315 in 1977, $450 in 1978, and $550 by February 1979. This trend of escalating rents meant more tenants became permanent renters, unable to break into the housing market of cities. David Morrison, formerly of the California Department of Housing and Community Development, declared that renters had become second-class citizens. They were victims of rent gouging and faced eviction without good cause. According to Koeppel, a tenant movement began to push for rent control legislation, a long overdue action given that less than five percent of America's tenants lived under rent control laws. She lamented that only a few cities were fortunate enough to have rent controls—New York City since World War II, Boston, Washington, DC, Miami Beach, and others in more recent years.[50]

In the wake of Proposition 13, city councils in Los Angeles and Beverly Hills passed "stop-gap rent freezes" while Berkeley and Davis voters won rent rollback initiatives, and Santa Cruz approved an anti-speculation tax in November. In May 1979, there were enough Santa Monica voters to approve rent control. Yet, most initiatives attempted in other California cities failed. Supporters of rent control, such as David Morrison, were upset by how opponents defeated their efforts with expensive public relations campaigns: "If you have unlimited funds you can buy talent and run a very sophisticated propaganda campaign—and win." By Koeppel's calculation, the San Francisco rental industry outspent tenant organizations $500,000 to $11,000. As she explained, the words "rent control" sent "shivers down the spines of landlords from Long Island to Los Angeles."[51]

Were rent controls effective? Koeppel acknowledged the example of New York City that showed skyrocketing rents despite long-standing rent controls. There were several key arguments against rent controls: they reduced new construction; they triggered unemployment for construction workers; and they caused "property decline, abandonment, severe housing shortages and higher taxes." If the real estate tax base does not rise enough to support government spending, homeowners are hit with higher taxes.

Opponents of rent control called for more construction as the solution for housing shortages and high rents. It was uncomplicated, stated Ted Dienstfrey of the California Housing Council: "Builders must be allowed to build—what they know how to do best."[52] The differing solutions came down to opposing views on what government could achieve. Koeppel and politicians wanting rent controls saw government intervention as essential. The *Nation's* focus on rent control offered a better story than any discussion of job creation in the aftermath of Proposition 13. The doom predicted by liberals was incorrect, including UCLA economists who forecast a job loss of 450,000. Instead, there was a gain of about a half million jobs and 18 months of economic growth after the passage of Proposition 13. Surprising too was the climb in aggregate tax revenues.[53]

The *New Republic* was another forum for progressive analysis of the economy. Irving Howe lamented the William Buckley-types who never had to worry about getting a job and were too willing to promote conservative economic solutions that reduced the size of government. For Howe, it was honorable to defend government regardless of the financial cost: "If a dose of bureaucracy is the price we must pay for humane social arrangements, then the price is worth paying." Howe's concern for vulnerable Americans in financial need was genuine, and he was ready to demonstrate on the streets "against the current menace from the right."[54]

Perhaps unaware of the financial struggles of Milton Friedman's early life, Anne Colamosca wrote of Friedman's privileged life preventing him from understanding the shortcomings of the free market. She claimed that Friedman would be wiser if he was a female academic fighting to get tenure, raising a family, and keeping the home in order: "[U]nfortunately he does not have to cope with free-market malfunctions on such a personal level."[55]

New Republic writers had faith in and wanted "aggressive" government, particularly a "liberal inflation program" that could bring "a government-guaranteed job for anyone who can work, and a guaranteed decent minimum annual income for everyone."[56] The benefits of a "stiff tax" on energy, "say a dollar a gallon on gasoline," would be rebates for the poor and money for "massive government" research to solve the energy crisis.[57] Taking the position that government controls "look very appealing," the *New Republic* saw Edward (Ted) Kennedy, who wanted widespread controls, as "the only leading presidential candidate who offers a serious inflation program."[58]

Economist Lester Thurow's argument that "planners possess all the technical tools for implementing whatever form of recovery the political system might settle upon" earned the praise of *New Republic* book reviewer Herbert Gintis, economics professor at the University of Massachusetts, Amherst. Gintis was hopeful that America would witness the coming of "social democratic politics" soon with Thurow as its "economic guru."[59] In defending Keynesian or democratic socialist economic models, intellectuals were clear on one point: supply-side economics was a bad option that for the most part benefited the rich at the expense of other Americans.

As the economy struggled, some radicals distanced themselves from left politics to become professionals in law, academics, journalism, medicine, and business. A well-known leader of the New Left during the 1960s, Todd Gitlin wrote that as "the movement's moral imperatives grew more burdensome, many wearied of the life of the professional radical." It was time to move one. One of those who "set out on the track that middle-class upbringing and education had prepared us for before Sixties politics intervened," Gitlin returned to graduate school to study sociology at the University of California, Berkley.[60] What happened? According to Gitlin, the "millennial, all-or-nothing moods of the Sixties proved to be poor training for practical politics." Moreover, he said idealistic leftists had "no clean hands. The idea of a unitary Left destined to save the world because it was born on the side of the angels is grotesque blindness. Even benign social democracy … loses much of its allure if for no other reason than that capital goes on strike and a weak economy cannot satisfy the demands an aroused democracy makes."[61] Whether progressives changed their politics or not, new ideas about the economy were worthy of examination for some exploring why Keynesianism fell short in correcting a faltering economy.

III

Irving Kristol's economic articles of the 1970s published in the *Wall Street Journal*, *Commentary*, and *The Public Interest* influenced many to take supply-side ideas seriously.[62] A former Trotskyite—"a member in good standing of the Young People's Socialist League"—who graduated from City College in New York in 1940, Kristol had a wry sense of humor and a sharp intellect that scored points for the conservative movement he found himself supporting. One of his definitions of a liberal was a person who approved the work of an 18-year-old girl in a pornographic film on the condition that she received, at least, the minimum wage.[63]

Kristol believed that the survival of capitalism hinged on whether businessmen could go beyond a stark, self-seeking approach to business and practice genuine "social responsibility" and "business ethics." Although flawed as all economic theories were, supply-side economics appeared to Kristol to offer a legitimate path where capitalism and the wealth it generated made room for noble aims. Key was economic growth: the creation of wealth that allowed the financing of necessary programs to help Americans. Supply-side economics also meant lower taxes and the number of economists who held that higher taxes were good for the economy was declining.[64]

By the late 1970s, supply-side economic theory was attractive and straightforward. The reduction of income taxes and investment taxes put more money in people's hands and encouraged job-creating investments. As former leftist Michael Novak wrote: "Lower tax rates tease money out of bank vaults, where it sits uninvested and unused. Lower tax rates awaken 'animal spirits'—keen-eyed spirits, eager to invest in new businesses in order to bring new technologies to market and create new jobs."[65] Those who embraced this argument cited President John F. Kennedy's surprising tax cuts of the previous decade that ushered in a stronger economy. In 1977, the think tank AEI invited Novak, a Catholic theologian, to join its team. There the Democrat Novak found the arguments of Irving Kristol and other pioneer supply-siders compelling. He remembered Kennedy's statement that captured the logic behind supply-side economics: "It is a paradoxical truth that tax rates are too high today and tax revenues are too low, and the soundest way to raise the revenues in the long run is to cut the rates now.... The purpose of cutting taxes now is not to incur a budget deficit, but to achieve the more prosperous, expanding economy that can bring a budget surplus."[66]

When Novak met Republican congressman Jack Kemp, who invited him to a Young Republicans meeting in Minnesota in 1979, he gained additional knowledge of economics. Novak looked to the former Buffalo Bills star quarterback as "an extraordinarily gifted teacher." Kemp took economic theory and explained it in an understandable manner: "I believe in incentives. I trust you with your own money." He asked his constituents: "If you do hard, sweaty work in the mills your whole life so your kids can go to college, do you want the government to take a big chunk of it, just to give it to people who maybe did not sacrifice as much as you have?"[67] Kemp told the story of his garbage man who stopped him at the curb to encourage him to keep fighting the Democrats and prevent them from changing the rules "just as my kids start to get ahead."[68]

With the tempting incentives of lower taxes and a more welcoming climate of business, entrepreneurs eagerly jumped to invest in businesses and advance new technologies, all of which generated new jobs. A notable feature of supply-side economics was its rejection of the "limits of growth" viewpoint held in Keynesian circles. Conservative Republicans were confident of getting the country on track, whereas liberal Democrats "took on the crabbed countenance of Herbert Hoover."[69]

Milton Friedman was no supply-side economist, but he by and large was supportive of the bill forwarded by Jack Kemp and William Roth that would reduce tax rates over a three-year period. He understood that federal tax rates as high as 70 percent resulted in taxpayers buying tax shelters even if this denied them investing in more profitable activities. Simply put, taxpayers were willing to buy shelters for 50 cents on the dollar to avoid paying a federal tax of 70 cents on the dollar. By sharply reducing individual and corporate taxes, the Kemp-Roth bill would result in more taxpayers paying the tax and investing "their funds in the most profitable ventures."

In the end, the supply-siders believed the government would generate more revenue, although Friedman was not as confident on this point. More significantly, Friedman argued that the bill needed to take an extra step—a limit on government spending. Given that the "total tax burden on the American people is what the government spends, not those receipts called 'taxes,'" it was important to have both tax reduction and spending reduction. American economic history demonstrates that governments "will spend whatever the tax system will raise—plus a good deal more." Greater revenue for the government to continue wasteful spending was not the answer.[70]

From the vantage point of the late 1970s, economists were aware that the Kennedy tax was a resounding success when implemented during the Johnson administration. Nonetheless, supply-side theory, referred to some as "economic snake oil," had a tough fight to convince political leaders raised on Keynesianism. Victories were incremental. Kemp became the first supply-side politician in 1975. The following year, the Republican National Committee was cool on any revolutionary ideas on tax cutting, favoring instead a more traditional approach of balancing expenses and revenues. Certainly, few policymakers believed tax cuts could revitalize the economy; if there were tax cuts, they would come after other policies ushered in a stronger economy.[71]

Economist Paul Craig Roberts was a major pioneer who charted the rise of supply-side ideas within the Republican Party. With an economics Ph.D. and after being a fellow at Stanford's Hoover Institution, he joined Jack Kemp's staff in 1975. He had a soft voice, but opponents who tangled with him discovered that he was tenacious and had a high standard of intellectual integrity.[72] Roberts marked February 23, 1977, as key to the emergence of supply-side policy and the resurrection of the Republican Party. With a booming voice, Republican John Rousselot introduced a substitute amendment on the floor of the House of Representatives that gave every American "a simple across-the-board tax reduction." In the past, Republicans had acted on rising deficits by voting against Democratic spending and promising fiscal sanity when they returned to power.

Surprising both Democrats and many Republicans, Rousselot did not offer the typical balanced-budget talk of the Republican Party but instead focused on a permanent tax reduction he believed would stimulate productivity and investment more effectively than the Democrat's proposed stimulus package of a one-year $50 rebate. Keynesian theory held that a good economy relied on healthy government spending, but here was a Republican amendment adding to the deficit (although not as much as the Democrats' proposal). Much drama and irony followed as Democrats, aware of the Republican soft spot, criticized Rousselot for risking a bigger deficit with a permanent tax cut. The explanation for the Democratic Party's double standard was its opposition to any tax cuts, in part because Keynesian analysis viewed that "a dollar of tax cuts results in less additional demand than a dollar of spending."

In addition to the issue of demand, Democrats argued that a tax reduction favored the rich over lower-income Americans. "Battling Jim" Wright, the Democratic majority leader, cited Budget Committee numbers to push the narrative of "the old trickle-down economic theory."[73] It did not matter that in the field of economics there was no such thing as a trickle-down economic theory.[74] Nevertheless, no one could deny that an equal cut in taxes meant a family earning $50,000 would see a larger percentage of saving than a family earning $25,000.

At the same time Democrats resisted supply-side thinking, Republicans hurt their cause with internal squabbles. The day before Rousellot presented his amendment, Arthur Laffer advised Jack Kemp not to support it because Rousellot did not go far enough and make the argument that tax cuts would pay for themselves. Roberts worried that the exaggerations of Laffer and Jude Wanniski blanketed "the supply-side movement with hyperbole" thus causing disunity between congressional insiders and outsiders. Roberts rushed over to Kemp's office and convinced him to stay in the game with Rousellot. Still, friction remained because of Wanniski's editorial "JFK Strikes Again" (Kemp had the same initials as Kennedy) that gave no credit to other House Republicans who worked hard to advance tax cuts. When Roberts challenged Wanniski for his "tactless editorial," the *Wall Street Journal* editor replied: "We will sacrifice you to the revolution."[75]

Despite this friction, five months later Kemp and Senator William Roth took an important step and introduced their bill proposing the reduction of personal income tax rates by 30 percent in stages. There were several reasons for the progress of supply-side economics. People began to speak up. Freshman Senator Orrin Hatch (Republican) on the Joint Economic Committee (JEC) became an unpopular figure because of his opposition to the rise of spending and the growth of government. He found it irresponsible that lawmakers continued to oppose lowering personal income tax rates: "Each time those of us who pushed for a tax reduction were told that there was no room in the budget. There was not any room in the budget for the spending programs either. But that did not keep us from spending."[76]

Keynesians stonewalling Republican Hatch was one thing, but doing the same to a powerful Democrat was another thing. Democratic Senator Russell Long, chairman of the Senate Finance Committee, not only wanted to cut the tax on capital gains but he also challenged the Treasury's argument that higher taxes resulted in more revenue for government. In June 1977 at a hearing of the Subcommittee on Taxation, he stated: "It would be my guess if you would reduce your top rate to 50 percent, you actually would make money." It was a remarkable development that a powerful Democrat spoke supply-side language. Senator Long's decision to give entrepreneur Michael Evans the task of creating a supply-side model to get more accurate revenue estimates for the Senate Finance Committee opened the floodgates.[77]

The tide turned as the worsening economy of Carter's final two years spurred interest in supply-side ideas.[78] One advantage for its proponents was the shortcomings of Keynesian economic models, devised by Lawrence Klein and Otto Eckstein, that stressed spending and did not consider the role of incentives in economic growth. Consequently, they forecast that tax cuts would cause a decline of the Gross National Product (GNP). But then again, how reliable was a model that failed to have a good answer to the problem of stagflation? Other Keynesian ideas appeared suspect.

Economist Lester Thurow reasoned that people would work regardless of the level of taxation until they reached a targeted amount of wealth. If there were high taxes, they worked harder and longer. But such thinking put Keynesians in a bind. For example, if a Keynesian economist called for a tax cut to stimulate higher spending, by Thurow's logic people with lower taxes would work less. This would decrease the total production of goods and services—the opposite goal of Keynesianism.[79]

In contrast to Keynesian claims, there was evidence that a high marginal tax rate discouraged people from working longer. Once workers approached income earnings that put them in a higher tax bracket, there was less incentive to earn additional taxable income. In commonsense terms, supply-side proponents stated additional examples of deterrents. Even a modest marginal tax rate put a drag on the economy. For example, if a worker had a 25 percent marginal tax rate, he kept $75 of the $100 he earned that day. But he faced a decision if he wanted his house painted and the cost of a painter for the day was $80. Painting the house himself meant a saving of $5, but this option shrunk the tax base by $180. Lost to the government was the tax revenue from the $100 that the worker chose not to earn and the $80 that he did not pay the painter.[80]

Supply-side economists explained that a progressive income tax rate designed to "soak the rich" was also "a barrier to upward mobility" for many Americans. Why strive for your best if the rewards were progressively less? Keynesians began to lose the debate as more people saw the logic of supply-side analysis. Their argument that higher taxes would compel Americans to work harder and longer seemed to be backward thinking. By 1978 there was more evidence of Democrats flirting with supply-side ideas. In the fall, Democratic Senator Sam Nunn saw his amendment to reduce the personal income tax rate and to limit the growth of federal spending receive three-to-one support in the Senate.[81]

In addition, the 1979 report of the JEC under the leadership of Senator Lloyd Bentsen embraced a supply-side approach that, in the words of Paul Craig Roberts, "created a new ballgame." Remarkably, the title of the JEC's 1980 report was "Plugging in the Supply Side"; here was "Reganomics before Reagan."[82] Facing the challenges of the Congressional Budget Office (CBO) and econometric models protecting Keynesian thinking, supply-side economics had gained strength on both sides of the aisle.

IV

America was on the brink of an economic revolution and the most serious threat to Keynesian politicians was Ronald Reagan. The Californian was the key transformative figure putting political clothing on supply-side theory; he was one the first Republican leaders to embrace the Kemp-Roth bill.[83] There are, however, various interpretations on the timing and how specifically Reagan embraced supply-side ideas. After the 1978 midterm election, supply-sider Jude Wanniski wanted Jack Kemp to pursue the GOP presidential nomination because Reagan and the other candidates were "traditional austerity Republicans." Reagan's subsequent speeches praising Kemp and supply-side ideas proved Wanniski wrong. In early summer 1979, Kemp met with Reagan at a dinner party held at Arthur Laffer's home in California. After probing Reagan's understanding of economics and commitment to supply-side ideas, Kemp pledged his allegiance to Reagan. As Laffer admitted to Wanniski, Reagan was "eighty-five percent with us on the issues, which doesn't give me reason to go against him."[84]

Nevertheless, Wanniski was skeptical, and he believed Reagan gave too much attention to traditional Republican economic ideas. It took months before he was comfortable that Reagan's commitment to supply-side economics was genuine. With a group of 25 meeting in Los Angeles in January 1980, Wanniski witnessed Reagan's impressive discussion of economics: "Reagan was so thoroughly in tune with the day's discussion that the thought struck me with full force that he had the basic model before we arrived, indeed before any of the Kemp group was born."[85] Wanniski appeared to relish the limelight and he either exaggerated his role in advancing the supply-side movement or made inconsistent statements. Keeping with his reputation as a "wildman," he gave a curious interview to the *Village Voice* in April, stating that Reagan lost focus on supply-side economics without the encouragement of Kemp.[86]

David Stockman's version is that "Reagan had been successfully 'converted'" in Los Angeles by Kemp and other supply-siders in attendance. Stockman, who viewed Reagan as a "cranky obscurantist," was unhappy with the news that Kemp had given his allegiance to Reagan. He was unsure whether to laugh or kick his desk.[87] If he had no confidence in Reagan as a supply-side champion, he probably had not read Reagan's articles over the years calling for lower taxes. Critics called Reagan many things, but Stockman was the only person in America who labeled him "cranky." Flirting with supply-side theory for a short term and serving in Reagan's administration even more briefly, Stockman garnered the attention of cartoonists who portrayed him as a cold and bloodless policymaker.[88]

Political journalists Rowland Evans and Robert Novak appeared to want it both ways, presenting analyses that Reagan was and was not an ardent supply-sider. They wrote that Reagan was "ambivalent" about his support for the Kemp-Roth tax bill, but they also stated that he viewed it as "serious policy" and that he "began to unveil himself as the political leader of the supply-side movement."[89] According to Evans and Novak, even though Reagan's commitment to supply-side theory was "nearly" as strong as Jack Kemp's, the Californian was "vague" on details, causing Kemp and other supply-siders some concern.[90]

Edward Meese, one of Reagan's closest friends and political confidants, took issue with those implying Reagan was a passive figure with no economic policy who had had supply-side thinking foisted on him. Reagan's philosophy of limited government, his wide-ranging reading of economic literature, and his life experiences shaped him to be a "'supply-sider' long before the term was invented." Rather than converting Reagan, Kemp "was basically pushing on an open door."[91]

Martin Anderson agreed, calling the drama over the question of supply-side economics a "great myth" pushed by those who wanted to discredit supply-side economics by claiming there was a major rift between supply-siders and other economists advising Reagan.[92] Anderson knew that someone fed the media this false narrative, but he was unable to discover the person's identity: "Reporters will go to extreme lengths to protect the identity of their sources, including going to jail, even when they have been lied to. And that is why someone can betray or misrepresent the views of colleagues with virtual impunity."[93] Paul Craig Roberts also disputed the idea of Reagan falling into the hands of "Lafferite snake-oil salesmen" who supposedly filled a void when other Republicans kept their distance from "a right-wing contender for the Republican nomination."[94] Forgotten was the reality that a broad range of Republican politicians began to see supply-side economics as a winning political issue.

As a Hollywood star reaching the 94 percent tax bracket during the 1940s, Reagan understood the negative upshot of high taxes. Why take extra work for only 6 cents of each dollar? It may have been easier to do fewer films, but others were hurt when he worked less: "If I decided to do one less picture, that meant other people at the studio in lower tax brackets wouldn't work as much either; the effect filtered down, and there were fewer total jobs available." Reagan concluded that as the government took more for taxes, people lost the incentive to do extra work and businesses lost motivation to maximize profits and instead found tax shelters and loopholes that did little for economic growth. It was a lesson Reagan never forgot and his support of supply-side thinking made sense: "If, on the other hand, you reduce tax rates and allow people to spend and save more of what they earn, they'll be more industrious; they'll have more incentive to work hard, and money they earn will add fuel to the great economic machine that energizes our national progress." The result, he explained, was "more prosperity for all—and more revenue for government."[95] This was no somber economic message.

Before he became a candidate for the Republican nomination, Reagan delivered numerous radio addresses to the nation about taxes. In October 1977, he told listeners there would be more tax revenues and jobs if the government lowered the tax rates for businesses and individuals. The economists he cited included Arthur Laffer, and the politician he wanted the people to support was Jack Kemp. The following year he spoke of the good work of Kemp and William Steiger in attempting to give all Americans "a real tax break." Still, the White House pushed Democrats in Congress to block those promoting tax relief of the wrong kind.

Carter wanted to increase the progressivity of income taxes so that those making more than $20,000 paid more. But Reagan worried about the consequences of steepening the tax brackets for those who worked, earned, and made the country run. Without citing the Laffer curve in another radio message, he outlined the effect of high taxation on working people who faced less employment opportunities when business leaders withdrew capital from productive businesses.[96] By arguing for lower taxes as an antidote to inflation, Reagan was on track for reaching blue-collar Democrats dissatisfied with the economy and willing to hear a new message that sounded more appealing than the traditional austerity ideas of past Republicans.[97]

The health of the bond market was one of many markers of economic trouble. Having an inverse relationship with interest rates, bond prices fall when interest rates rise. In the final stage of the Carter government, there was gloom in the bond market. Setting time aside for a meeting with the press, one senior officer at a bond-trading house told his secretary to hold all telephone calls. He only lasted 30 minutes before bolting to the trading room: "I have to see how much money we've lost while we were talking. The way things are going, it could easily be $2 million or $3 million." In February 1980, the *Wall Street Journal* reported that the high interest rates led to "a staggering $400 billion in paper losses on bondholdings."[98] Double-digit inflation resulted in a stunning drop of bond prices in 1979 and 1980. Bondholders discovered that inflation and taxation wiped out the fixed rate of interest of the bond.[99] Books on the woeful economy were big sellers, notably Howard J. Ruff's *How to Prosper During the Coming Bad Years* (1979) and Douglas R. Casey's *Crisis Investing: Opportunities and Profits in the Coming Depression* (1980).[100]

The issue of high taxes reduced faith in Keynesian theory, and Henry C. Wallich, a governor of the Federal Reserve Board, predicted that within a decade "universities and government will be overrun with monetarists and neo-classical economists devoted to free markets and deeply skeptical of activist macroeconomic management." Many Keynesians bristled at the claim that their ideas were incorrect. Well-known Arthur Okun of the

Brookings Institution responded: "I'm nobody's vestigial remnant."[101] In the *New Republic*, both Okun and Lester Thurow argued that the answer to inflation was government intervention. Okun wanted incentive tax benefits for those who voluntarily held down wages and prices, and Thurow sought wage subsidies to employers who hired minorities because it was an "unequal structure of unemployment" that promoted stagflation.[102] In another *New Republic* article, John Kenneth Galbraith reminded readers that "God is a Keynesian Democrat"; he opposed tax cuts opting instead for the proper "use of the powers of the state."[103]

The problem Keynesian economists faced was the growing number of people who believed the economic theory had had one failure after another. The good Keynesian decades of the 1950s and 1960s were history. The focus was now on Carter's economic programs driven by Keynesian thinking. "We were good Keynesians once, but we had to change our minds," acknowledged Thomas Sargent of the University of Minnesota. Sargent witnessed rhetoric undermined by reality: "The raw fact that hits everybody is that the economy has just not behaved according to the best Keynesian models."[104]

By the late 1970s, tax reduction and deregulation became key Republican planks while liberals failed to achieve a consensus on how best the government could legislate an objective society.[105] Tom Bethel argued that it was long overdue for economic commentators and politicians to acknowledge the role rewards and incentives played in generating economic growth. Another advantage of supply-side theory for Republicans was that it allowed the party to move away from the balancing-budget focus of the past and the heavy political cost that often followed. The tools of the budget-balancers were cutting spending and raising taxes. Unless you had dozens of lawmakers like Senator Orrin Hatch, Bethel stated, one could forget the "pipe dream" of Congress cutting spending. Besides, raising taxes was not a winning strategy. High tax rates did not win votes, were not effective revenue collecting devices, and stifled commerce. On the other hand, the supply-side argument was politically feasible, Bethel said: "Politicians won't cut spending, but they don't mind cutting taxes—cutting tax *rates*, I should stress."[106]

The constant ace card for Reagan and supply-siders was the poor performance of Keynesianism. An increasing number of Americans faced money problems as both inflation and unemployment rose. What mattered for average citizens was whether the economy functioned—that is, whether one could make a living with a good job, have money to buy things, and keep the fruits of their labors.[107] Stagflation left them to wonder whether Carter knew what he was doing. Were conservatives correct when they described Democrats as foolish for thinking that employees stood to benefit if employers became poorer? America was on the brink of an economic revolution, but first the people needed to decide with their votes. Perhaps there could be a victory for a presidential candidate who embraced the Hayekian slogan: "We can get government off our backs, out of our pockets."[108]

Notes

1. Tom Bethel, "The Death of Keynes: Supply-Side Economics," *National Review*, December 31, 1980, 1560.
2. Ibid., 1560, 1562.
3. Friedrich Hayek, *New Studies in Philosophy, Politics, Economics and the History of Ideas* (London: Routledge & Kegan Paul, 1978), 23, 29.
4. Brian Domitrovic, *Econoclasts: The Rebels Who Sparked the Supply-Side Revolution and Restored American Prosperity* (Wilmington, DE: ISI Books, 2009), 192.
5. Walter H. Waggoner, "Ira Corn Jr., Executive and Bridge Devotee, is Dead," *New York Times*, April 29, 1982: http://www.nytimes.com/1982/04/29obituaries/ira-corn-jrexecutive (accessed May 17, 2016).
6. Ira G. Corn, Jr., "Personal and Economic Freedom: Yesterday, Today, and Tomorrow," *Imprimis*, 9, no. 1 (1980): 1–2.
7. Ibid., 2–4.
8. Kenneth W. Thompson, ed., *The Carter Presidency: Fourteen Intimate Perspectives of Jimmy Carter* (Lanham, MD: University of Press of America, Inc., 1990), 88.
9. Corn, Jr., "Personal and Economic Freedom," 4–5.
10. Walter E. Williams, "The Poor as First Victims of the Welfare State," *Imprimis*, 9, no. 7 (1980): 2–3, 6.
11. Walter E. Williams, *Up from the Projects: An Autobiography* (Stanford, CA: Hoover Institution Press, 2010).
12. For a defense of regulations, see John Tirman, "Business Wars on the Regulators, *Nation*, December 30, 1978, 730–733.
13. On Stigler's ideas, see Mark Skousen, *Vienna & Chicago: Friends or Foes?: A Tale of Two Schools of Free-Market Economics* (Washington, DC: Regnery Publishing, Inc., 2005), 208–211.
14. Michael Novak, *Writing from Left to Right: My Journey from Liberal to Conservative* (New York: Image, 2013), 178–179.

15. See "The Regulation Mess," *Newsweek*, June 12, 1978, 86–87.
16. W. Carl Biven, *Jimmy Carter's Economy: Policy in an Age of Limits* (Chapel Hill: The University of North Carolina Press, 2002), 219.
17. Lee Iacocca, *Iacocca: An Autobiography* (New York: Bantam Books, 1986), 134. Paul Ingrassia and Joseph B. White, *Comeback: The Fall and Rise of the American Automobile Industry* (New York: Simon & Schuster, 1994), 64–66, 68–69.
18. William Tucker, "The Wreck of the Auto Industry," *Harper's*, December 1977, 58.
19. Auto industry leaders often made this argument during the 1970s. See Henry Ford II, "The High Cost of Regulation," *Newsweek*, March 20, 1978, 15. Phillip Caldwell, "Getting Our Share," *Newsweek*, April 16, 1979, 16. Meg Jacobs, *Panic at the Pump: The Energy Crisis and the Transformation of American Politics in the 1970s* (New York: Hill and Wang, 2017), 66.
20. Tip O'Neill with William Novak, *Man of the House: The Life and Political Memoirs of Speaker Tip O'Neill* (New York: Random House, 1987), 324.
21. Jimmy Carter, *A Full Life: Reflections at Ninety* (New York: Simon & Schuster 2015), 152–153. "Bankruptcy of Bail-Out?," *Saturday Review*, January 1, 1980, 30–31.
22. Iacocca, *Iacocca*, 239.
23. Milton Friedman, "Chrysler: Are Jobs the Issue?," *Newsweek*, September 10, 1979, 66.
24. William E. Simon, *A Time for Truth* (New York: Reader's Digest Press, 1978), 99.
25. Steven F. Hayward, *The Age of Reagan: The Fall of the Old Liberal Order, 1964–1980* (New York: Three Rivers Press, 2001), 609.
26. Ken Auletta, *The Streets Were Paved with Gold* (New York: Random House, 1979), 317–318.
27. Charles Murray, *Losing Ground: American Social Policy, 1950–1980* (New York: Basic Books, 1984), 64–65.
28. Auletta, *The Streets Were Paved with Gold*, 91, 274, 278.
29. Stephen Woolcock, "The Economic Policies of the Carter Administration," in M. Glenn Abernathy et al., eds., *The Carter Years: The President and Policy Making* (New York: St. Martin's Press, 1984), 44.
30. Alan S. Blinder, *Economic Policy and the Great Stagflation* (New York: Academic Press, 1979), 217. Blinder explains that "the 1971–1974 controls program constituted a remarkable act of national self-flagellation. More remarkable still is the American public's eagerness to try for a repeat performance at any time" (132–133).
31. Quoted in Bruce J. Schulman, *The Seventies: The Great Shift in American Culture, Society, and Politics* (Boston: Da Capo Press, 2002), 134, 288n49.

32. Quoted in Burton I. Kaufmann and Scott Kaufman, *The Presidency of James Earl Carter Jr.*, Second Edition, Revised (Lawrence: University Press of Kansas, 2006), 168.
33. Quoted in Kaufman, *The Presidency of James Earl Carter Jr.*, 168–169.
34. Quoted in Biven, *Jimmy Carter's Economy*, 191.
35. Ibid., 192–193. Prior to 1983, the consumer index measured housing costs of new houses and current mortgage rates, thus hitting only a small portion of homeowners.
36. Quoted in Kaufman, *The Presidency of James Earl Carter Jr.*, 203.
37. Ibid., 204.
38. Henry J. Aaron, *Politics and the Professors: The Great Society in Perspective* (Washington, DC: The Brookings Institution, 1978), 146–147, 167.
39. Victor S. Navasky, *A Matter of Opinion* (New York: Farrar, Straus and Giroux, 2005), 198.
40. Bertram M. Gross, "Welcome to Stagflation," *Nation*, August 11–18, 1979, 99–100. Bertram M. Gross, "Anti-Inflation for Progressives," *Nation*, June 23, 1979, 750–755.
41. Robert Lekachman, "The Polls Say: Price Control," *Nation*, March 3, 1979, 236. Robert Lekachman, "Saving Chrysler," *Nation*, August 25–September 1, 1979, 133.
42. Lekachman reviewed Podhoretz's book *Breaking Ranks*. See "Books & the Arts," *Nation*, November 10, 1979, 469–470.
43. Lekachman reviewed Peter Steinfels, *The Neoconservatives: The Men Who are Changing America's Politics*. See "Books & the Arts," *Nation*, July 14–21, 1979, 53–54.
44. E. L. Doctorow, "The Rise of Ronald Reagan," *Nation*, July 19–26, 1979, 65, 82.
45. In January 1980, James Buchanan, future Nobel Prize-winner in economics, wrote of Sowell's book, *Knowledge and Decisions*: "You have written a great book, and I do not recall ever having said that to anyone." See Thomas Sowell, *A Man of Letters* (New York: Encounter Books, 2007), 161.
46. Ralph Nader, "Corporate Power in America," *Nation*, March 29, 1980, 367.
47. Robert Engler, "Letting Big Oil Do It," *Nation*, October 25, 1980, 412.
48. William K. Tabb, "Playing Productivity Politics, *Nation*, January 5–12, 1980, 18–19.
49. James Crotty, "From Keynes to Where We Are Now," *Nation*, October 14, 1978, 366–367, 369.
50. Barbara Koeppel, "A Tenant Revolt," *Nation*, May 26, 1979, 597–598, 600.
51. Ibid.," 597–598.
52. Ibid., 598–599.

53. "Taxquake Tremors," *Newsweek*, June 26, 1978, 23. Jude Wanniski, *The Way the World Works*, Fourth Edition (Washington, DC: Regnery Publishing, Inc., 1998), 347. John Ehrman, *The Eighties: America in the Age of Reagan* (New Haven: Yale University Press, 2005), 38.
54. Irving Howe, "The Right Menace," *New Republic*, September 9, 1978, 14, 18.
55. Anne Colamosca, "Capitalism and Housework," *New Republic*, March 29, 1980, 18–19.
56. "Liberals and Inflation," *New Republic*, January 20, 1979, 12–13.
57. "Energy Economics," *New Republic*, July 7 and 14, 1979, 5.
58. "Time for Controls?," *New Republic*, February 23, 1980, 5, 8.
59. "Books and Arts," *New Republic*, April 12, 1980, 31, 33.
60. Todd Gitlin, *The Sixties: Years of Hope, Days of Rage* (New York: Bantam Books, 1989), 432.
61. Ibid., 437.
62. One example is "Towards a 'New' Economics?" published in 1977 in the *Wall Street Journal*. See Irving Kristol, *The Neoconservative Persuasion: Selected Essays, 1942–2009*, ed. Gertrude Himmelfarb (New York: Basic Books, 2011), 151–154.
63. See Irving Kristol, "Memoirs of a Trotskyist," in Irving Kristol, *Neoconservatism: The Autobiography of an Idea* (Chicago: Elephant Paperbacks, 1999), 469–480. John Micklethwait and Adrian Woolridge, *The Right Nation: Conservative Power in America* (New York: Penguin Press, 2004), 76.
64. See Irving Kristol, "No Cheers for the Profit Motive" (1979) and "Ideology and Supply-Side Economics" (1981) in Kristol, *The Neoconservative Persuasion*, 155–170.
65. Novak, *Writing from Left to Right*, 175–176.
66. Quoted in Novak, *Writing from Left to Right*, 176.
67. Ibid., 177–178.
68. Ibid., 176, 178.
69. Hayward, *The Age of Reagan*, 526.
70. Milton Friedman, "The Kemp-Roth Free Lunch," *Newsweek*, August 7, 1978, 59.
71. Paul Craig Roberts, *The Supply-Side Revolution: An Insider's Account of Policymaking in Washington* (Cambridge, MA: Harvard University Press, 1984), 4.
72. Domitrovic, *Econoclasts*, 135, 138.
73. Roberts, *The Supply-Side Revolution*, 7–8, 10–11, 14–15, 20, 24.
74. See Thomas Sowell, *Intellectuals and Society*, Revised and Enlarged Edition (New York: Basic Books, 2011), 148–150.
75. Roberts, *The Supply-Side Revolution*, 27–30.

76. Ibid., 46.
77. Ibid., 46–47.
78. For brutal economic numbers, see Domitrovic, *Econoclasts*, 175–176.
79. Roberts, *The Supply-Side Revolution*, 34–35, 41.
80. Ibid., 37–38.
81. Ibid., 7, 38, 41.
82. Ibid., 61–63.
83. Bob Colacello, *Ronnie & Nancy: Their Path to the White House 1911 to 1980* (New York: Warner Books, 2004), 472.
84. Wanniski, *The Way the World Works*, 349.
85. Ibid., 350.
86. Domitrovic, *Econoclasts*, 207–208.
87. David A. Stockman, *The Triumph of Politics: The Inside Story of the Reagan Revolution* (New York: Avon, 1987), 53–54.
88. Lou Cannon, *President Reagan: The Role of a Lifetime* (New York: PublicAffairs, 2000), 218.
89. See Rowland Evans and Robert Novak, *The Reagan Revolution* (New York: E. P. Dutton, 1981), 2, 66, 69–71.
90. Ibid., 78–79, 85.
91. Edward Meese III, *Reagan: The Inside Story* (Washington, DC: Regnery Publishing, Inc., 1992), 121, 124.
92. Martin Anderson, *Revolution* (New York: Harcourt Brace Jovanovich, 1988), 157–158.
93. Anderson referred to the matter of a wedge that arose at the beginning of Reagan's presidency. See Anderson, *Revolution*, 265.
94. Roberts, *The Supply-Side Revolution*, 87–88.
95. Ronald Reagan, *Ronald Reagan: An American Life* (New York: Pocket Books, 1990), 231–232.
96. Reagan, *In His Own Hand*, 274–279. Also, see Domitrovic, *Econoclasts*, 205–206.
97. Lou Cannon, *Governor Reagan: His Rise to Power* (New York: PublicAffairs, 2003), 447.
98. Biven, *Jimmy Carter's Economy*, 6–7.
99. Domitrovic, *Econoclasts*, 177.
100. Ibid., 178.
101. "The New Economists," *Newsweek*, June 26, 1978, 59.
102. TRB, "Jimmy in Wonderland," *New Republic*, January 7, 1978, 2.
103. John Kenneth Galbraith, "The Trouble with Economists," *New Republic*, January 14, 1978, 21.
104. "The New Economists," 59.
105. David T. Courtwright, *No Right Turn: Conservative Politics in a Liberal America* (Cambridge, MA: Harvard University Press, 2010), 5, 15.

106. Bethel, "The Death of Keynes," 1565–1566.
107. Meese, *Reagan*, xviii.
108. Nicholas Wapshott, *Keynes Hayek: The Clash That Defined Modern Economics* (New York: W. W. Norton & Company, 2011), 261.

CHAPTER 10

The Presidential Campaign of 1980

In the early summer of 1980, President Carter was "quietly confident" about winning a second term. One Carter advantage was the media. As press secretary Jody Powell acknowledged, most reporters were liberal Democrats. For the Carter years, missing in media sessions was the level of bitterness and tension of the Richard Nixon and Gerald Ford era.[1] Even those journalists who were unenthusiastic about Carter often failed to grasp basic economics in their reports on the economy, so, consequently, Carter did not receive the criticism that conservative economists believed was necessary.[2] Meetings with Wall Street leaders reassured Carter that his economic policies were on the right track. It also pleased Carter that Ronald Reagan became the Republican nominee: "At the time, all my political team believed that he was the weakest candidate the Republicans could have chosen."

Carter looked forward to the challenge of the 69-year-old former actor and his "ridiculous theory" of enormous tax cuts and other proposals that "defied economic logic."[3] The *Nation* wrote of Reagan's "radicalism," and of Republicans "determined to commit political suicide" in choosing him as their leader.[4] James Reston of *The New York Times* was another who thought the choice of Reagan was a gift to Democrats: "Seldom in the history of American politics has a party out of power shown so much generosity to a President in so much difficulty."[5]

Carter's "managerial penchant for rationality and problem-solving" had not led to governing that was any better than his immediate predecessors.

E. R. Crouse, *America's Failing Economy and the Rise of Ronald Reagan*,
https://doi.org/10.1007/978-3-319-70545-3_10

His technocratic approach combined with unrealistic deadlines failed to inspire confidence. Politicians with less enthusiasm for economic management bided their time. The 1978 midterm elections ushered in a more conservative Senate body, and by 1980 conservatism became a powerful force in American politics.[6] Often intemperate with his language, economist William Simon described the modern Keynesian mindset as one that had experienced a drastic change since the FDR days: "Today our state is simply a redistributionist machine run amok…." He said that the "political curse of the era" is the "coercive egalitarianism" that sought "to level all people" in the hope of creating a better, humanitarian society.[7]

Even if this assessment of Keynesianism was unfair, the American people knew that Ronald Reagan's conservative version of smaller government offered a new path for them. As Carter declared at the Democratic Convention three months before the election: "This election is a stark choice between two men, two parties, two sharply different pictures of America and the world. But it is more than that. It is a choice between two futures."[8]

I

James M. Wall, editor of the *Christian Century*, declared Carter "a good president" with many accomplishments at a time when any leader regardless of party could not escape the reality of an inflationary economy.[9] A growing number of commentators were less effusive of Carter and linked the worsening economy with key decisions, including his choice for chairman of the Federal Reserve (the Fed).

Conservatives argued the Carter's policies of excessive government spending and stifling regulation had caused deep-seated distortions in the economy that would take significant time to reverse. The record of the Fed was not much better. Milton Friedman's consistent criticism was its propensity to react in the extreme, one way or another, increasing the quantity of money too quickly or too slowly.[10] When Carter entered the White House, Paul Volcker was the president of the number one bank in the Federal Reserve System—the New York Federal Bank. Many bankers spoke highly of him and he was a logical candidate to become the chairman of the Fed eventually.

Carter did not know Volcker existed, but others convinced him he was the best choice to replace William Miller. The six-foot seven-inch Volcker smoked stinking cigars and kept mostly to himself; he was not wealthy, having spent his career as a civil servant, and there were no tennis or golfing dates with other Washington movers and shakers.[11] When Volcker met with Carter, he said in effect, "now look, I'll tell you, in no uncertain terms, that I'm going to be independent. If you don't like that, then I am not your man."[12] Neither William Miller nor Charles Schultze were enthusiastic with Carter's choice.

Milton Friedman wrote that Volcker "has his job cut out for him if he is going to end the Fed's 65-year-old addiction to an unstable monetary policy." In the most recent years, the Fed only gave lip service to controlling the quantity of money; it instead attempted to control interest rates without success.[13] In a secret meeting on October 6, 1979, Volcker and the Federal Reserve Board decided to change the procedure on monetary policy. In the past, the Fed targeted interest rates or the quantity of money in order to exercise control of the economy. When it raised interest rates, the creation of new money slowed.[14] Volcker, however, identified a shortcoming—that is, even with the best staff "and all the computing power we could give them, there could never be any certainty about just the right level of the federal funds [interest] rate to keep the money supply on the right path and to regulate economic activity." A better approach, he argued, was for the Federal Reserve to focus on the quantity of money and thus give Americans a clearer message: "People don't need an advanced course in economics to understand that inflation has something to do with too much money; if we could get out the message that when we say we're going to control money, we mean we're going to deal with inflation, then we would have a chance of affecting ordinary people's behavior."[15] After Volcker's October 6 announcement of changes in the Fed's policy, Friedman was cautiously hopeful. "Could it be that the Federal Reserve truly changed course and had become more accountable to its promises of monetary restraint?"[16]

Friedman told his *Newsweek* readers that Carter faced difficult choices; if the Fed correctly restrained monetary growth, there would be less inflation but not in time for the November 1980 election. Moreover, monetary tightness would cause higher unemployment in the months before the election. With pressure from Democratic lawmakers to increase government spending and the realization that the inflation crisis would take years to fix, the temptation was great for Carter to adopt quick-fix answers.[17] According to Alan Greenspan, Volcker's rejection of any attempts to manage the economy with short-term interest rates and his decision to tighten the money supply "was arguably the most important change in economic policy in fifty years."[18]

Strict monetary policy was a courageous step to take. Certainly, the consequences for Carter were profound. What followed by mid-1980 were astronomical interest rates above 20 percent and high unemployment, nearly 9 percent. Symbols of the pain caused by high interest rates came when building contractors mailed "two-by-fours" to the Federal Reserve. To his credit, Carter supported the Fed's new direction, at least in the beginning.[19]

In the eyes of his progressive critics, Carter's incompetence seemed to deepen and observers, such as Arthur Schlesinger Jr., declared in February 1979 that Carter was wrong for the presidency.[20] A few weeks earlier, Schlesinger wrote: "While Democrats don't much like him, they don't dislike him enough, for the moment anyway, to start organizing against him."[21] Yet, months later there was a serious challenge by Senator Ted Kennedy. At the dedication of the nine-story John F. Kennedy Library in October 1979, Jackie Onassis appeared to recoil when Carter kissed her. It was too much for her: "He acts if the presidency carries with it the *droit du seigneur*."

The New England liberals were critical of Carter for sharing in his speech that Kennedy's assassination caused him to cry in a manner not since the death of his own father.[22] They were no happier with Carter's speech, delivered to the 7000 in attendance, focusing on the theme of limits: "After a decade of high inflation and growing oil imports, our economic cup no longer overflows. Because of inflation, fiscal restraint has become a matter of simple public duty. We can no longer rely on a rising economic tide to lift the boats of the poorest in our society."[23] Even though Carter was in no way adopting conservative economics, his talk of limits appeared to threaten the spending programs that the progressive wing of the Democratic Party demanded to care for the poor.

Unfortunately, 1980 began on a rough note for the administration when the Office of Management and Budget (OMB) forecast a deficit 50 percent greater than the original target for the fiscal year. With financial markets reacting dramatically, Carter decided in February to reopen the 1981 Fiscal Year budget already submitted to Congress. After several intense days of cutting, the administration produced a revised and balanced budget in March 1980.[24] Nonetheless, encouraging economic news was in short supply. The voluntary program of wage and price standards showed no signs of success and unemployment numbers were bad. From March to May, the rise in unemployment was 1.6 percent, the largest two-month rise in more than 45 years.[25] High inflation continued.

Milton Friedman saw Carter's anti-inflation program as a cosmetic measure "designed more to quiet public outcry than to resolve our serious economic problem." Missing was the political will to adopt tough but effective methods to solve the problems of inflation and declining production. The president proposed a cut of $14 billion in spending for fiscal 1981, but a more sensible cut would be in the range of $60–100 billion. Friedman was blunt: "Carter has not proposed a meaningful cut in spending. He has simply proposed a slightly smaller *increase*."[26]

Friedman cut through the misleading advertisements of the proposed balanced budget for 1981. "Have you no shame?," he asked Carter and members of Congress, knowing full well that the balance was only on paper and achieved by a "strenuous accounting sleight of hand." With the policies in place there was no real chance of a balanced budget: "The talk is of fiscal restraint, austerity and the like, but the paper balance was achieved only by providing for a massive increase in taxes combined with a continued increase in government spending (in real terms, after allowing for inflation)."[27]

II

There was no shortage of drama in the 12-month period leading up to the election as presidential hopefuls jockeyed for victory. The most serious Democratic threat for Carter was Kennedy who announced his candidacy on November 7, 1979, three days after Iranian militants took Americans hostage in Tehran. Journalist Elizabeth Drew characterized the competition between Carter and Kennedy as a virtual "civil war."[28] There was much press interest in Kennedy with an exceptionally large number of journalists signing on to accompany him on the campaign trial. Both Carter and Kennedy had liabilities, and no one could confidently predict the outcome, even though Carter's approval rating was only 19 percent in an early fall Associated Press-NBC Poll.

A few days before the 47-year-old Kennedy formally announced his candidacy, he performed badly in a CBS television interview special, talking in semicoherent half sentences and stumbling to explain why he wanted to be president. Kennedy's choice for campaign chairman was his brother-in-law Stephen Smith whose low and monotone voice was difficult to follow. Visiting an Iowa farm with his wife Joan in January 1980, Kennedy appeared uncomfortable with small talk about hog prices and feed, but it was important to get the necessary "visuals" for television.[29]

His economic position was that there were no problems government could not deal with: "What we need is not more government or less government but better government." Economic solutions came by drawing on the "best minds," whether it was national health insurance or any program for "those shunted aside in our society."[30]

In January, the Kennedy campaign was low in money and some expected an imminent collapse. After the Iowa caucus, the campaign stopped leasing a 727 airliner equipped with communications technology that only presidential nominees generally used.[31] Beginning his campaign with a large plane sent a message as did the switch to less-expensive commercial and charter flights.

Not able to control the economy, Carter turned to the task of defeating Kennedy, planning strategy as early as the fall of 1978 with the expectation of a Kennedy challenge. By early 1979, Carter had field organizations in Iowa, New Hampshire, and Florida, putting in place a renomination strategy that focused on Carter as presidential and Kennedy as one with questionable moral character. In February 1980, the day before the New Hampshire primary, Carter attempted to put a brave face on the issue of the troubling economy, informing journalists that his economic policies were fine.

The plan was to avoid making economic decisions that might upset Democrats who favored Kennedy. Once Kennedy dropped out of the race, the White House would focus on mending those angered by Carter's policies, notably labor unions and city mayors who wanted greater government action.[32] Kennedy's victories in New York and Connecticut on March 25 clarified the precariousness of the Carter campaign hoping to build unified support amid discouraging economic news. At least Carter did not have to worry about contender Jerry Brown, governor of California, who folded his campaign in April after poor results.

As the final primaries approached, Carter's lead in delegate numbers was large and Kennedy could not mathematically win the nomination. But the Kennedy campaign fought for a strong finish, hoping the Democratic Party would deny Carter the nomination. On the campaign trail, journalist Elizabeth Drew reported in June: "This is not a scrap between a couple of old pols who realize that it is in part a game; it appears that Kennedy and Carter really dislike each other and what each thinks the other stands for—and that this dislike has deepened as the campaign has gone on."

Kennedy told his audiences that it was time for the country to move "closer to the ideal of economic democracy and social progress and social justice."[33] In the *New Republic*, Arthur Schlesinger's explanation for "Carter's horrible failure in economic policy" was his denial of Democratic principles: "On such matters he is not a Democrat—at least in anything more recent than the Grover Cleveland sense of the word."[34]

On May 29, with the last primaries only days away, Carter campaigned in Columbus, Ohio, with a rally at a plaza outside Nationwide Insurance. Removing his jacket, showing his listeners that he was one of them, Carter promised that inflation would go down in the second half of 1980: "We have no fear of the future. In my judgment, the greatest nation on earth, with your help, will be greater in the years to come."[35] Carter did win enough delegates on June 3 to give him the nomination, but Kennedy won California, New Jersey, and Rhode Island, and he remained defiant: "Today Democrats from coast to coast were unwilling to concede the nomination to Jimmy Carter. And neither am I."[36] He felt victory was possible at the Democratic Convention if it was an "open convention."[37]

The Democratic National Convention took place in New York City in early August when Carter's popularity stood at 21 percent, the lowest for any president in the 45-year history of the Gallup Poll. Despite the poor numbers, most politically active unions supported Carter over Kennedy whose 1146 delegates fell short of Carter's delegate number by almost 1000.[38] At the convention, a plus for Carter was the speech by Vice President Mondale who believed in "strong, efficient, compassionate government" and the Democrats' "good, solid, progressive record."[39] Wrestling with despair the previous year, Mondale had considered resigning. One year later, he was ready to fight Reagan and prevent him from repealing the accomplishments of Roosevelt, Truman, Kennedy, Johnson, and two generations of Americans who built "a more just and hopeful society."[40]

The gap between what appealed to Democratic and Republican leaders widened significantly. Whereas the platform declared that the "Democratic Party has long stood for an active, responsive, and vigorous government," the Republican platform read: "[Democrats] believe that every time new problems arise beyond the power of men and women as individuals to solve, it becomes the duty of government to solve them, as if there were never an alternative…."[41] Having an apartment close to Madison Square Garden, conservative author William A. Rusher dropped in on the convention with his press credentials to hear Mondale ask 3000 delegates if they could "*afford*" four years of Ronald Reagan. Noting their passionate "NO-O-O," Rusher made the point that most of the delegates depended on government for their paychecks.[42] Carter pointed out in his convention speech that the Democrats represented economic security and justice, whereas Reagan promised despair and risk. It was unfortunate, however, that Carter committed a blooper when he praised "Hubert Horatio Hornblower – er, Humphrey!" and chased a reluctant Kennedy on the stage hoping for a photo-op of their arms linked in a victory clasp.

Despite what Kennedy and other progressives thought, Carter was no conservative. Two weeks earlier, he shot down a request by his economic advisors to adopt a tax reduction and moderate spending program to stimulate the economy.[43] Philip M. Klutznick, his second Secretary of Commerce, articulated Carter's faith in government: "The most important thing that we need is elimination of the notion that the government is our enemy."[44] Liberals were not out of the game. Even in California where Howard Jarvis had led the successful tax revolt two years earlier, California voters turned against Proposition 9, which called for a major reduction of state income tax rates.[45] If partly discredited, Keynesian ideas persisted as did reservations about conservative economic theory and Ronald Reagan who read books such as Freidrich Hayek's *The Road to Serfdom*.

III

When Reagan announced his candidacy for the Republican presidential nomination on November 13, 1979, he included an emotional pledge: "I cannot and will not stand by while inflation and joblessness destroy the dignity of our people."[46] Considered the front runner, Reagan had a target on his back as Howard Baker, Robert Dole, Philip Crane, John Anderson, John Connally, and George Bush looked for any mistakes from the Californian. Missing in late 1979 were signs of the "terrible divisiveness of 1976" that many believed was the reason the Republicans lost the White House. There was speculation among Republicans that Gerald Ford might take on another run, but he found life on the outside much more enjoyable.

Senate Minority Leader Howard Baker was a moderate Republican who some believed might save the party from the conservatives. Announcing his candidacy, Baker declared that "government by ideological reflex, left or right, will not bring the unity we need."[47] His task of overtaking Reagan seemed hopeless; Dole and Crane were also long shots. Anderson's strategy was to corner the market on Republican moderates; however, his public statement that he would choose Ted Kennedy rather than Reagan as president was a serious mistake.[48]

Although Texan John Connally raised the most money of any Republican candidate, his campaign showed little progress.[49] By March 1979, a Gallup Poll had Connally at 15 percent. Economist Arthur Burns viewed John Connally as a dishonest politician, who had "the prejudices of the business world but none of the convictions."[50] One difficulty was his heated rivalry with another Texan who actually was a Connecticut transplant.

Surprising many was the rise of George Bush who began planning a run for president in 1977 and spent more than 300 days on the political trail in 1979. When he declared his candidacy on May 1, 1979, he had visited every state of the union, only missing eight.[51] A tall man with a crooked smile, Bush at age 55 had an impressive resume—successful businessman, representative from Texas, director of the C.I.A., Ambassador to the United Nations, and Republican Party chairman, but in October 1979 he was nowhere in the polls. Campaign manager James Baker III wrote of Bush's early "microscopic" numbers: "When he later cracked the polls, the campaign staff made some celebratory lapel pins that trumpeted our number, 'three percent.'"[52]

Not a natural and compelling speaker, Bush attempted to generate enthusiasm with bold predictions to the Washington press: "I know I'm going to win this nomination. You just watch."[53] He believed it was good politics not to label himself a conservative, instead letting people come to their own conclusions.[54] Certainly, Bush's opposition to the Kemp-Roth plan of tax cuts set him apart from Reagan.[55]

But then again could a moderate defeat Reagan? Taking a page from Carter's 1976 campaign playbook, Bush spent far more time in Iowa than any other Republican running for president, and he scored a surprising win there giving him momentum for New Hampshire and greater media attention. His 31.6 percent over Reagan's 29.5 percent was a narrow victory, but it was a victory. Forgetting that Reagan had done no campaigning in Iowa but almost won, NBC's Tom Pettit asserted on the *Today Show* that "Ronald Reagan is dead."[56] It was a hectic episode as dozens of reporters clamored to secure a seat on the Bush campaign's old 19-passenger turboprop Fairchild.[57]

Edward Meese claimed that the "establishment news media and politicians" were thankful to see the Republican race "come back into the hands of more 'appropriate' contenders."[58] Gerald Ford believed Reagan was "too conservative" to win.[59] Reagan did not panic: "Let George have the Fortune

500," he declared at a January meeting. "I've got to be the candidate of the farmer, the small businessman, the independent, the entrepreneur."[60]

The emergence of Reagan as a genuine contender for president could only take place in a climate ripe for change. His choice of national headquarters was symbolic. Rather than Washington, DC, or New York City, he chose an ordinary office building within earshot of the Los Angeles International Airport. There the senior advisors discussed policy, including an economic direction distinct from Carter's. Key components were a reduction of federal tax rates, regulation, and spending; indexing of federal income tax brackets; and balancing the federal budget.[61] Among those who endorsed Reagan's economic approach was economist Arthur Burns, who had advised President Nixon. Martin Anderson gave Burns high marks as one of the few genuinely great men he knew. Dignified and a slow talker, he possessed "a brain with [the] power and speed of a large computer."[62]

As someone who said the federal government was too interventionist, Reagan embraced the conservative label, though with an optimistic twist: "I would like nothing better than to be the leader of this country, a leader whose idea was to remove the shackles and the roadblocks that hold down this great people by government and turn the genius of America once again to be the great country that we were."[63] Reagan's use of humor often softened hard economic truths. One quip exposed the problem with inflation: "I visited my doctor the other day and when he told me I was sound as a dollar I fainted dead away."[64] Noting the failure of price controls during the reign of Roman emperor Diocletian, Reagan declared: "I'm one of the few persons old enough to remember that."[65]

Reagan's messages were often uplifting, but no amount of positive words and excellent presentation by him could erase all the damage by campaign manager John Sears, the 39-year-old chain-smoking, "brooding Machiavelli with uncertain or dubious ideological conviction," who miscalculated by not allowing Reagan to campaign in Iowa.[66] After losing Iowa, Reagan fired Sears who had turned into a "megalomaniac."[67] According to Lyn Nofziger, Reagan did not like Sears and said: "He never looks me in the eye; he looks me in the tie."[68] Sears's political intrigue and his shutting out of key Reagan supporters of the past had earned him the nickname "Rasputin."[69]

The turning point of the primaries was Reagan's performance in New Hampshire where he rebuffed organizers who attempted to stop him from talking at a scheduled leaders' debate.[70] His subsequent victory in New

Hampshire—50 percent to Bush's 23—was good news for Democrats; they expected Reagan's eventual Republican nomination would ensure a presidential win for the Democratic Party. After Iowa, the Reagan campaign aired half-minute and one-minute television commercials with him presenting supply-side-type points. His economic message of growth rather than austerity was revolutionary: "If we reduce paperwork and unnecessary regulations, if we cut tax rates deeply and permanently, we'll be removing many of the barriers that hold everyone back." Not only would all Americans benefit, but poorer people would experience the largest gains. "If we put incentives back into society, everyone will gain," Reagan explained to his television audience. It was essential to move ahead without leaving "anyone" behind. Used heavily from February to May, the commercials were successful in giving Reagan a "spurt in the polls."[71]

By late May, Reagan's competitors were out of the race with Howard Baker, John Connally, and Robert Dole gone in early March; Philip Crane in April; and George Bush, the last competitor to quit, a victim to depleting finances. Attending the Western Deserts Gospel Sing at the San Bernardino County Fairgrounds in Victorville, California, Reagan told journalists the day after Bush's withdrawal that Carter was the only person he campaigned against. It was time to build Republican unity.[72] The hostility of some journalists likely encouraged Republicans to set aside their differences and support their new leader. In his *New Republic* article "Preferring Jimmy," John Osborne wrote: "Ronald Reagan is an ignoramus, a conscious and persistent falsifier of fact, a deceiver of the electorate and, one suspects, of himself."[73]

At the Republican Convention in July, held at the Joe Louis Arena in Detroit, the program included a wide range of well-known people supporting Reagan, including Hollywood stars Jimmy Stewart and Michael Landon, NASCAR legend Richard Petty, Olympic skater Dorothy Hamill, and pop stars Donny and Marie Osmond. In charge of press relations for Reagan, Lyn Nofziger was a bald, "wry, rumpled man" with a constant five-o'clock shadow, "an ideological conservative who made special effort to be helpful to the press."[74] The best drama for the media cycle was Reagan's choice for vice presidential nominee.

Initially, Reagan was unhappy with Bush and viewed him as a wimp and one apparently tone deaf to the call of supply-side economics (something Bush called "voodoo economics"). Stronger candidates included Senator Paul Laxalt, a Reagan friend and ardent supporter; Howard Baker; and Jack Kemp. Since Representative William Steiger's shocking death in

December 1978, Kemp had become the leading Republican in the House fighting for lower tax rates.[75] The most intriguing name on the list was Gerald Ford. The Ford option derailed when a Walter Cronkite interview of him gave the impression that Ford sought a "co-presidency" role.[76] When Reagan heard what he said, he asked Michael Deaver to go to Ford's suite and request a meeting. After talking his way past the Secret Service, Deaver faced Henry Kissinger who told him he could not see Ford because he was in bed. Deaver responded: "Somebody is going to have to get him, or Ronald Reagan is going to go on television and pull the plug on this."

Ford met with Reagan and their conversation included laughter and jokes; both agreed that Ford as the vice president nominee would not work and was not the right thing to do. Within one hour, Reagan announced his pick was George Bush, who had two valued characteristics: he was a gentleman and team player. It would take many months before the Bush camp discovered whether it had been right or wrong about "voodoo economics."[77] Almost lost in the drama of Reagan's choice for running mate was a very conservative GOP platform that stressed economic opportunity in contrast to the government entitlement of Democrats.[78] Certainly, Reagan's acceptance speech had much supply-side flavor. Supply-siders were content except for those who wanted Reagan's speech to champion a gold standard rather than using the tamer language of a "monetary standard."[79]

One more addition to the team was James Baker III, a former Marine and successful Texas lawyer who was campaign chairman for Gerald Ford's run in 1976 and George Bush's run in 1980. For Baker, the "sense of adventure and high challenge" of political life was a welcome change from the daily practice of law. He was no ideological economic conservative. While working in the Ford administration, he persuaded Richard Cheney to choose the politics of protectionism over policy for a Ford speech addressing the American textile industry and Chinese competition. When Baker met Henry Kissinger for the first time, Kissinger, who had argued for the free-trade position on the textiles issue, remarked "so you're Textile Baker."[80]

Many in the Reagan camp were suspicious of Baker; Campaign aide Max Hugel called him "the biggest phony who ever lived."[81] William Casey, an old-looking 67, was already Reagan's campaign chairman and Baker took the title "senior advisor." Baker described Casey as a "chronic mumbler" whose clothes were either rumpled or disheveled.[82] Later, the short and profane Stuart Spencer, "almost a cartoonist's dream of a political operative," joined the campaign to provide tactical expertise.[83]

If the campaign was to press economic issues, it needed a balance of Reagan's economic instincts and competent economic advisors. Reagan's college degree in economics, his study of economic theory throughout the 1970s, and an excellent distillation of economics in his popular articles and radio broadcasts all gave him an economic foundation that surpassed most politicians. Reagan read widely, drawing on authors, such as Freidrich Hayek, which explains his 1976 point that "Fascism was really the basis for the New Deal."[84] It was wrong for anyone to assume Reagan was talking about storm troopers and dictators. Rather, he was repeating Hayek's analysis in *The Road to Serfdom* that FDR's National Planning Board "devoted a good deal of attention to the example of planning" found in Italy and other dictatorships.[85]

To guide his economic statements, Reagan had a formidable economic advisory group ranging from monetarist Milton Friedman to supply-sider Jack Kemp. Other well-known advisors included Alan Greenspan; Paul McCracken, former chairman of the Council of Economic Advisors; Charles E. Walker, former deputy secretary of the treasury; Murray L. Weidenbaum, world-class scholar on regulation; James T. Lynn, former director of the OMB; William E. Simon, former Treasury secretary; and Walter Wriston, chairman of Citibank/Citicorp. In total, Reagan had 74 advisors on economic policy alone for the 1980 presidential campaign.[86]

When journalists questioned Reagan's belief that his proposed tax cuts would not raise the deficit, he pointed to the Kennedy cuts of the 1960s and the analysis of Jack Kemp and William Roth. Reagan set himself apart from the "'Eisenhower-Nixon-Ford-Bush' Republican economic orthodoxy" by presenting economics points that made sense to his listeners. His audiences found it stunning when informed that General Motors required 24,800 of its employees to work full time to fill out government regulatory paperwork; government regulations were out of control.[87] Stating that no energy crisis existed "from the days of the horseless carriage until 1971," Reagan declared the government's intervention in the oil industry a disaster. There was no energy problem: "Two-thirds of the oil is still down there ... but government won't let them charge the price."[88]

Reagan received big cheers from a large crowd at a shopping mall when he gave his assessment of government control: "We have a group of elitists in Washington who have no more faith and trust in the American people, and they think they must control our destiny, make all the rules, tell us how to run our lives and our businesses." A better approach, Reagan argued, was "to have a President who will take the government off the people's backs and turn the great genius of the American people loose once again."[89] Those aware of the writings of the Austrian School may have detected the Hayekian flavor of Reagan's words.

Speaking at a Teamsters luncheon in Columbus, Ohio, Reagan claimed that American workers had "been shattered by a new Depression—the Carter Depression." As bad as the economy was, it was not technically a depression and the media questioned Reagan's choice of words. John Chancellor of NBC complained: "Depression is the wrong term." Was this another case when Reagan confused his facts? Actually, he inserted the word in his speech deliberately and the controversy that ensued allowed him to score political points: "As far as I am concerned, the line between recession and depression cannot be measured in the strict economists' terms but must be measured in human terms."

Workers experiencing "the worst misery" since the Great Depression could be excused for referring to the economy in 1980 as a depression.[90] Always good for a cheer from audiences was Reagan's articulation of this point: "A recession is when your neighbor loses his job. A depression is when you lose your job. And recovery is when Jimmy Carter loses his!"[91] Slow to receive the approval of big business executives, Reagan made a stronger connection with working people with "calluses on their hands" than Fortune 500 companies.[92]

It was not always smooth sailing for Reagan's economic message, especially when the media looked for any sign of weakness to exploit with the candidate they saw as insensitive to the poor. Reagan ran into trouble in early August when he gave a speech in a South Bronx community. While he addressed the failure of Carter's promises to improve the lives of those living in poor communities, a large crowd of locals gathered and began shouting and heckling. Reagan was vulnerable to the charge he was "anti-poor, anti-black and anti-disadvantaged." Fortunately for Reagan, the evening television news of the encounter captured his "command presence" of controlling the angry black crowd. According to journalist Lou Cannon, he won the respect of those who shouted at him.[93]

On September 8, 1980, Martin Anderson, Reagan's chief domestic policy advisor, received an angry phone call 35,000 feet in the air aboard a United 727 airliner going from Philadelphia to Chicago. An electronic marvel, the ground-to-air communication link allowed James Baker, phoning from the national headquarters in Los Angeles, to warn of a potential media disaster. The problem began months earlier as Reagan's economic team struggled to articulate a grand economic strategy that would stand up to intense scrutiny from the media expecting specific details. Could Reagan make a good argument for a tax cut and an increase in defense spending without running large deficits? Using the well-respected Congressional Budget Office (CBO) economic forecast figures made sense, but Reagan's advisors had to deal with CBO's predicted deficit of $44 billion for 1981.

The economic speech Reagan was to give in Chicago the following day called for a large deficit. He was to pitch a plan to American voters that called for a deficit of $50 billion a year.[94] The phone connection was a little scratchy, but Anderson understood Baker's message: "We just can't go with these $50 billion deficits. There must be something you can do."[95] Anderson faced other problems—that is, most of the other economic advisors would not be in Chicago, and there was less than one day to adjust Reagan's speech.[96]

Soon after landing in Chicago, Anderson contacted Robert Boyd, the Senate Budget Committee's top expert, to inquire about other economic forecasts. Much to Anderson's delight, Boyd's latest numbers indicated a major increase in federal tax receipts. Reagan's economic advisors, staying at the old, prominent Palmer House hotel, had to work fast. Although the speech was not until the next morning, Anderson and his team only had a few hours before the 8:00 p.m. scheduled briefing of the national press corps. Allan Greenspan, who over the years had earned the respect of many journalists, cautioned Anderson about giving numbers at the press briefing.

Nevertheless, Anderson forged ahead with calculations based on the Senate's Budget Committee numbers. His new estimates called for a $27 billion deficit for year one, a balanced budget by year three, followed by large surpluses. He used one of the typewriters located in the press room and pounded out Reagan's economic program on a single sheet of paper that a secretary copied for the press along with a fact sheet.[97] At the press briefing Anderson began with a joke: "[W]e had originally planned to do this briefing using blue smoke and mirrors [in reference to political opponent John Anderson's claims that the Reagan numbers did not add up], but we couldn't find any smoke or mirrors and decided to use facts instead."[98]

Greenspan and William Van Cleave, both brilliant Reagan advisors, answered tough questions accurately and clearly. One huge hurdle was behind the Reagan team. The following morning Reagan delivered what some believed was "the most crucial speech of his campaign."[99] With a commitment to tax cuts and balancing the budget, Reagan offered a good mix of supply-side economics and traditional Republican concern for the Democrats' zealous government spending.[100]

IV

In September, the inflation rate was 13 percent and the unemployment rate was eight percent, putting the misery index at a woeful 21. Carter faced internal divisions and much work was needed to unite the Democratic Party, which had been battered by Senator Kennedy's challenge for the nomination. Carter had a strained relationship with some labor leaders, but by Labor Day organized labor support was stronger than was the case four years earlier.[101] Reagan had a seven percent advantage in the polls, a margin Carter believed he could close as the electorate learned the differences between Carter's sensible restrained budget and the uncertainty of Reagan's ideas. At a town hall meeting in September, Carter stated: "Reagan is different from me in almost every basic element of commitment and experience and promise to the American people."[102] Because he most likely could not win on his economic record, he had to make Reagan the issue.[103]

The difficulty for Carter was greater media attention on ordinary Americans unhappy with his policies. At a campaign meeting in Flint, Michigan, trucker Clarence Murphy asked Carter why laid-off autoworkers received generous governments benefits while he received nothing. It was "too costly" to provide benefits for Murphy and other truckers who hauled cars for the auto industry, Carter responded. Laid-off Kenneth McMillan, whose employer supplied the sheet metal for the auto industry, was likewise angry with Carter's inaction. McMillan's wife stated: "The denial of benefits stinks. As far as I'm concerned, we have just as much right to the money as the autoworkers. After all, the cars get made out of steel, don't they?"[104]

If Carter sought to argue on the campaign trail that he was fiscally prudent, observers, such as Milton Friedman, did not buy it. His policies spelled higher government spending, higher taxes, "still more and more intrusive government regulation and intervention, still more 'fine-tuning.'" The reelection of Carter would foretell a willingness to keep Keynesianism that denied more freedom and prosperity. Friedman also was critical of Reagan's campaign rhetoric of supporting the Chrysler bailout and approving some restrictions on imports, but at least Reagan's record demonstrated "his long-held philosophical commitment" to smaller government and individual freedom.[105]

When asked in September 1980 about the decline in American productivity, Friedman responded that the sharp drop in productivity accompanying the recession of recent months was not serious. Rather, the bigger problem was the gradual economic decline since 1976 that Carter's policies could not solve. The culprits remained excessive taxes, regulations, and price control measures. America needed "a freer market and more competition, not a pale imitation of Mussolini's corporate state." Bad government policy had been experienced during the last four years, but Friedman was hopeful: "A strong dose of good government is all that it will take to produce healthy and vigorous economic growth."[106]

The other factor in the election campaign was John Anderson, a 10-term member of the House of Representatives, who withdrew from the Republican contest in late April. Deciding to run as an Independent, he chose Democrat Patrick J. Lucey as his running mate. A 58-year-old, slight man who smoked cigarillos and preferred Scotch, Anderson was a liberal Republican known for his independent style in Congress.[107] Journalists began to sing his praises and a list of influential people were enthusiastic, including Paul Newman, Norman Lear, Gloria Steinem, and Kurt Vonnegut.[108]

Anderson supported a government bailout of the auto industry and had reservations about tax cuts. A *Washington Post* poll in mid-September had him at 13 percent, about one-third of where both Carter and Reagan stood. When Carter boycotted a scheduled debate on September 21, Anderson and Reagan met at the Baltimore Convention Center, each gaining valuable free airtime.[109]

By October, time was running out for Carter to provide evidence that his economic policies could turn the economy around. To a Pennsylvania audience, he disclosed his disappointment with the Federal Reserve's attack on inflation: "My own judgment is that the strictly monetary approach to the Fed's decision on the discount rate and other banking policies is ill-advised.... I think that the Fed ought to look at the adverse consequences of increased interest rates on the general economy as a major factor in making their own judgments."[110] It was difficult for him to escape a Keynesian mindset.

Still, there was hope because Carter's polls had him almost even with Reagan three weeks before the election.[111] There were many undecided voters and his team anticipated a possible swing of support when more

Americans considered the consequences of a Reagan presidency. John Anderson polled near 15 percent, which was enough to affect the outcome even without winning a single state. Because the Carter camp expected it would lose more voters to Anderson than Reagan would, it told Democratic organizers to attack him directly.[112] Influential progressive leaders expressed more doubt than hope for Anderson, but they were glad to see him campaign.

The conclusion of the *Nation's* Symposium on the Anderson Candidacy was: "Let Anderson run. Let a thousand flowers bloom. The more disruption the man can cause, the better. To the degree that America is divided, disrupted and disunified, the world is that much safer."[113] Although this was too radical for the mainstream media, most journalists were upset with Carter for not taking his large majorities in Congress and delivering a more activist government.[114]

One important task for the Reagan campaign was to show Americans that the Democrats' portrayal of Reagan as dangerous was off base. Initially wary, the Reagan campaign agreed to debate Carter on television, hoping to build on what it believed was a slight lead over him. There was growing confidence because even though some polls had Carter in the lead, what mattered more was the Electoral College vote, which looked promising for Reagan. William Casey expected that the publication of the Consumer Price Index (CPI) in late October would show a rise in inflation: "Between that and the debate, we'll ride the economic issue all the way home."[115] When the CPI numbers arrived, the price of food was up and the annual rate for all goods neared a 13 percent rise, causing "huge, unlegislated tax increases for most individual taxpayers."[116] Carter wisely avoided talking about the economy for months, whereas Reagan repeatedly drew attention to Carter's inability to answer "for the economic misery he's caused."[117]

On the evening of October 28, alone with James Baker, Reagan asked for privacy as he prayed to God minutes before taking the stage to debate Carter.[118] In the televised debate watched by approximately 100 million, Reagan drove hard on the economy, lamenting that "this nation has been portrayed for too long a time to the people as being energy-poor when it is energy-rich," that the reason behind inflation was that "the government is living too well." Building on this line of attack, Reagan asked Americans to consider their circumstances under the Carter administration: "Are you better off than you were four years ago? Is it easier for you to go and buy things in the stores than it was four years ago? Is there more or less unemployment in the country than there was four years ago?"[119] After the successful debate, the Reagan camp expected him to win as many as 320 electoral votes, 50 more than the number predicted by an NBC survey.[120]

The day after the debate, Carter wrote in his diary: "... I had a list of things [to say], which we believe ... will become preeminent in the public's mind as they approach the point a week from now of actually going to the polls to decide on a leader for the nation for the next four years. Both sides felt good after the debate."[121] Carter's poll had him about even with Reagan on the weekend before the election. Martin Anderson worried since the polls did not have Reagan in the lead: "I changed my view a day or two before the election, when Wirthlin got on the plane and, instead of looking concerned and harried, he looked relaxed and happy."[122] Indeed, by Monday evening the numbers looked bad for Carter and Stuart Eizenstat burst into tears as Pat Caddell's poll data indicated the prospects for victory were gone.[123] In preparing to tell the president the bad news, Jody Powell poured himself a stiff drink and waited until Carter had a double martini before he gave him the polling numbers.[124]

In the face of gloomy economic news, there was little the Carter campaign could do. At Reagan's last campaign event, he asked the San Diego crowd: "Are you more confident that our economy will create productive work for our society or are you less confident? Do you feel you can keep the job you have or gain a job if you don't have one?" Citing actual numbers, Reagan scored good points: "Are you satisfied that inflation at the highest rates in thirty-three years were the best that we could do? Are interest rates at 14½ percent something you are prepared to live with?"[125] There were many other issues for voters to consider, but the economy was the number one concern for countless Americans.

On the rainy and cold Election Day in Washington, Caddell shared with political journalist Elizabeth Drew that it was over for Carter as Reagan was ahead as much as 10 points. As the polls closed, the results came quickly. Drew wrote: "This isn't an election, it's an earthquake. Carter is being handed a staggering defeat.... The networks are telling us tonight that according to their exit polls the results stem largely from dissatisfaction with the economy, especially inflation, and there's probably a great deal to that."[126] In its coverage, *Time* magazine offered two photographs side by side—one of Ronald and Nancy smiling, the other of Jimmy and Rosalynn looking shell-shocked: "Yes, landslide—stunning, startling, astounding, beyond the wildest dreams and nightmares of the contending camps, beyond the furthest ken of the armies of pollsters, pundits, and political professionals."[127]

With exit polls showing that the economy was the most important issue for most voters, the final popular vote was Reagan 51.6 percent, Carter 41.7 percent, and Anderson 6.7 percent. The electoral vote total was 489 for Reagan and a devastating 49 for Carter. In addition, the Republicans gained 12 Senate seats—winning their first majority since 1950—and 33 House seats. The last time a Democratic president lost his bid for another term was in 1888 when President Grover Cleveland lost to Benjamin Harrison.

Even though White House staffer Stuart Eizenstat expected the loss, the finality of it was brutal: "[I]t was like preparing yourself for the death of a family member: when it comes, it's still devastating." Hamilton Jordan called Carter "the world's worst loser." Worried that people might think he was a poor loser sulking in the White House, Carter gave the "earliest concession by a presidential candidate since 1904." The response of many Democratic leaders was anger because the early concession before polls closed on the West Coast jeopardized Democratic politicians in the west. Tip O'Neill's phone message to Carter's congressional liaison captured the frustration of those never satisfied with his inner circle: "You guys came in like a bunch of jerks, and I see you're going out the same way."[128] Joe Rauth likewise pulled no punches: "If I hated Jimmy Carter yesterday, I hate him twice as much today when I see what he has done to the Democratic party." It was Arthur Schlesinger's opinion that the "long national nightmare" was over but at the price of many fine Democrats—George McGovern and other prominent liberals—who lost their elections.[129]

Schlesinger struggled to understand the loss to Republicans: "No intellectual phenomenon has been more surprising in recent years than the revival in the United States of conservatism as a respectable social philosophy." William Rusher argued that Schlesinger and others dismissive of conservative gains were "victims of their own excellent propaganda." Liberal commentator Max Lerner explained that conservatives "gave plenty of notice, if the liberals had kept their eyes and ears open."[130] They should have known of the depth of discontent of Americans toward a variety of economic policies. Regular Americans appeared to be more in tune with an economy they believed was in shambles; they wondered whether they would keep their jobs and be able to afford what they needed to buy.[131]

Others who assessed Carter's presidency pointed to his "misfortune to be president during a deeply troubled time in our history."[132] Nonetheless, the American people did not want excuses; they wanted someone who confronted hard times and made changes for the better. *Time* reported that inflation, affecting every paycheck and pocketbook, was the number one concern for voters, and unemployment the prime worry of countless others. Many Democratic voters went to Reagan and the example of New Yorker Joe Augeri is revealing: "I voted for Reagan today because I think the country needs a change, a new direction, a new management team running the Government. It was the inflation rate going up again and the country falling into a worse recession that changed my mind about Carter two or three weeks ago."[133] As bad as unemployment, inflation, and interest rates were, Reagan saw something worse: "[I]t seemed to me that America was losing faith in itself. Almost every day, the president was sending a message to the American people that America had passed its prime, that Americans were going to have to get used to less in the future, that we should not have the same hopes for the future that we once did, and that we had only ourselves to blame for it."[134]

The failure of Keynesian thinking to solve inflation was a shock for many Democrats, but Carter's economic advisors did not blame their Keynesian policies. Eizenstat claimed their biggest mistake was misjudging inflation and responding with a policy that overstimulated the economy. He also stated that economic advisors "pushed" Carter to embrace a Keynesian approach. Schultze acknowledged their "excessive demand stimulus," but this mistake was not significant. In essence, what hurt the Carter administration was unfortunate timing.[135] Lyle Gramley was one Carter advisors who took a more critical view of what government could achieve with government planning: "If there was any very large mistake that we made in terms of belief in accepted wisdom and what it implied about the way things were going, it was that one could measure the full employment–unemployment rate with sufficient precision so that one could feel fairly sure that, if the unemployment rate were at 5½ percent or above, the inflation surely ought to rewind."[136]

The postelection analysis covered much ground, but often missing was any appreciation of the influence of Reagan's ideas. The media was slow to recognize that most voters found his ideals appealing. In the month before the election, conservative thinker James Q. Wilson challenged the standard media narrative: "[T]he Reagan candidacy is a candidacy based on *issues*, issues which the candidate has developed over the better part of two decades and which now, taken as a whole, command the assent of a very large proportion of the American people."[137]

Yes, Carter was weak and Reagan was a good communicator, but that was only part of the story. Conservative theory consisting of monetarism, supply-side theory, and Austrian School ideas presented by Friedrich Hayek in the 1940s offered compelling analysis on the impact of high taxes on investments, the erosion of worker productivity, and the punitive effects of regulations. If conservatives won most intellectual debates on the economy, more important was the realization of ordinary Americans that the economic policies of the past had not worked.

As Reagan wrote: "After a half century that had given them the New Deal and the 'Great Society' and produced a government that took an average of forty-five percent of the national wealth, people were just fed up."[138] Without using economic jargon, Reagan delivered a conservative economic message in a commonsense way. When Democratic leaders argued that Reagan was successful with voters because he "appealed to their greedy instincts," they revealed a degree of blindness to the economic struggles of many ordinary Americans.[139] Of course, few Keynesian Democrats wanted to concede that their ideas were inferior to what Reagan offered. Paul Samuelson admitted much of Keynesianism collapsed, but this was because of stagflation rather than the merit of free-market theories.[140] On December 17, Carter wrote that the economy was "going surprisingly well. Unemployment, inflation, retail sales, gross national product, value of the dollar, trade balance—all these things, even housing starts—are holding up very nicely."[141]

The twentieth century witnessed, in Milton Friedman words, "a major increase in the role of the state and a major decline in the freedom of individuals to conduct their own affairs." Central planning at its worst was the triumph of communism in the Soviet Union and China that brought tyranny and misery. India and most Third World countries also languished economically under some form of central planning. In the West, the welfare state grew first in Britain followed by the United States with the introduction of FDR's New Deal. Although the British and American social programs were noble, they came at a price of "crushing" taxation, inflation, and weak growth. Friedman said all this at the time of Reagan's defeat of Carter.[142] Reagan's victory was the political outcome of a conservative "movement building for many years in the United States and, to a less[er] extent, throughout the world."[143]

When Jimmy Carter entered the White House, many Americans appreciated his apparent technocratic competency. Historian Robert Collins wrote that "Americans had at last found an omniscient problem-solver, someone who seemed to know something about everything."[144] With many Keynesians guiding his presidency, Carter's failure was an economic failure that was a major blow to the psyche of Democrats who expected the experts to revive Keynesianism and propel America to better economic fortunes. Keynesianism stumbled in academic circles, but its fall as an economic policy was especially brutal, something ordinary Americans experienced day to day as they adapted to employment setbacks and paid higher taxes.

If economist Thomas Sowell's analysis is correct, there are two major philosophies on the role of government. A progressive vision has faith in sweeping government schemes devised by men and women of special talents. On the other hand, conservatives are wary of the promises and ability of the government to "legislate bliss," arguing that one only needed to study the record of Keynesianism since the 1960s. Beginning with the work of Austrian School economists, such as Friedrich Hayek, followed by the Chicago School analysis of Milton Friedman and the rise of supply-siders, free-market economists and politicians delivered a serious blow to Keynesianism.[145]

In 1980, President Carter seemed pessimistic, a sharp contrast to the optimism of Reagan and others who championed economic growth. Carter's missteps, the revival of conservatism, and the dissemination of free-market ideas opened the door for the most conservative Republican to reach the White House since the 1920s. One of Reagan's campaign slogans was "Let's make America Great Again." Voters knew that America ailed and most welcomed Reagan's economic medicine.

Notes

1. Jody Powell, *The Other Side of the Story* (New York: William Morrow and Company, Inc., 1984), 38. Robert Locander, "Carter and the Press: The First Two Years," *Presidential Studies Quarterly* 10, no. 1, Politicizing the Presidency, 1789–1980 (Winter 1980): 110.
2. William Simon wrote: "Certainly the average citizen who received his briefings about the economy from the general press, particularly from the networks, scarcely knew what was happening." See William E. Simon, *A Time for Truth* (New York: Reader's Digest Press, 1978), 88.
3. Jimmy Carter, *Keeping Faith: Memoirs of a President* (Fayetteville: University of Arkansas Press, 1995), 539–540, 542. Ann Mari May argues that except for his last year, the economic record of the Carter years was not as bad as most Americans believed. See Ann Mari May, "Economic Myth and Economic Reality: A Reexamination of the Carter Years," in *The Presidency and Domestic Policies of Jimmy Carter*, eds.

Herbert D. Rosenbaum and Alexej Ugrinsky (Westport, CT: Greenwood Press, 1994): 649–666.
4. "The Anderson Candidacy," *Nation*, May 17, 1980, 586. Richard J. Walton, "Now Is the Time….," *Nation*, May 10, 1980, 556.
5. Quoted in Edward Meese III, *Reagan: The Inside Story* (Washington, DC: Regnery History, 1992), 40.
6. Dilys M. Hill and Phil Williams, "Introduction," in *The Carter Years: The President and Policy Making*, eds. M. Glenn Abernathy et al. (New York: St. Martin's Press, 1984), 1–3.
7. William E. Simon, "Inflation: Made and Manufactured in Washington, D.C.," *Imprimis*, 8, no. 7 (1979): 3.
8. Quoted in Elizabeth Drew, *Portrait of an Election: The 1980 Presidential Campaign* (New York: Simon & Schuster, 1981), 259.
9. "'God Help Me, I love It,'" *Christian Century*, November 26, 1980, 1151.
10. Milton Friedman, "The Fed: At It Again," *Newsweek*, February 19, 1979, 65.
11. Alan Greenspan, *The Age of Turbulence: Adventures in a New World* (New York: Penguin Press, 2007), 84. One colleague wrote: "Many of us would give him better cigars simply so we could stand to work with him." See "Big Man for a Big Job," *Newsweek*, August 6, 1979, 59.
12. Quoted in W. Carl Biven, *Jimmy Carter's Economy: Policy in an Age of Limits* (Chapel Hill: The University of North Carolina Press, 2002), 238.
13. Milton Friedman, "Volcker's Inheritance," *Newsweek*, August 20, 1979, 65.
14. Biven, *Jimmy Carter's Economy*, 240.
15. Quoted in Biven, *Jimmy Carter's Economy*, 241.
16. Milton Friedman, "Has the Fed Changed Course?" *Newsweek*, October 22, 1979, 39.
17. Milton Friedman, "President Carter's Trilemma," *Newsweek*, October 1, 1979, 54.
18. Greenspan, *The Age of Turbulence*, 85.
19. Ibid., 85–86.
20. Arthur M. Schlesinger Jr., *Journals 1952–2000*, eds. Andrew Schlesinger and Stephen Schlesinger (New York: Penguin Press, 2007), 461.
21. Ibid., 453.
22. Ibid., 478.
23. Quoted in Biven, *Jimmy Carter's Economy*, 260.
24. Ibid., 204.
25. Milton Friedman, "Monetary Overkill," *Newsweek*, July 14, 1980, 62.
26. Milton Friedman, "Carter's Anti-Inflation Plan," *Newsweek*, March 24, 1980, 33.

27. Milton Friedman, "Balance on Paper," *Newsweek*, June 23, 1980, 68.
28. Drew, *Portrait of an Election*, 13.
29. Ibid., 42, 52.
30. Ibid., 56, 62–63.
31. Ibid., 49, 65.
32. Ibid., 123–124, 137–139.
33. Ibid., 164, 166.
34. Arthur Schlesinger Jr., "The Great Carter Mystery," *New Republic*, April 12, 1980, 21.
35. Quoted in Drew, *Portrait of an Election*, 183.
36. Ibid., 187.
37. Steven F. Hayward, *The Age of Reagan: The Fall of the Old Liberal Order, 1964–1980* (New York: Three Rivers Press, 2001), 659.
38. Drew, *Portrait of an Election*, 222, 224, 254.
39. Ibid., 257.
40. Peter G. Bourne, *Jimmy Carter: A Comprehensive Biography from Plains to Postpresidency* (New York: A Lisa Drew Book/Scribner, 1997), 443, 462.
41. Quoted in Hayward, *The Age of Reagan*, 673.
42. William A. Rusher, *The Rise of the Right* (New York: William Morrow and Company, Inc., 1984), 304.
43. Jimmy Carter, *White House Diary* (New York: Farrar, Straus and Giroux, 2010), 446–447.
44. Quoted in Kenneth W. Thompson, ed. *The Carter Presidency: Fourteen Intimate Perspectives of Jimmy Carter* (Lanham, MD: University Press of America, Inc., 1990), 113.
45. Richard A. Viguerie, *The New Right: We're Ready to Lead* (Falls Church, VA: The Viguerie Company, 1981), 142.
46. Quoted in Craig Shirley, *Reagan Rising: The Decisive Years, 1976–1980* (New York: Broadside Books, 2017), 284.
47. Drew, *Portrait of an Election*, 24, 26, 30–31.
48. Lou Cannon, *Governor Reagan: His Rise to Power* (New York: PublicAffairs, 2003), 467.
49. Kim Phillips-Fein, *Invisible Hands: The Making of the Conservative Movement from the New Deal to Reagan*, (New York: W. W. Norton, 2009), 239.
50. Schlesinger Jr., *Journals 1952–2000*, 462–463.
51. James A. Baker III, *"Work Hard, Study … and Keep Out of Politics!"* (Evanston, IL: Northwestern University Press, 2008), 81–83. Bush and James Baker began hatching a campaign plan during a 1977 trip in China. Before the end of the year, they "set up a political action committee called the Fund for Limited Government."

52. Ibid., 85.
53. Drew, *Portrait of an Election*, 25–26.
54. Ibid., 106–107.
55. Hayward, *The Age of Reagan*, 625.
56. Ibid., 629–630, 635.
57. Baker, *"Work Hard, Study … and Keep Out of Politics,"* 85–86, 88.
58. Meese, *Reagan*, 3.
59. "Reagan's TV Politics," *New Republic*, March 22, 1980, 3. Shirley, *Reagan Rising*, 311.
60. Jude Wanniski, *The Way the World Works*, Fourth Edition (Washington, DC: Regnery Publishing, Inc., 1998), 351.
61. Martin Anderson, *Revolution* (New York: Harcourt Brace Jovanovich, 1988), 111, 116–121.
62. Ibid., 144.
63. Quoted in Drew, *Portrait of an Election*, 120.
64. Hayward, *The Age of Reagan*, 613.
65. Meese, *Reagan*, 41.
66. Hayward, *The Age of Reagan*, 630.
67. This was the opinion of Martin Anderson. See Deborah Hart Strober and Gerald S. Strober, *The Reagan Presidency: An Oral History of the Era* (London: Thistle Publishing, 2015), 13.
68. Ibid., 16.
69. Bob Colacello, *Ronnie & Nancy: Their Path to the White House 1911 to 1980* (New York: Warner Books, 2004), 480–481.
70. Brian Domitrovic, *Econoclasts: The Rebels Who Sparked the Supply-Side Revolution and Restored American Prosperity* (Wilmington, DE: ISI Books, 2009), 204.
71. Rowland Evans and Robert Novak, *The Reagan Revolution* (New York: E. P. Dutton, 1981), 61–62, 78. Also, see Wanniski, *The Way the World Works*, 351.
72. Drew, *Portrait of an Election*, 173.
73. John Osborne, "Preferring Jimmy," *New Republic*, June 14, 1980, 10.
74. Drew, *Portrait of an Election*, 208.
75. Domitrovic, *Econoclasts*, 203.
76. Baker, *"Work Hard, Study … and Keep Out of Politics,"* 98–99, 103.
77. Strober and Strober, *The Reagan Presidency*, 22–24. Also, see Ronald Reagan, *Ronald Reagan: An American Life* (New York: Pocket Books, 1990), 215–216.
78. Donald T. Critchlow, *The Conservative Ascendancy: How the Republican Right Rose to Power in Modern America*, Second Edition, Revised and Expanded (Lawrence: University Press of Kansas, 2011), 173–174.

79. Evans and Novak, *The Reagan Revolution*, 80, 105. Over the years, Reagan embraced the idea of a gold standard, but to avoid any negative reaction from the financial establishment, Reagan's advisors did not want to hear the "four-letter [gold] emotive word" (105).
80. Baker, *"Work Hard, Study ... and Keep Out of Politics,"* 22, 35.
81. Strober and Strober, *The Reagan Presidency*, 17.
82. Baker, *"Work Hard, Study ... and Keep Out of Politics,"* 101. Also, see Cannon, *Governor Reagan*, 483.
83. Cannon, *Governor Reagan*, 483–485.
84. "I've Had a Bum Rap," *National Review*, May 17, 1976, 15.
85. For a discussion on this issue, see Hayward, *The Age of Reagan*, 681–682. On the political economy link between the New Deal and Mussolini, see Wolfgang Schivelbusch, *Three New Deals: Reflections on Roosevelt's America, Mussolini's Italy, and Hitler's Germany, 1933–1939* (New York: Picador, 2006).
86. Anderson, *Revolution*, 170.
87. Drew, *Portrait of an Election*, 113, 117.
88. Quoted in Drew, *Portrait of an Election*, 114.
89. Ibid., 116.
90. Cannon, *Governor Reagan*, 494–495. Hayward, *The Age of Reagan*, 681.
91. Quoted in Hayward, *The Age of Reagan*, 683.
92. Phillips-Fein, *Invisible Hands*, 247.
93. Cannon, *Governor Reagan*, 478–479.
94. Anderson, *Revolution*, 122, 125, 127.
95. Quoted in Anderson, *Revolution*, 129.
96. Ibid., 130.
97. Ibid., 130–132, 134.
98. Quoted in Anderson, *Revolution*, 137.
99. Ibid., 137–138.
100. According to Brian Domitrovic, Reagan's statement missed two supply-side assumptions. See Domitrovic, *Econoclasts*, 211.
101. Gary M. Fink, "Fragile Alliance: Jimmy Carter and the American Labor Movement," in *The Presidency and Domestic Policies of Jimmy Carter*, 800.
102. Douglas Brinkley, *The Unfinished Presidency: Jimmy Carter's Journey Beyond the White House* (New York: Viking, 1998), 3.
103. Cannon, *Governor Reagan*, 490.
104. "Jobless Muddle," *Time*, October 27, 1980, 74.
105. "Election Perspective," *Newsweek*, November 10, 1980, 94.
106. Milton Friedman and Paul A. Samuelson, "Productivity: Two Experts Cross Swords," *Newsweek*, September 8, 1980, 68–69.
107. Drew, *Portrait of an Election*, 149, 154.

108. Hayward, *The Age of Reagan*, 646.
109. Baker, *"Work Hard, Study … and Keep Out of Politics,"* 111, 113.
110. Quoted in Biven, *Jimmy Carter's Economy*, 245–246.
111. Carter, *Keeping Faith*, 554, 562.
112. Drew, *Portrait of an Election*, 305.
113. "The Anderson Candidacy," *Nation*, May 17, 1980, 587.
114. Mark J. Rozell, "President Carter and the Press: Perspectives from White House Communications Advisors," *Political Science Quarterly*, 105, no. 3 (1990): 420.
115. Drew, *Portrait of an Election*, 310–312, 316.
116. W. Elliot Brownlee, *Federal Taxation in America: A Short History* (Cambridge: University of Cambridge Press, 1996), 133.
117. Drew, *Portrait of an Election*, 319–320.
118. Baker, *"Work Hard, Study … and Keep Out of Politics,"* 108.
119. Quoted in Drew, *Portrait of an Election*, 325.
120. Ibid., 332, 334.
121. Carter, *Keeping Faith*, 565.
122. Strober and Strober, *The Reagan Presidency*, 35.
123. Carter, *Keeping Faith*, 568.
124. "When Jimmy Knew," *Time*, November 17, 1980, 25.
125. Quoted in Cannon, *Governor Reagan*, 508–509.
126. Drew, *Portrait of an Election*, 337–338.
127. "Reagan Coast-to-Coast," *Time*, November 17, 1980, 16.
128. Brinkley, *The Unfinished Presidency*, 1–2, 24.
129. Schlesinger Jr., *Journals 1952–2000*, 506.
130. Rusher, *The Rise of the Right*, 307–308.
131. H. W. Brands, *Reagan: The Life* (New York: Doubleday, 2015), 220.
132. Mike Wallace with Gary Paul Gates, *Between You and Me* (New York: Hyperion, 2005), 47.
133. "Anatomy of a Landslide," *Time*, November 17, 1980, 26.
134. Reagan, *Ronald Reagan*, 205–206.
135. Biven, *Jimmy Carter's Economy*, 206.
136. Quoted in Biven, *Jimmy Carter's Economy*, 206–207.
137. Quoted in Hayward, *The Age of Reagan*, 616.
138. Reagan, *Ronald Reagan*, 207.
139. For example, Secretary of Commerce Bob S. Garland in Carter's government later made this point in reference to Reagan and grain growers. See Thompson, ed., *The Carter Presidency*, 128.
140. Sylvia Nasar, *Grand Pursuit: The Story of Economic Genius* (New York: Simon & Schuster Paperbacks, 2011), 425. Paul Samuelson stated that he resisted the temptation to move rightward as mainstream economics did in the 1980s, but in the early 1990s he appeared to acknowledge

government's limitations: "My enhanced skepticism about government ownership of the means of production or the efficacy of planning is not a reflection of ossifying sympathies and benevolence, but rather is a response to the testimony of proliferating real-world experiences." See Samuelson, "My Life Philosophy," 238.

141. Carter, *White House Diary*, 497.
142. Friedman, "Election Perspective," 94.
143. Anderson, *Revolution*, 7.
144. Robert M. Collins, *Transforming America: Politics and Culture in the Reagan Years* (New York: Columbia University Press, 2007), 19.
145. WHayward, *The Age of Reagan*, 686–687.

Index[1]

[1] Note: Page number followed by 'n' refers to notes.

E. R. Crouse, *America's Failing Economy and the Rise of Ronald Reagan*,
https://doi.org/10.1007/978-3-319-70545-3

Printed by Printforce, the Netherlands